W9-CBW-541

CREATIVITY 37
Annual Awards

CREATIVITY 37
Annual Awards

COLLINS | **DESIGN**

An Imprint of HarperCollins*Publishers*

CREATIVITY 37
Copyright © 2008 by COLLINS DESIGN and CRESCENT HILL BOOKS

All rights reserved. No part of this book may be used or reproduced in any manner whatsoever without written permission except in the case of brief quotations embodied in critical articles and reviews. For information, address Collins Design, 10 East 53rd Street, New York, NY 10022.

HarperCollins books may be purchased for educational, business, or sales promotional use. For information, please write: Special Markets Department, HarperCollins*Publishers*, 10 East 53rd Street, New York, NY 10022.

First Edition

First published in 2008 by:
Collins Design
An Imprint of HarperCollins*Publishers*
10 East 53rd Street
New York, NY 10022
Tel: (212) 207-7000
Fax: (212) 207-7654
collinsdesign@harpercollins.com
www.harpercollins.com

Distributed throughout the world by:
HarperCollins*Publishers*
10 East 53rd Street
New York, NY 10022
Fax: (212) 207-7654

Cover design by Scott Gilbertson, Folio Design Studio.

Book design by Designs on You!
Anthony and Suzanna Stephens.

Additional photography provided by Renee Murphy.

Library of Congress Control Number: 2008924806

ISBN: 978-0-06-158276-9

All images in this book have been reproduced with the knowledge and prior consent of the individuals concerned. No responsibility is accepted by producer, publisher, or printer for any infringement of copyright or otherwise arising from the contents of this publication. Every effort has been made to ensure that credits accurately comply with information supplied.

Produced by Crescent Hill Books, Louisville, KY.

Printed in China by Everbest Printing Company.

First Printing, 2008

NC
998
.C7
V. 37

Table of Contents

FOREWORD

Now in its 38th year, The Creativity Annual Awards is one of the oldest and most widely respected design competitions in the world. This book showcases the winners of the 2007 competition.

For years, one design in each category has been voted the 'Best in Category' and received our prestigious Platinum Award for this recognition. For the first time, we are devoting an entire page to each of the seventy-eight Platinum Award winners, and providing the story behind each design.

With over 1,000 winning designs from over twenty-nine countries, The Creativity Annual Awards is proud to continue our tradition of bringing awareness and well-deserved recognition to the world's most imaginative design firms, both large and small.

MEDAL DESIGNATIONS

 Platinum—This symbol designates a Platinum Award winning design. Our most prestigious award is reserved for the Best in Category. Only one design is awarded per category.

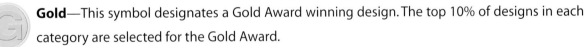 **Gold**—This symbol designates a Gold Award winning design. The top 10% of designs in each category are selected for the Gold Award.

 Silver–This symbol designates a Silver Award winning design. The top 25% of designs in each category are selected for the Silver Award.

CREATIVITY
Annual Awards

Register online.
creativityawards.com

MedlinePlus

medlineplus.gov/salud

YELLOW BUS

Creative Firm: **CRABTREE + COMPANY - FALLS CHURCH, VA**
Creative Team: **SUSAN ANGRISANI, ROD VERA**
Client: **NATIONAL LIBRARY OF MEDICINE**

Creative Firm: **CJ DESIGN - SANTA CRUZ, CA**
Creative Team: **CHRIS MARK**
Client: **YELLOW BUS ADVERTISING**

HARRIETTE'S
SONG

Category: **RULE29 - GENEVA, IL**
Creative Team: **JUSTIN AHRENS, JOSH JENSEN**
Creative: **HARRIETTE'S SONG**

Focusing on Laboratory Supplies and Equipment

Creative Firm: **DEVON ENERGY - OKLAHOMA CITY, OK**
Creative Team: **TIM LANGENBERG**
Client: **DEVON ENERGY CORPORATION**

Creative Firm: **DESIGNSKI L.L.C. - TOLEDO, OH**
Creative Team: **DENNY KREGER**
Client: **CHIRON SCIENTIFIC**

MARK RICHEY
woodworking

Creative Firm: **RAINCASTLE COMMUNICATIONS - NEWTON, MA**
Creative Team: **ROTEM MELLER, PAUL REGENSBURG**
Client: **MARK RICHEY WOODWORKING**

RIVER SPRINGS

Creative Firm: **PEAK SEVEN ADVERTISING - DEERFIELD BEACH, FL**
Creative Team: **BRIAN TIPTON, DARREN SEYS**
Client: **WITHLACOOCHEE PARTNERS**

CARMEN

Creative Firm: **RASSMAN DESIGN - DENVER, CO**
Creative Team: **JOHN RASSMAN**
Client: **OPERA COLORADO**

everything
but the dog

Creative Firm: **WINSPER INC. - BOSTON, MA**
Creative Team: **STEVE BAUTISTA, BRIAN FANDETTI, KEVIN CIMO, KAITY MALONEY**
Client: **EVERYTHING BUT THE DOG**

BAYTOWNE
W H A R F
YAMAHA WATERCRAFT
2008 PRODUCT PREMIER

Creative Firm: **VITRO/ROBERTSON - CARLSBAD, CA**
Creative Team: **PAUL LAMBERT, TRACY SABIN**
Client: **YAMAHA WATERCRAFT**

Creative Firm: **MCGUFFIE DESIGN - NORTH VANCOUVER, BC**
Creative Team: **STEVE MCGUFFIE**
Client: **SKANA CAPITAL CORP.**

Creative Firm: **HORNALL ANDERSON DESIGN WORKS - SEATTLE, WA**
Creative Team: **JACK ANDERSON, ANDREW WICKLUND, ELMER DELA CRUZ,**
PETER ANDERSON, NATHAN YOUNG
Client: **SEATTLE SEAHAWKS**

Creative Firm: **KIMBERLY HOPKINS, DESIGN & ILLUSTRATION - NOTTINGHAM, MD**
Client: **BAREFOOT BAROQUE**

Creative Firm: **HELENA SEO DESIGN - SUNNYVALE, CA**
Creative Team: **HELENA SEO**
Client: **REALITY DIGITAL**

Creative Firm: **COASTLINES CREATIVE GROUP - VANCOUVER, BC**
Creative Team: **BYRON DOWLER, CHRIS FREEMAN,**
JOSLI ROCKAFELLA, KIRKLAND ROBINSON
Client: **DIRTY LAUNDRY TEES**
HTTP://WWW.ILOVEDIRTYLAUNDRY.COM

 Creative Firm: **SNAP CREATIVE - ST. CHARLES, MO**
Creative Team: **ANGELA NEAL, DANIELLE WALZ**
Client: **INFORMED WORKPLACE**

Creative Firm: **HBO OFF-AIR CREATIVE SERVICES - NEW YORK CITY, NY**
Creative Team: **VENUS DENNISON, ANA RACELIS**
Client: **HBO U.S COMEDY ARTS FESTIVAL**

 Creative Firm: **PALIO - SARATOGA SPRINGS, NY**
Creative Team: **GUY MASTRION, TODD LAROCHE, RAFAEL HOLGUIN,**
JENNIFER ASSELTA, MIREK JANCZUR, PETER O'TOOLE
Client: **PALIO**

Creative Firm: **BRANDOCTOR - ZAGREB, CROATIA**
Creative Team: **MOE MINKARA, IGOR MANASTERIOTTI, DAVOR RUKOVANJSKI**
Client: **PUB GAJBA (MEANING CRATE OF BEER)**

Creative Firm: **UQAM ÉCOLE DE DESIGN - MONTRÉAL, QC**
Creative Team: **HASSAN AZIZ, LYNE LEFEBVRE**
Client: **TRANSITION TV**

Creative Firm: **PETERSON RAY & COMPANY - DALLAS, TX**
Creative Team: **MILER HUNG**
Client: **THE GECKO LOUNGE**

COUTURE

LOONGBAR

Creative Firm: **TAMAR GRAPHICS - WALTHAM, MA**
Creative Team: **TAMAR WALLACE**
Client: **POSH+FUNK COUTURE**

Creative Firm: **DESIGN OBJECTIVES PTE LTD - SINGAPORE**
Creative Team: **RONNIE S C TAN**
Client: **JW MARRIOTT BEIJING**
FTP.DESIGNOBJECTIVES.COM.SG

wordland

DESIGNER'S

LUNCHEON

Creative Firm: **KF DESIGN - TAKASAKI, JAPAN**
Creative Team: **KEVIN FOLEY**
Client: **WORDLAND**

Creative Firm: **GEE + CHUNG DESIGN - SAN FRANCISCO, CA**
Creative Team: **EARL GEE**
Client: **STORA ENSO NORTH AMERICA**

PAINTING

Creative Firm: **KINESIS - ASHLAND, OR**
Creative Team: **KATHLEEN SANCHEZ, BRANDY SHEARER**
Client: **APOGEE PAINTING**

Creative Firm: **PETERSON RAY & COMPANY - DALLAS, TX**
Creative Team: **SCOTT RAY**
Client: **CROSSROADS COFFEEHOUSE & MUSIC COMPANY**

active ingredient

IGNITING IDEAS

Creative Firm: **TORRE LAZUR MCCANN - PARSIPPANY, NJ**
Creative Team: **CHRISTOPHER BEAN, JENNIFER ALAMPI,**
MARCIA GODDARD, JENNIFER DEE, BRETT NICHOLS
Client: **TL ACTIVE INGREDIENT**

Fallingwater

Creative Firm: **FITTING GROUP - PITTSBURGH, PA**
Creative Team: **TRAVIS NORRIS, VICTORIA TAYLOR**
Client: **WESTERN PENNSYLVANIA CONSERVANCY**

Creative Firm: **SABINGRAFIK, INC. - CARLSBAD, CA**
Creative Team: **MICHELE TRAVIS, TRACY SABIN**
Client: **SHEPHERD'S RANCH**

Creative Firm: **DESIGN OBJECTIVES PTE LTD - SINGAPORE**
Creative Team: **RONNIE S C TAN**
Client: **MY HUMBLE HOUSE**
FTP.DESIGNOBJECTIVES.COM.SG

BYRNE **URBAN SCHOLARS**

SUPPORT | ADVOCATE | INSPIRE

Creative Firm: **RASSMAN DESIGN - DENVER, CO**
Creative Team: **LYN D'AMATO, JOHN RASSMAN**
Client: **BYRNE URBAN SCHOLARS**

Creative Firm: **HORNALL ANDERSON DESIGN WORKS - SEATTLE, WA**
Creative Team: **JACK ANDERSON, YURI SHVETS**
Client: **ENTREPRENEURS AND INNOVATORS FOR THE ENVIRONMENT**

Creative Firm: **A3 DESIGN - CHARLOTTE, NC**
Creative Team: **AMANDA ALTMAN, ALAN ALTMAN, LAUREN GUALDONI, CARBONHOUSE**
Client: **CARBONHOUSE**

Creative Firm: **A3 DESIGN - CHARLOTTE, NC**
Creative Team: **AMANDA ALTMAN, ALAN ALTMAN**
Client: **TARGET CARE**

Creative Firm: **BRIGHT RAIN CREATIVE - ST. LOUIS, MO**
Creative Team: **MATT MARINO, KEVIN HOUGH**
Client: **TRAINWRECK SALOON**

Creative Firm: **RAINCASTLE COMMUNICATIONS - NEWTON, MA**
Creative Team: **ROTEM MELLER, PAUL REGENSBURG**
Client: **ARTIZAN DESIGN CENTRE**

Creative Firm: **HORNALL ANDERSON DESIGN WORKS - SEATTLE, WA**
Creative Team: **DAVID BATES, JAVAS LEHN**
Client: **SPACE NEEDLE**

Latcha+Associates was asked to create the annual report for the Boys Scouts of America, Detroit Area Council. The task was to share key statistics for the 2006 year, in addition to reiterating the organization's mission and membership activities. The design intent was to remind or inform current and potential benefactors of what it means to be a Scout.

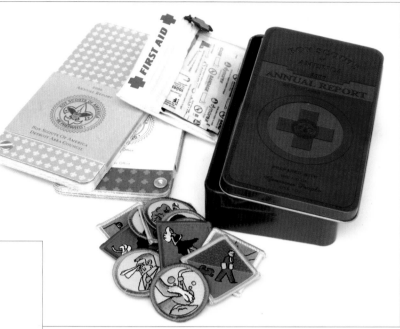

Latcha+Associates decided to take a lighthearted approach, wanting to connect with the benefactors in a fun and unexpected way. The final design was inspired by a vintage First Aid Kit, carried by Boy Scouts in the 1940's.

The kit is a tin containing a 17-panel "deck." One side shows the requisite details—numbers, financials, statistics, etc. (typical annual report information). The flip side of the deck serves as a useful yet lighthearted look at First Aid for the Office.

It covers everything from puncture wounds (think stapler wars) to nosebleeds (time to lay off the nasal spray). While the technical instructions were accurately pulled from a current Boy Scout First Aid Guide, the reader is advised to "seek real help" in an emergency. To top it off, the tin also contains a real mini first aid kit, just in case.

This alternative approach to a simple annual report reminds us not only what it means to be a Scout, but also that life shouldn't be all work and financial statistics.

Creative Firm: **LATCHA+ASSOCIATES—FARMINGTON HILLS, MI**
Creative Team: **RYAN MCCARTHY, TAMMY GARDELL, BOB MAAS, ARMAND ARCHAMBAULT**
Client: **BOY SCOUTS OF AMERICA**

The ⓟ symbol designates a Platinum Award Winner, our Best in Category.

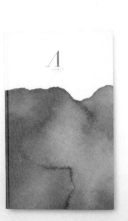

Creative Firm: **BRUKETA & ZINIC OM - ZAGREB, CROATIA**
Creative Team: **DAVOR BRUKETA, NIKOLA ZINIC, IVANKA MABIC,
MIREL HADZIJUSUFOVIC, IMELDA RAMOVIC**
Client: **ADRIS GRUPA**

Creative Firm: **COATES AND COATES - NAPERVILLE, IL**
Creative Team: **WADE NIDAY, RON COATES**
Client: **CORN PRODUCTS INTERNATIONAL, INC.**
WWW.COATESANDCOATES.COM

Creative Firm: **FUTURA DDB - LJUBLANA, SLOVENIA**
Creative Team: **ZARE KERIN**
Client: **TELEKOM SLOVENIJE**

Creative Firm: **CMG DESIGN INC. - PASADENA, CA**
Creative Team: **CHRIS HAMILTON, BERMUDA JOHN EWAN, GREG CRAWFORD**
Client: **MERCURY GENERAL CORPORATION**

reliable energy...

365

kWh

OG&E 36447

Creative Firm: **COATES AND COATES - NAPERVILLE, IL**
Creative Team: **CAROLIN COATES, RON COATES, JIM SCHNEPF, CHARLIE SIMOKAITIS**
Client: **OGE ENERGY CORPORATION**
WWW.COATESANDCOATES.COM

Creative Firm: **RUDER FINN DESIGN - NEW YORK, NY**
Creative Team: **LISA GABBAY, SALVATORE CATANIA, KAVEN LAM**
Client: **NEW YORK THEATER WORKSHOP**

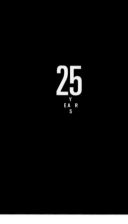

25 YEARS

VISION
DRIVE
UNIQUE

From the Managing Director

HEDIA
GRABBER

life
MATTERS

family

Creative Firm: **VOICEBOX CREATIVE - SAN FRANCISCO, CA**
Creative Team: **KRISTIE WISE, JACQUES ROSSOUW,**
MARK TUSCHMAN, SUSAN SHARPE, SARAH KATZ O'HARA,
TUCKER AND HOSSLER
Client: **PALO ALTO MEDICAL FOUNDATION**

Creative Firm: **LEVINE & ASSOCIATES - WASHINGTON, DC**
Creative Team: **MONICA SNELLINGS, GREG SITZMANN, STEVE HERNDON**
Client: **INTERNATIONAL YOUTH FOUNDATION**

joining FORCES

touching LIVES

REALIZING THE
power
AND
promise
OF YOUNG PEOPLE

youth voices
FROM 70 COUNTRIES AND TERRITORIES

S Creative Firm: **AAC SAATCHI & SAATCHI - HAMILTON, BERMUDA**
Creative Team: **SHEILA WOODBRIDGE, PENELOPE DULLAGHAN, STEPHEN RAYNOR, LINDSEY SIMS**
Client: **TOKIO MILLENNIUM RE**

Creative Firm: **VOICEBOX CREATIVE - SAN FRANCISCO, CA**
Creative Team: **KRISTIE WISE, JACQUES ROSSOUW, MARK TUSCHMAN, SARAH KATZ O'HARA, TUCKER AND HOSSLER**
Client: **PALO ALTO MEDICAL FOUNDATION**

Creative Firm: **COATES AND COATES - NAPERVILLE, IL**
Creative Team: **CAROLIN COATES, RON COATES, CHARLIE SIMOKAITIS**
Client: **ROHM AND HAAS COMPANY**
WWW.COATESANDCOATES.COM

Creative Firm: **EMERSON, WAJDOWICZ STUDIOS - NEW YORK, NY**
Creative Team: **JUREK WAJDOWICZ, LISA LAROCHELLE, YOKO YOSHIDA, MANNY MENDEZ**
Client: **ARCUS FOUNDATION**

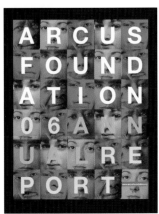

"THE CALM BEFORE THE *STORM* "

DMX TECHNOLOGIES GROUP LIMITED annual report 2006

The ancient Greeks

held the first Olympic Games in honour of Zeus, the Greek gods and goddesses in the year 776 were held in Olympia, Greece thereafter for every A.D 393, when they were abolished.

FOR I KNOW, YOU WILL PUSH ME TO MY LIMITS OF HUMAN ENDURANCE.

Creative Firm: **Q-PLUS DESIGN PTE LTD - SINGAPORE**
Creative Team: **DILLON DEVAN, MARK SIDWELL**
Client: **DMX TECHNOLOGIES GROUP LIMITED**

Creative Firm: **AAC SAATCHI & SAATCHI - HAMILTON, BERMUDA**
Creative Team: **SCOTT WILLIAMS, RHONA EMMERSON, MARK EMMERSON, RALPH RICHARDSON, KIP HERRING, STEPHEN RAYNOR**
Client: **MAXRE**

MaxRe

Creative Firm: **SAYLES GRAPHIC DESIGN - DES MOINES, IA**
Creative Team: **JOHN SAYLES**
Client: **MID-IOWA HEALTH FOUNDATION**

Creative Firm: **BCN COMMUNICATIONS - CHICAGO, IL**
Creative Team: **HARRI BOLLER, ROTH & RAMBERG, TED STOIK**
Client: **CN**

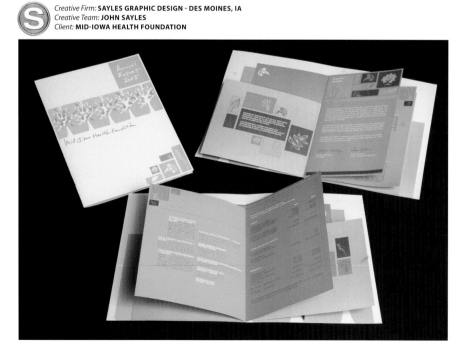

global leverage
at work

Sara Lee Fresh Bakery Breads *Based on the consumer insight that children want to eat white bread, but parents want them to get the nutrition of whole grains, we developed Sara Lee Soft & Smooth bread, a whole grain white bread that looks and tastes every bit as good as traditional white bread. Sara Lee Soft & Smooth Made with Whole Grain White bread quickly became the top-selling bread in the nation, helping Sara Lee become the leading fresh bread brand in America. To capitalize on this innovation platform, we launched Sara Lee Made with Whole Grain White hot dog and hamburger buns just in time for grilling season.*

Creative Firm: **DD+A - OMAHA, NE**
Client: **VALMONT INDUSTRIES**

Creative Firm: **COATES AND COATES - NAPERVILLE, IL**
Creative Team: **CAROLIN COATES, RON COATES, STEVEN MCDONALD, JIM SCHNEPF**
Client: **SARA LEE CORPORATION**
WWW.COATESANDCOATES.COM

Creative Firm: **MAD DOG GRAPHX - ANCHORAGE, AK**
Creative Team: **KRIS RYAN-CLARKE**
Client: **FOOD BANK OF ALASKA**

Creative Firm: **TAYLOR & IVES INCORPORATED - NEW YORK, NY**
Creative Team: **ALISA ZAMIR**
Client: **BOWERY RESIDENTS' COMMITTEE, INC.**

Creative Firm: **EPIGRAM - SINGAPORE**
Creative Team: **KELVIN LOK, LOUISSA LEE, FRANK PINCKERS, RUSSELL WONG, SHARON LAM**
Client: **CAPITALAND LIMITED**

Creative Firm: **CROXSON DESIGN - HOUSTON, TX**
Creative Team: **STEPHEN CROXSON, KENNETH WEAVER**
Client: **SUPERIOR ENERGY SERVICES**

Creative Firm: **CREDENCE PARTNERSHIP PTE LTD - SINGAPORE**
Creative Team: **FRANCIS SKG, WER 1**
Client: **LOTTVISION LIMITED**

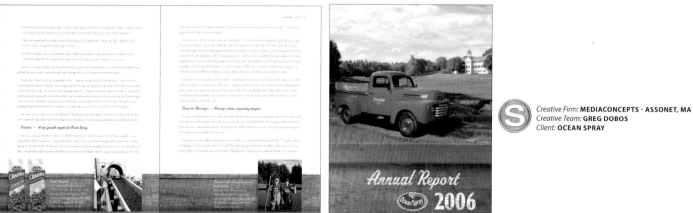

Creative Firm: **MEDIACONCEPTS - ASSONET, MA**
Creative Team: **GREG DOBOS**
Client: **OCEAN SPRAY**

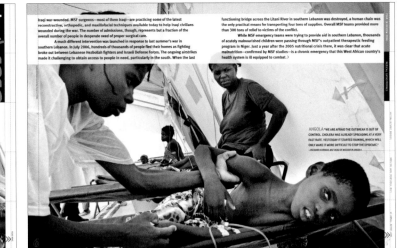

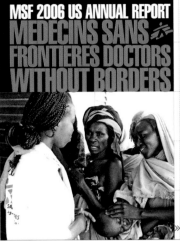

Creative Firm: **EMERSON, WAJDOWICZ STUDIOS - NEW YORK, NY**
Creative Team: **JUREK WAJDOWICZ, LISA LAROCHELLE, MANNY MENDEZ, YOKO YOSHIDA, ESPEN RASSMUSEN, ALEXANDER GYADELOW, DIETER TELEMANS, CARLOS TOMASI, OMAR ODEH, THOMAS DWORZAK, PAOLO PELLEGRINI, KADIR VAN LOHUIZEN, TON KOENE**
Client: **MEDECINS SANS FRONTIERES/DOCTORS WITHOUT BORDERS**

Creative Firm: **COATES AND COATES - NAPERVILLE, IL**
Creative Team: **CAROLIN COATES, RON COATES**
Client: **PROLOGIS**
WWW.COATESANDCOATES.COM

Creative Firm: **SGDP - CHICAGO, IL**
Creative Team: **AUGUSTA TOPPINS, CLAUDINE GUERTIN**
Client: **MORRIS ANIMAL FOUNDATION**
WWW.SGDP.COM

Creative Firm: **BCN COMMUNICATIONS - CHICAGO, IL**
Creative Team: **JIM PITROSKI, ROB MILEHAM, TED STOIK**
Client: **GENERAL MOTORS CORPORATION**

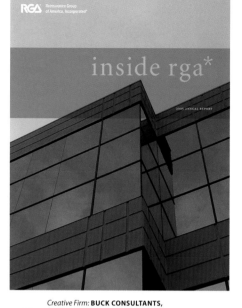

inside rga*

2005 ANNUAL REPORT

How We See the World

Impact

The Rockefeller Foundation 2006 Annual Report

Creative Firm: **EMERSON, WAJDOWICZ STUDIOS - NEW YORK, NY**
Creative Team: **JUREK WAJDOWICZ, LISA LAROCHELLE, MANNY MENDEZ, YOKO YOSHIDA, JONAS BENDIKSEN**
Client: **THE ROCKEFELLER FOUNDATION**

Creative Firm: **BUCK CONSULTANTS, AN ACS COMPANY - ST. LOUIS, MO**
Creative Team: **JENNIFER WHITLOW, BILL GORMAN, GREG RANNELLS, CHRISTINE DONNIER-VALENTIN, HENRY WESTHEIM**
Client: **REINSURANCE GROUP OF AMERICA, INC.**

Creative Firm: **RTS RIEGER TEAM WERBEAGENTUR GMBH - DÜSSELDORF, GERMANY**
Creative Team: **MICHAELA MÜLLER, FRANCISCO NAVARRO Y GOMES, KERSTIN OYDA**
Client: **THYSSENKRUPP ELEVATOR AG**

Creative Firm: **PARAGRAPHS DESIGN - CHICAGO, IL**
Creative Team: **RACHEL RADTKE, CARY MARTIN, CARRIE CERESA**
Client: **ASSURANT**

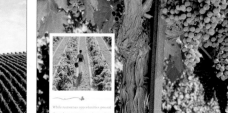

Creative Firm: **PARAGRAPHS DESIGN - CHICAGO, IL**
Creative Team: **CARRIE CERESA, GRETCHEN NORMAN**
Client: **CAREER EDUCATION CORPORATION**

Creative Firm: **TAYLOR & IVES INCORPORATED - NEW YORK, NY**
Creative Team: **ALISA ZAMIR**
Client: **BLACKROCK, INC.**

Creative Firm: **GRAFIK MARKETING COMMUNICATIONS - ALEXANDRIA, VA**
Creative Team: **ARUTHER HSU, MELISSA WILETS, KRISTIN MOORE**
Client: **VOLUNTEERS OF AMERICA**

Creative Firm: **SUKA DESIGN - NEW YORK, NY**
Creative Team: **BRIAN WONG, BUD GLICK**
Client: **VISITING NURSE SERVICE OF NEW YORK**
WWW.VNSNY.ORG

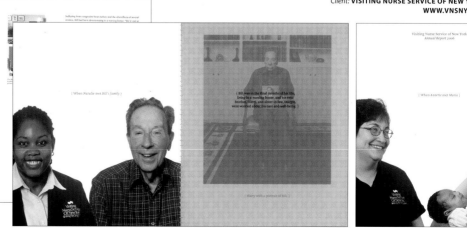

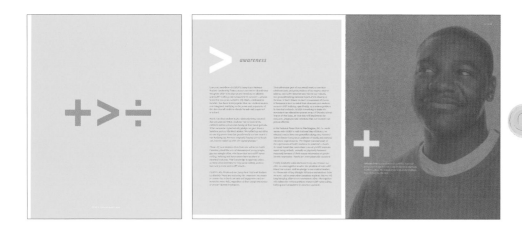

Creative Firm: **SUKA DESIGN - NEW YORK, NY**
Creative Team: **BRIAN WONG, CONRAD VENTUR**
Client: **GAY, LESBIAN AND STRAIGHT**
EDUCATION NETWORK
WWW.GLSEN.ORG

Creative Firm: **PARAGRAPHS DESIGN - CHICAGO, IL**
Creative Team: **DORA RODRIGUEZ, RACHEL RADTKE**
Client: **ALLSCRIPTS**

Creative Firm: **ORANGESEED DESIGN - MINNEAPOLIS, MN**
Creative Team: **DAMIEN WOLF, ERIC JUDYCKI, REBECCA AVIÑA, MARK OSTOW**
Client: **HARVARD DIVINITY SCHOOL**

Creative Firm: **SPLASH PRODUCTIONS PTE LTD - SINGAPORE**
Creative Team: **STANLEY YAP, BRICE LI, TERRY LEE, JOSHUA TAN**
Client: **ECS HOLDINGS LTD**

Creative Firm: **TAYLOR & IVES INCORPORATED - NEW YORK, NY**
Creative Team: **ALISA ZAMIR**
Client: **THE HERSHEY COMPANY**

Creative Firm: **PARAGRAPHS DESIGN - CHICAGO, IL**
Creative Team: **RACHEL RADTKE, DORA RODRIGUEZ, CARY MARTIN**
Client: **CITIZENS REPUBLIC BANCORP**

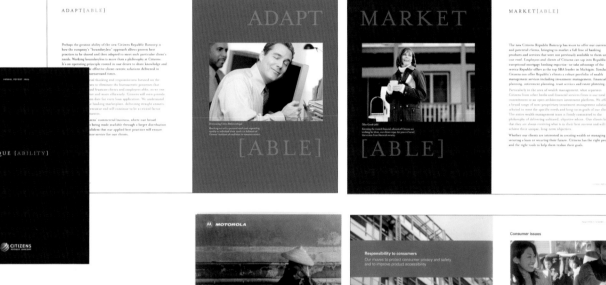

Creative Firm: **LISKA + ASSOCIATES - CHICAGO, IL**
Creative Team: **STEVE LISKA, DEBORAH SCHNEIDER, SABINE KRAUSS**
Client: **MOTOROLA**

Creative Firm: **COASTLINES CREATIVE GROUP - VANCOUVER, BC**
Creative Team: **BYRON DOWLER, PAUL EDWARDS, BROOKE THORSTEINSON, JOSLI ROCKAFELLA**
Client: **URASIA ENERGY INC**

Creative Firm: **SUKA DESIGN - NEW YORK, NY**
Creative Team: **BRIAN WONG**
Client: **ICSC**
WWW.ICSC.ORG

Creative Firm: **FATHOM CREATIVE - WASHINGTON, DC**
Creative Team: **ANJEANETTE AGRO, TOM GAMERTSFELDER,
SHERI GRANT, CRAIG HILL, DREW MITCHELL, ANNE MORRIS**
Client: **ARCHITECT OF THE CAPITOL**

Creative Firm: **KOR GROUP - BOSTON, MA**
Creative Team: **JIM GIBSON, ANNE CALLAHAN, BILL GALLERY, JOEL HASKELL,
ALEXANDRA MOLLOY, ERIN DYM**
Client: **BETH ISRAEL DEACONESS MEDICAL CENTER**

Creative Firm: **SIGNI - MEXICO**
Creative Team: **RENE GALINDO, ODETTE EDWARDS**
Client: **COCA-COLA FEMSA**

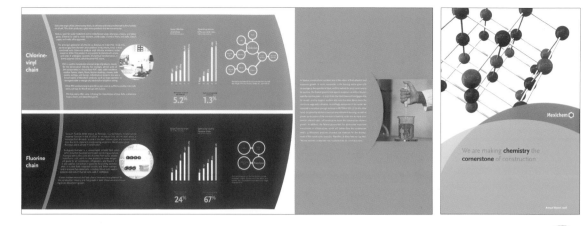

Creative Firm: **SUKA DESIGN - NEW YORK, NY**
Creative Team: **JEN PRESSLEY-THOMAS**
Client: **FUND FOR PUBLIC HEALTH**
WWW.FPHNY.ORG

Creative Firm: **SIGNI - MEXICO**
Creative Team: **RENE GALINDO, FELIPE SALAS**
Client: **MEXICHEM**

Creative Firm: **SUKA DESIGN - NEW YORK, NY**
Creative Team: **JEN PRESSLEY-THOMAS, BUD GLICK**
Client: **INNER-CITY SCHOLARSHIP FUND**
WWW.INNERCITYSF.ORG

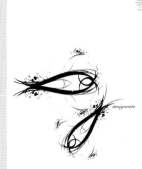

Creative Firm: **CREDENCE PARTNERSHIP PTE LTD - SINGAPORE**
Creative Team: **FRANCIS SKG, ADELINE MAH**
Client: **AMARA HOLDINGS LIMITED**

Creative Firm: **HEYE & PARTNER GMBH - UNTERHACHING, GERMANY**
Creative Team: **NORBERT HEROLD, HELMUT HUSCHKA, STEFAN ELLENBERGER,**
SEBASTIAN HACKELSPERGER, MANUELA KUNZE, CAMILLO BUECHELMEIER
Client: **MCDONALD'S GERMANY**

Creative Firm: **FUTURA DDB - LJUBLANA, SLOVENIA**
Creative Team: **ZARE KERIN, ANDRAZ FILAC**
Client: **NATIONAL GEOGRAPHIC**

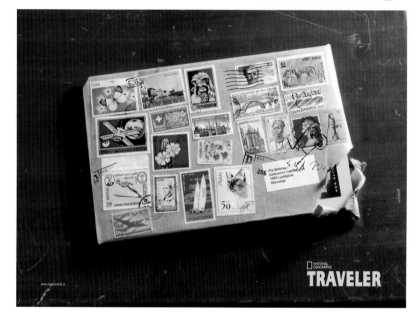

Creative Firm: **WINSPER INC. - BOSTON, MA**
Creative Team: **STEVE BAUTISTA, BRIAN FANDETTI, KEVIN CIMO,**
BOB CLINTON, KAITY MALONEY, CAROLINE BISHOP
Client: **TIMBERLAND PRO**

Creative Firm: **BRAINCHILD CREATIVE - NOVATO, CA**
Creative Team: **DAVID SWOPE, JEF LOEB, LAURA LINDOW, CURTIS MYERS**
Client: **FLEX YOUR POWER**

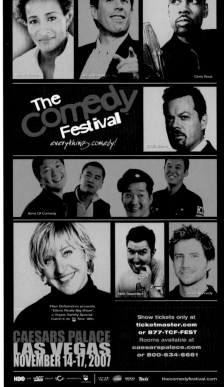

Creative Firm: **HBO OFF-AIR CREATIVE SERVICES - NEW YORK CITY, NY**
Creative Team: **VENUS DENNISON, ANA RACELIS, RON ACQUAVITA**
Client: **HBO U.S COMEDY ARTS FESTIVAL**

The Smithsonian Latino Center

(SLC) functions as a collaborative partner with the Smithsonian Institution. It helps ensure Latino culture is represented in exhibitions, collections, and lecture and research series.

The creative firm Grafik was asked to create a fresh, energetic "face" for SLC that would capture the essence of Latino culture—a big challenge since the Latino culture is so diverse.

Another challenge is that SLC is a brand within a brand in that it must embody the Smithsonian brand of quality, scholarship and credibility. Equally important, SLC wanted to avoid stereotyping Latino culture as strictly "Mexican" or "Columbian-centric", but instead needed to broaden the scope.

Grafik's approach was to provide a set of brand guidelines that stipulated font choices, color and texture applications, as well as designing initial key communication tools such as large-format newsletters, a media kit and a'"vision brochure" that allowed the board of directors a unified way to speak about SLC and its vision and goals.

The ⓟ symbol designates a Platinum Award Winner, our Best in Category.

32

Creative Firm: **GRAFIK MARKETING COMMUNICATIONS - ALEXANDRIA, VA**
Creative Team: **MILA ARRISUENO, GREGG GLAVIANO, LYNN MURPHY**
Client: **SMITHSONIAN LATINO CENTER**

Creative Firm: **GRAPHICULTURE - MINNEAPOLIS, MN**
Creative Team: **CRYSTAL BARLOW, BRYAN POHL, TIFFANY MOORE**
Client: **MINNESOTA CENTER FOR PHOTOGRAPHY**

Creative Firm: **KAA DESIGN GROUP, INC. - GRAPHICS STUDIO - LOS ANGELES, CA**
Creative Team: **MELANIE ROBINSON, LOUIS-PHILIPPE CARRETTA, DEVANEE NIEDNAGEL**
Client: **BEAUVALLON**

Creative Firm: **WYLER WERBUNG - ZÜRICH, SWITZERLAND**
Creative Team: **FELIX STREULI, CLAUDIO DUSCHLETTA, ALEXANDRA STOCKER, RUEDI WYLER, ANDREAS KONRAD, CHRISTINE GUARNIERI**
Client: **ENGADIN ST. MORITZ**
WWW.WYLERWERBUNG.CH

Creative Firm: **PRIMARY DESIGN, INC. - HAVERHILL, MA**
Creative Team: **JULES EPSTEIN, SHARYN ROGERS, ALLISON DAVIS, JEN DEMORE, VITA MIRONOVA**
Client: **PRIMETIME COMMUNITIES**
WWWW.SOCO146.COM

Creative Firm: **GOLD - PONTE VEDRA BEACH, FL**
Creative Team: **KEITH GOLD, BRIAN GOLD, PETER BUTCAVAGE, JAN HANAK**
Client: **SYNCHRONICITYLIVE.COM**

Creative Firm: **CROXSON DESIGN - HOUSTON, TX**
Creative Team: **STEPHEN CROXSON, RICHARD BYRD, LAURIE CROXSON**
Client: **BAKER PETROLITE**

Creative Firm: **THE BAILEY GROUP - PLYMOUTH MEETING, PA**
Creative Team: **DAVE FIEDLER, STEVE PERRY, CHRISTIAN WILLIAMSON, JESSICA GLEBE**
Client: **THE P.I.N.K. SPIRITS COMPANY**

This was the first international conference on social entrepreneurship in India. The client, UN Ltd. UK, asked UMS Design Studio to create an innovative and visually memorable identity for the conference that would be adaptable as a souvenir, print collateral and venue branding. The objective was to generate awareness of the work in which social entrepreneurs around the world are involved.

UMS Design Studio composed a concept to show how a small seed can result in a great transformation in society. The agency's biggest hurdle was interpreting how the kinetic attributes of growth and transformation could be conveyed in a brochure while also showing movement in space and time. The concept had to be easily and accurately interpreted in any language or culture.

A hand drawn mandala-like growth motif was chosen as the main visual element. This organic image is meant to represent the grassroots work that is taken on by social entrepreneurs. The mandala-like structure and pattern (taken from Indian iconography) expands outwards, which conveys growth and positive radiance.

The design uses a stark black and green color palette for visual impact. The small green dot in the center of the brochure represents a small seed sown by a social entrepreneur. (It also represents the "bindu" or the "origin of creation" in Indian thought.) The thought that a small seed can grow and create positive transformation in society is reflected through Indian symbols.

The organic motif has been printed on several pages, and concentric circles are cut into the pages, so the idea of growth is visually experienced as the person turns the pages.

Creative Firm: **ULHAS MOSES DESIGN STUDIO - MUMBAI, INDIA**
Creative Team: **ULHAS MOSES**
Client: **UN LTD UK**
WWW.ULHASMOSES.COM

The (P) *symbol designates a Platinum Award Winner, our Best in Category.*

Every Swinerton office is involved in their community, working with organizations such as Habitat for Humanity, Rebuilding Together and Project Mercy. We are very proud of our employee volunteerism because we believe it reflects the generosity and commitment of everyone within the Swinerton Family. Swinerton's Non-Profit Foundation identifies worthy causes (youth, health, human services, environmental, construction education and cultural programs) throughout our geographic territories and responds with financial grants.

Serving Our Community

Creative Firm: **SWINERTON INCORPORATED - SAN FRANCISCO, CA**
Creative Team: **MARK GUDENAS, BILL LABRANCHE**
Client: **SWINERTON INCORPORATED**

Creative Firm: **ULHAS MOSES DESIGN STUDIO - MUMBAI, INDIA**
Creative Team: **ULHAS MOSES**
Client: **BRITISH COUNCIL**
WWW.ULHASMOSES.COM

Creative Firm: **BBK STUDIO - GRAND RAPIDS, MI**
Creative Team: **YANG KIM, MICHELE CHARTIER, DEAN VAN DIS, KRISTIN TENNANT, SVH PRINTING**
Client: **IZZYDESIGN**

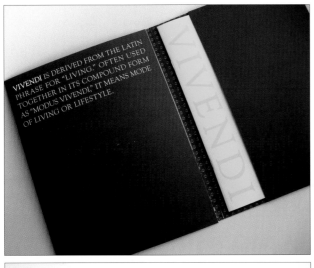

zeitgeist
DESIGN+BUILD+MARKET+SELL

Creative Firm: **HELENA SEO DESIGN - SUNNYVALE, CA**
Creative Team: **HELENA SEO, NANCY TOMKINS, BILL FLEMING**
Client: **VIVENDI DEVELOPMENT**

Creative Firm: **FRANK. - MIAMI, FL**
Creative Team: **TODD HOUSER**
Client: **ZEITGEIST**

Creative Firm: **PROTOBRAND - BOSTON, MA**
Creative Team: **VASSIA ALAYKOVA, KRISTIN ANDREOTES**
Client: **SELF-PROMOTION**

THE MYTH

Creative Firm: **BRIAN J. GANTON & ASSOCIATES - CEDAR GROVE, NJ**
Creative Team: **BRIAN J. GANTON, JR., MARK GANTON,**
CHRISTOPHER GANTON, PAT PALMIERI, JOHN HOVELL
Client: **OLDCASTLE GLASS**

Creative Firm: **GRAFIK MARKETING COMMUNICATIONS - ALEXANDRIA, VA**
Creative Team: **JOHNNY VITROVITCH, MICHAEL MATEOS**
Client: **GHT**

Creative Firm: **GRAPHICAT LTD. - WANCHAI, HONG KONG**
Creative Team: **COLIN TILLYER**
Client: **NOBLE GROUP LIMITED**

Creative Firm: **Q - WIESBADEN, GERMANY**
Creative Team: **THILO VON DEBSCHITZ, MATTHIAS FREY**
Client: **ARJOWIGGINS**

Creative Firm: **PEAK SEVEN ADVERTISING - DEERFIELD BEACH, FL**
Creative Team: **JONATHAN BERG**
Client: **THE PUGLIESE COMPANY**

Creative Firm: **CSC'S P2 COMMUNICATIONS SERVICES - FALLS CHURCH, VA**
Creative Team: **TERRY WILSON, AARON KOBILIS, JIM MCDERMOTT, JENNIFER VOLTAGGIO**
Client: **CSC ABD**

Creative Firm: CSC'S P2 COMMUNICATIONS SERVICES - FALLS CHURCH, VA
Creative Team: TERRY WILSON, AARON KOBILIS, JENNIFER VOLTAGGIO, JOHN FARQUHAR
Client: CSC TMG

 Creative Firm: MUELLER DESIGN - OAKLAND, CA
Creative Team: KYLE MUELLER, CHARMIAN NAGUIT
Client: OMNIVISION

Creative Firm: COASTLINES CREATIVE GROUP - VANCOUVER, BC
Creative Team: BYRON DOWLER, PAUL EDWARDS, JOSLI ROCKAFELLA
Client: SUPERFEET WORLDWIDE
HTTP://WWW.SUPERFEET.COM/

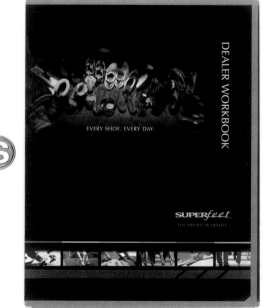

Creative Firm: **BIG MOON MARKETING - TOWSON, MD**
Creative Team: **MARIAN MATTHIS, LITHOGRAPHICS PRINTING**
Client: **THOMAS NELSON, INC.**

MAX LUCADO
3:16
THE NUMBERS OF HOPE

APRIL 2007
■ Product Partner Gathering – Gather core product partners to firm overall strategy and plans
■ 3:16 style guide available at www.thomasnelson.com/styleguide316

JULY 2007
■ Retail Partner Vision Cast – Convenes at ICRS and will introduce the core product partners and invite retailers to participate in the 3:16 project

JUNE - AUGUST 2007
■ Pre-release campaign
  • Initiating with ICRS, begin billboard mass transit advertising campaign to create pre-release buzz
  • Web/viral campaign launched

AUGUST 14, 2007
■ Product ship date, including:
  • 3:16 trade book with in-book 40-day devotional
  • Hope, Pure and Simple
  • 3:16 Small Group Study
  • 3:16 Spanish edition, with other languages quickly following, including German, Swedish, Dutch, Korean, Japanese, and Chinese
  • 3:16 consumer music CD (bonus CD-Rom included with digital study of book of John)
  • 3:16 church musical
  • 3:16 web program site launch

SEPTEMBER 11, 2007
■ Product publishing date

Creative Firm: **TOYOTA FINANCIAL SERVICES - TORRANCE, CA**
Creative Team: **DANIEL KO**
Client: **TOYOTA FINANCIAL SERVICES**

Creative Firm: **THE MONOGRAM GROUP - CHICAGO, IL**
Creative Team: **HAROLD WOODRIDGE, CHIP BALCH**
Client: **WILDMAN HARROLD**
WWW.WILDMAN.COM

TOXIC TORT.

THE CHALLENGE: Defending manufacturers from multi-district class action lawsuits alleging personal injury and/or property damage.

THE APPROACH: Crafting an industry-wide strategy to challenge class certification and demystifying the complex scientific issues for judges and juries to make informed decisions.

In cases filed in various states, our lawyers have taken the lead in formulating and coordinating an aggressive, methodical and unified defense strategy that has resulted in the defeat of class certification and dismissal of suits by summary judgment in a number of jurisdictions. In instances where our clients have gone to trial, every jury verdict in the last decade has been for the defense.

In Florida, when plaintiffs abandoned personal injury claims to focus on allegations that the preservative chromated copper arsenate (CCA) impacted their properties, the district court denied class certification and agreed with our argument that the individualized nature of any class member's property claim

In recent years, the plaintiffs' bar has attempted to create the next wave of litigation by setting its sights on the CCA-treated wood industry.

In Colorado state court, our attorneys defended Osmose, Inc., a leading manufacturer, when the plaintiff, a carpenter, claimed that he had suffered illnesses after breathing sawdust from the wood, and that he had received no safety information about the product. This was the first CCA case to go to verdict in a decade and was scrutinized by the industry, the plaintiffs' bar and the media.

Result! Our client won a defense verdict by demonstrating to the jury that the injuries were not caused by inhaling the sawdust, that the product was safe when used as recommended, and that the safety information had been prominently displayed.

Our formula for success in these cases — and in many toxic tort lawsuits—is

and the need for product identification made class certification improper.

straightforward. Our lawyers have immersed themselves in the complex scientific issues so that they can identify and explain the critical issues of the case in a way that is understandable to the court or jury. We also have relationships with a cadre of well-respected experts whose persuasive testimony explains the true lack of causal connection.

Because of our scientific expertise and track record in these and similar cases, other law firms representing members of the industry have followed our recommendations and stood as one at the pre-trial and trial stages. This coordinated attack on inappropriate class certifications and, if necessary, the scientific merits of individual claims has preserved our clients' strong reputations and positions while demonstrating that when there's good chemistry among the lawyers defending in industry, the chances for success are greatly enhanced.

WILDMAN HARROLD | CASE STUDY

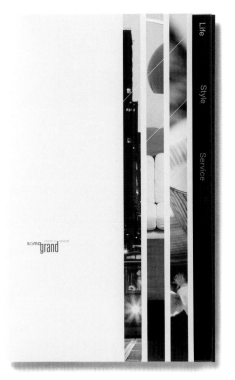

The first of its kind in San Francisco, Soma Grand is a 22-story condominium that boasts designer aesthetics, amazing views and boutique hotel-style services. The scope of work by Chen Design Associates included visual branding development, art direction, design, writing, project management and implementation of all print collateral, sales center visuals and print advertising.

It was important to distinguish Soma Grand from the pack of similar-looking real estate developments sprouting up in the same area. Chen Design Associates focused on the exciting location and the unique combination of sophisticated, yet affordable urban living with hotel-quality service.

Chen Design Associates drew inspiration from the architectural materials used in the design of Soma Grand for the brochure, including furnishing details, textures and fine artwork. The visual images were then used in expansive photographs with generous white space. The detailed imagery and modern typography were paired with sleek acetate overprinted with metallic silver and warm browns in a tall format that mimics the towering building.

Creative Firm: **CHEN DESIGN ASSOCIATES - SAN FRANCISCO, CA**
Creative Team: **JOSHUA CHEN, LAURIE CARRIGAN, MAX SPECTOR**
Client: **PACIFIC MARKETING ASSOCIATES**

The ℗ *symbol designates a Platinum Award Winner, our Best in Category.*

Creative Firm: **PEAK SEVEN ADVERTISING - DEERFIELD BEACH, FL**
Creative Team: **STACY MATHRANI, DARREN SEYS**
Client: **CYPRESS MAYFAIR**

Creative Firm: **STUDIO TWO - LENOX, MA**
Creative Team: **HEATHER ROSE, KEVIN SPRAGUE**
Client: **BERKSHIRE CREATIVE ECONOMY**

Creative Firm: **KOR GROUP - BOSTON, MA**
Creative Team: **ANNE CALLAHAN, JIM GIBSON, BILL GALLERY, LIBRETTO**
Client: **CAMBRIDGE SCHOOL OF WESTON**

Creative Firm: **E-GRAPHICS COMMUNICATIONS - TOKYO, JAPAN**
Creative Team: **TOMOHIRA KODAMA, YASUYUKI NAGATO, YOSHITAKA NONAKA,
TAKANORI UTSUMI, NOBUKO MURAKAMI, TONY NAGELMANN**
Client: **NISSAN MOTOR COMPANY**

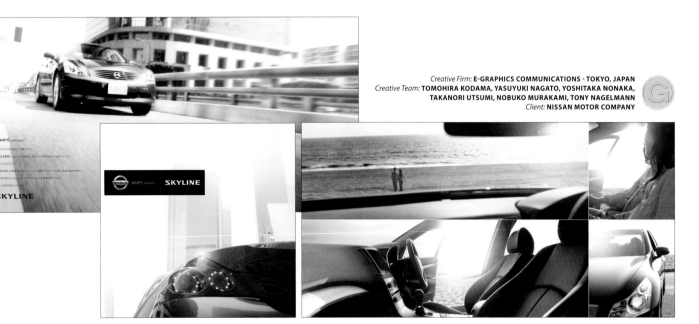

Creative Firm: **M/C/C - DALLAS, TX**
Creative Team: **GREG HANSEN, TODD BRASHEAR, HILLARY BOULDEN, AMANDA MYERS**
Client: **BIG THOUGHT**

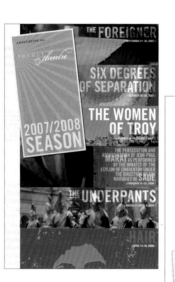

Creative Firm: **DAVIS DESIGN PARTNERS - HOLLAND, OH**
Creative Team: **MATT DAVIS, KAREN DAVIS**
Client: **PURDUE THEATRE, PURDUE UNIVERSITY**

Creative Firm: **KOR GROUP - BOSTON, MA**
Creative Team: **JAMES GRADY, MB JAROSIK, LEN RUBENSTEIN, PETER HOWARD, KATHLEEN THURSTON-LIGHTY, ROBERT THURSTON-LIGHTY**
Client: **EMERSON COLLEGE**

Creative Firm: **DD+A - OMAHA, NE**
Client: **HORNIG COMPANIES**

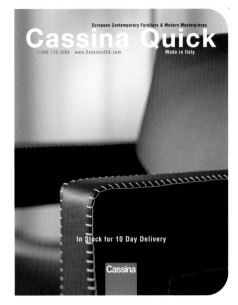

 Creative Firm: **KAA DESIGN GROUP, INC. - GRAPHICS STUDIO - LOS ANGELES, CA**
Creative Team: **MELANIE ROBINSON, CHRISTINA CHENG, LOUIS-PHILIPPE CARRETTA**
Client: **MADISONS FOUNDATION**

Creative Firm: **JONES STUDIO LIMITED - STATEN ISLAND, NY**
Creative Team: **PUI-PUI LI, ERIC JONES**
Client: **CASSINA USA**

Creative Firm: **PEAK SEVEN ADVERTISING - DEERFIELD BEACH, FL**
Creative Team: **JONATHAN BERG**
Client: **P&H INTERIORS**

Creative Firm: **E-GRAPHICS COMMUNICATIONS - TOKYO, JAPAN**
Creative Team: **TOMOHIRA KODAMA, SEIICHI YAMASHITA, CHIEKO IZUMI,
NOBUHIRO YAMAGUCHI, YUMIKO KAWASHIMA, KOUJI BABA**
Client: **NISSAN MOTOR COMPANY**

45

Creative Firm: **VOICEBOX CREATIVE - SAN FRANCISCO, CA**
Creative Team: **KRISTIE WISE, JACQUES ROSSOUW, AVIS MANDEL**
Client: **FOSTER'S WINE ESTATES**

Creative Firm: **KINDRED DESIGN STUDIO, INC. - HINESBURG, VT**
Creative Team: **STEVE REDMOND, JIM WESTPHALEN**
Client: **VASA, INC.**

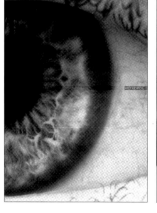

Creative Firm: **HORNALL ANDERSON DESIGN WORKS - SEATTLE, WA**
Creative Team: **JACK ANDERSON, KATHY SAITO, HAYDEN SCHOEN,
ELMER DELA CRUZ, CHRIS FREED, JOHN KOVAL**
Client: **CITATIONSHARES**

Creative Firm: **FUTURA DDB - LJUBLANA, SLOVENIA**
Creative Team: **ZARE KERIN**
Client: **METROPOLIS**

 Creative Firm: **E-GRAPHICS COMMUNICATIONS - TOKYO, JAPAN**
Creative Team: **TOMOHIRA KODAMA, FUYUKI OGINO, REIKO TASHIRO, ONE OR EIGHT GRAPHIC, CHIKARA KITABATAKE**
Client: **NISSAN MOTOR COMPANY**

Creative Firm: **SILVER CREATIVE GROUP - SOUTH NORWALK, CT**
Creative Team: **SUZANNE PETROW**
Client: **ROCKROSE DEVELOPMENT CORP.**

Creative Firm: **SIGNATURE ADVERTISING - DENVER, CO**
Creative Team: **DAVE PICCONE, LISA ORLOWSKI**
Client: **RIVERSTONE RESIDENTIAL**

Creative Firm: **DAVIS DESIGN PARTNERS - HOLLAND, OH**
Creative Team: **MATT DAVIS, KAREN DAVIS, GABRIEL AMADEAUS COONEY, JOSEPH W. DARWAL, SUSAN MOYSE, SUSAN SCHERVISH**
Client: **UNIVERSITY SCHOOL**

Creative Firm: **VOICEBOX CREATIVE - SAN FRANCISCO, CA**
Creative Team: **DAVID MURO, JACQUES ROSSOUW, GINA SATTA, GRADY MCFERRIN, TUCKER AND HOSSLER, ELLEN HALL**
Client: **CODORNÍU, S.A.**

Creative Firm: **E-GRAPHICS COMMUNICATIONS - TOKYO, JAPAN**
Creative Team: **TOMOHIRA KODAMA, YASUHIKO YOSHIDA, CHIEKO IZUMI, MINORU KAWASAKI, WOOD, YOSUKE NAKAJIMA**
Client: **NISSAN MOTOR COMPANY**

Creative Firm: **SUKA DESIGN - NEW YORK, NY**
Creative Team: **BRIAN WONG**
Client: **SOCIETY OF LINCOLN CENTER**
WWW.FILMLINC.COM

 Creative Firm: **E-GRAPHICS COMMUNICATIONS - TOKYO, JAPAN**
Creative Team: **TOMOHIRA KODAMA, YASUYUKI NAGATO, JUNICHI YOKOYAMA, HIROYUKI ARAI, NAOYA MIKI, CHIKARA KITABATAKE**
Client: **NISSAN MOTOR COMPANY**

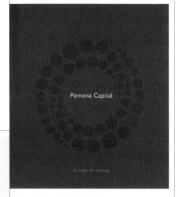

Creative Firm: **E-GRAPHICS COMMUNICATIONS - TOKYO, JAPAN**
Creative Team: **TOMOHIRA KODAMA, YOSHIHIRO MIMURA,**
MAO TAKAHASHI, LIVERO CREATIVE, EDDY KOHLI
Client: **NISSAN MOTOR COMPANY**

Creative Firm: **SUKA DESIGN - NEW YORK, NY**
Creative Team: **BRIAN WONG**
Client: **POMONA CAPITAL**
WWW.POMONACAPITAL.COM

Creative Firm: **HORNALL ANDERSON DESIGN WORKS - SEATTLE, WA**
Creative Team: **MICHAEL MARTINEZ, KATIE PHIPPS, SALLY BERGESEN**
Client: **VSP**

Creative Firm: **LISKA + ASSOCIATES - CHICAGO, IL**
Creative Team: **TANYA QUICK, JENN CASH, JASMINE PROBST, SEAN KENNEDY SANTOS**
Client: **LEVIEV FULTON CLUB**

Creative Firm: **DEFTELING DESIGN - PORTLAND, OR**
Creative Team: **ALEX WIJNEN**
Client: **CECILY INK**

As a brand new, start-up greeting card manufacturer, Portland, Oregon-based Cecily Ink faced a daunting task of creating budget-friendly business cards that would still reflect the artistic style of their greeting cards. They turned to creative firm Defteling Design for an innovative solution that wouldn't break the bank OR sacrifice style.

Defteling Design created business card concepts inspired by the patterns used in Cecily Ink's paper products. To save cost, they flooded one side of the business card with color and pattern while leaving the second side blank. This way, the business cards could be ganged up with the company's single-sided greeting card print run, making them cheaper to print.

The logo and main contact information were designed to print on label stock to they, too, could be printed more cheaply by being ganged up with labels used for product packaging. The narrow stickers were then applied by hand to the fount of the cards and wrapped to the back.

The overall result was a series of very economical, yet visually powerful business cards.

The Ⓟ *symbol designates a Platinum Award Winner, our Best in Category.*

Creative Firm: **TACTICAL MAGIC - MEMPHIS, TN**
Creative Team: **BEN JOHNSON, TRACE HALLOWELL**
Client: **FOLK INVESTMENT COMPANY**
WWW.TACTICALMAGIC.COM

Creative Firm: **THE UXB - BEVERLY HILLS, CA**
Creative Team: **NJ GOLDSTON, GLENN SAKAMOTO,**
MYLA ECONOMOUS
Client: **SWATFAME**

Creative Firm: **CYAN CONCEPT INC. - JONQUIÈRE, QC**
Creative Team: **VALÉRIE LAPORTE**
Client: **CYAN CONCEPT**

Creative Firm: **LEIBOWITZ COMMUNICATIONS - NEW YORK, NY**
Creative Team: **RICK BARGMANN, SHUO MENG**
Client: **LEIBOWITZ COMMUNICATIONS**

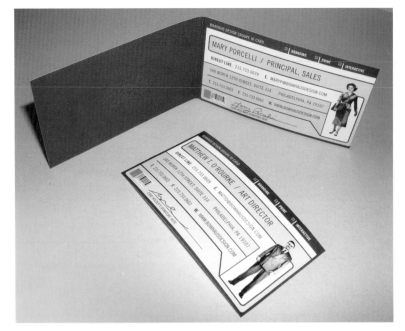

 Creative Firm: **BOWHAUS DESIGN GROUPE - PHILADELPHIA, PA**
Creative Team: **MATT O'ROURKE, MARY PORCELLI, CALHOUN**
Client: **BOWHAUS DESIGN GROUPE**

Creative Firm: **ELLEN BRUSS DESIGN - DENVER, CO**
Creative Team: **ELLEN BRUSS, JORGE LAMORA**
Client: **CHAMA COCINA MEXICANA Y TEQUILERIA**

 Creative Firm: **MEHUL DESIGNS - SUWANEE, GA**
Creative Team: **MEHUL PAREKH, NITA PAREKH**
Client: **MEHUL DESIGNS**

Creative Firm: **ELLEN BRUSS DESIGN - DENVER, CO**
Creative Team: **ELLEN BRUSS, CHARLES CARPENTER, BATZORIG CHIMEDDORJ**
Client: **INFINEUM**
WWW.INFINEUMPROPERTIES.COM

Creative Firm: **PALIO - SARATOGA SPRINGS, NY**
Creative Team: **GUY MASTRION, TODD LAROCHE, RAFAEL HOLGUIN, JENNIFER ASSELTA, MIREK JANCZUR, PETER O'TOOLE**
Client: **PALIO**

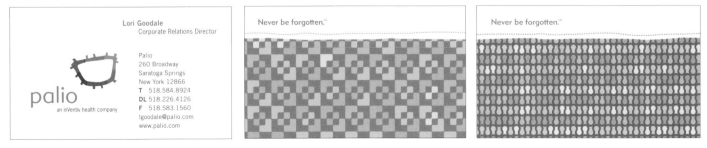

Creative Firm: **FRIBERGBASSETT - SAINT PAUL, MN**
Creative Team: **BARBARA BUHN FRIBERG, MICHELE BASSETT**
Client: **KEY SURGICAL, INC.**

Before updating Key Surgical's product catalog, creative firm FribergBassett created a new logo and identity system for the company. They then incorporated these items, along with a newly established color palette, into the product catalog.

The catalog features over 1,100 unique—and ever changing—products, as well as employee bios. The main intent was to create a catalog that was straightforward, yet engaging and easy to navigate. Certain products needed to be featured to scale so customers could easily identify size and shape, and orders would be more accurate.

FribergBassett admits that creating the pagination for 1,100 unique products was a challenge, especially since new products were constantly being added to the company's inventory. The fun part, they say, was reading the lively and revealing employee questionnaires, which were later adapted into employee bios.

The ⓟ symbol designates a Platinum Award Winner, our Best in Category.

Creativity 37 *Annual Awards* | **53**

Creative Firm: **CALAGRAPHIC DESIGN - ELKINS PARK, PA**
Creative Team: **RONALD J. CALA II, KATIE HATZ, JOE SCORSONE**
Client: **KATIE HATZ**

Creative Firm: **HBO OFF-AIR CREATIVE SERVICES - NEW YORK CITY, NY**
Creative Team: **VENUS DENNISON, CHRISTIAN MARTILLO**
Client: **HBO ENTERPRISES**

Creative Firm: **ROSKELLY, INC. - PORTSMOUTH, RI**
Creative Team: **THOMAS ROSKELLY, TIM SHIELDS**
Client: **CAPITAL MERCURY APPAREL**

Creative Firm: **BBK STUDIO - GRAND RAPIDS, MI**
Creative Team: **YANG KIM, MICHELE CHARTIER, ADAM RICE,
DEAN VAN DIS, KRISTIN TENNANT, JON POST**
Client: **IZZYDESIGN**

Creative Firm: **BRIAN J. GANTON & ASSOCIATES - CEDAR GROVE, NJ**
Creative Team: **BRIAN J. GANTON, JR., MARK GANTON, CHRISTOPHER GANTON**
Client: **OLDCASTLE GLASS**

Creative Firm: **ROSKELLY INC. - PORTSMOUTH, RI**
Creative Team: **THOMAS ROSKELLY, TIM SHEILDS**
Client: **CAPITAL MERCURY APPAREL**

Creative Firm: **ZUAN CLUB - TOKYO, JAPAN**
Creative Team: **AKIHIKO TSUKAMOTO, JUN HASEGAWA,**
NOBUHIRO NISHITAKATSUJI
Client: **DAZAIFU TENMANGU / TARO NASU GALLERY**

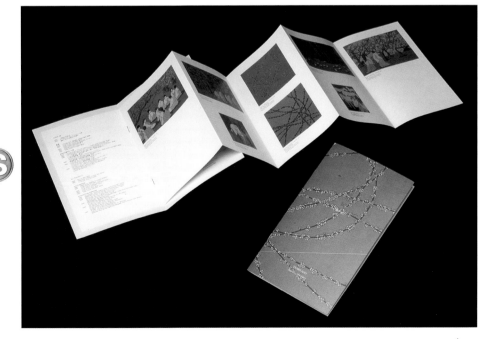

Creative Firm: **SCHOOL OF VISUAL ARTS - NEW YORK, NY**
Creative Team: **RICHARD WILDE, CHRISTOPHER AUSTOPCHUK,**
YELENA DEYNEKO, ADAM WAHLER
Client: **SCHOOL OF VISUAL ARTS**

The Senior Library 2006 is a collection of the best work created by seniors in the Advertising and Graphic Design department at the School of Visual Arts in New York.

In portfolio classes, students work with established professionals to develop concepts that are uniquely their own. The editor of the annual Senior Library selects from a wide variety of portfolios to create the book. It is mailed to members as well as current and prospective students.

This edition was designed by Christopher Austopchuck, a senior portfolio instructor, and includes work in several disciplines, including advertising, graphic design, typography, 3-D design and motion graphics.

The (P) *symbol designates a Platinum Award Winner, our Best in Category.*

Creative Firm: **CHEN DESIGN ASSOCIATES - SAN FRANCISCO, CA**
Creative Team: **JOSHUA CHEN, MAX SPECTOR**
Client: **STANFORD LIVELY ARTS**

Creative Firm: **Q - WIESBADEN, GERMANY**
Creative Team: **MATTHIAS FREY**
Client: **ANJA GOCKEL LONDON, ENGLAND**

Creative Firm: **ORANGESEED DESIGN - MINNEAPOLIS, MN**
Creative Team: **DAMIEN WOLF, TONJA LARSON, REBECCA AVIÑA,
ROB REBISCHKE, KELLY GORHAM, EMILY KREIS, KEITH LAUVER**
Client: **MONTANA LEGEND**

Creative Firm: **BACCARI/TANGRAM STRATEGIC DESIGN - NOVARA, ITALY**
Creative Team: **ALBERTO BACCARI, ENRICO SEMPI, ANNA GRIMALDI, ARCANGELO ARGENTO**
Client: **DAVIDE CENCI**

Creative Firm: **WALLACE CHURCH, INC. - NEW YORK, NY**
Creative Team: **STAN CHURCH, BIRD TUBKAM, RICH RICKABY**
Client: **WALLACE CHURCH, INC.**

This fun project involved designing an invitation to creative firm Wallace Church's annual summer Tuna Party, where fresh tuna is grilled for clients and friends.

For the 2006 Tuna Party, Wallace Church designed and "invitation" that featured an actual tuna can with a caricature of one of Wallace Church's two principals, Stan Church, printed on the label. They named the new product "Stan Kist Tuna."

Party details were printed to look like ingredients and nutritional facts. And sealed inside the can were five fun (but temporary) tattoos for guests to apply to themselves.

The (P) *symbol designates a Platinum Award Winner, our Best in Category.*

Creative Firm: **USE CREATIVE COMMUNICATION - HENDRIK IDO AMBACHT, NETHERLANDS**
Creative Team: **DENNIS BODMER, HENRIËTTE BODMER**
Client: **ACE EUROPEAN GROUP LTD**

Creative Firm: **ELLEN BRUSS DESIGN - DENVER, CO**
Creative Team: **ELLEN BRUSS, CHARLES CARPENTER**
Client: **MARK BROWN**

Creative Firm: **HILLTOP DESIGNS - TORONTO, ON**
Creative Team: **DAVID CORREIA**
Client: **MOIRA LAMB**

Creative Firm: **MAD DOG GRAPHX - ANCHORAGE, AK**
Creative Team: **KRIS RYAN-CLARKE**
Client: **WEST COAST PAPER**

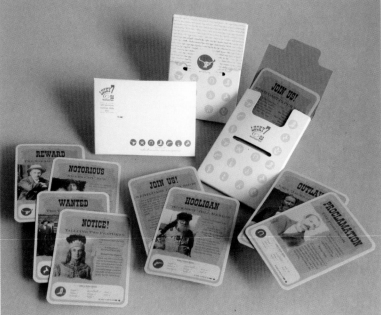

Creative Firm: **LEON MONTANA GRAPHIC DESIGN - BROOKLYN, NY**
Client: **TISCH**

THANKS FOR SENDING YOUR FRIENDS TO US
WE HOPE THAT THEY STILL SMILE WHEN THEY SEE YOU, WE DID SOME GOOD WORK ON THEM...

©CDN DENTAL ASSOCIATES

REMEMBER WHAT HAPPENED THE LAST TIME YOU MISSED YOUR DENTAL APPOINTMENT!?
JUST A FRIENDLY REMINDER FROM YOUR FRIENDLY DENTISTS.

©CDN DENTAL ASSOCIATES

HAVE YOU TRIED THE SQUEEZE-THE-NOZZLE METHOD... OR THE ROLL-FROM-END METHOD...
AND WHEN YOU GET TO THE BASH-WITH-HAMMER METHOD, YOU MIGHT CONSIDER MAKING AN APPOINTMENT.

©CDN DENTAL ASSOCIATES

DONUTS DONUTS SO NICE TO EAT LOVELY GOLDEN SOFT AND SWEET BUT THE NEXT TIME WHEN WE MEET YOUR ORAL HYGIENE WILL BE IN DEEP
HEY, WE'RE DENTISTS. MAKE AN APPOINTMENT.

©CDN DENTAL ASSOCIATES

Creative Firm: **MAD STUDIOS - HONG KONG**
Creative Team: **BRIAN YEE HUAN LAU, SARA PUI SIN LAIL**
Client: **CDN DENTAL ASSOCIATION**

Creative Firm: **LEVINE & ASSOCIATES - WASHINGTON, DC**
Creative Team: **GREG SITZMANN, LENA MARKLEY, MEGAN RIORDAN, KERRY MCCUTCHEON, TIERNEY SADLER**
Client: **LEVINE AND ASSOCIATES**

Creative Firm: **FITTING GROUP - PITTSBURGH, PA**
Creative Team: **TRAVIS NORRIS, ANDREW ELLIS**
Client: **WOMEN & GIRLS FOUNDATION**

Creative Firm: **QUIRST HAMILTON**
Creative Team: **SHEILA WOODBRIDGE**
Client: **ALYSON BURGESS & JOVICA MEDIC**

Creative Firm: **GEE + CHUNG DESIGN - SAN FRANCISCO, CA**
Creative Team: **EARL GEE, FANI CHUNG**
Client: **DCM**

Creative Firm: **CURIOSITY GROUP - PORTLAND, OR**
Creative Team: **YVONNE PEREZ-EMERSON, ALBERTO CERRITEÑO, LLOYD BAGTAS**
Client: **HEWLETT-PACKARD**

Creative Firm: **PEGGY LAURITSEN DESIGN GROUP - MINNEAPOLIS, MN**
Creative Team: **ANESSA MATTHEWS**
Client: **CHERYL VOLKMAN AND SCOTT KNIGHT**

Creative Firm: **WALLACE CHURCH, INC. - NEW YORK, NY**
Creative Team: **STAN CHURCH, JHONNY IRRAZABA**
Client: **WALLACE CHURCH, INC.**

Creative Firm: **BRIGHT RAIN CREATIVE - ST. LOUIS, MO**
Creative Team: **MATT MARINO, ANASTASIA HOLDWICK**
Client: **CHRIS & CHRISTINE MARSTALL**

Creative Firm: **TOM FOWLER, INC. - NORWALK, CT**
Creative Team: **ELIZABETH P. BALL, MARY ELLEN BUTKUS, BRIEN O'REILLY**
Client: **GUIDING EYES FOR THE BLIND**

Creative Firm: RASSMAN DESIGN - DENVER, CO
Creative Team: JENNIFER HARLOW, JOHN RASSMAN
Client: OPERA COLORADO

Creative Firm: FIDLER DESIGN INC. - MONCLOVA, OH
Creative Team: AMY FIDLER
Client: AMY & ANDREW FIDLER

Creative Firm: MTV NETWORKS - NEW YORK, NY
Creative Team: TERRY MCCORMICK, SUE KIM, JUNICHI NAKANE
Client: NICKTOONS NETWORK

Creative Firm: GEE + CHUNG DESIGN - SAN FRANCISCO, CA
Creative Team: EARL GEE, FANI CHUNG
Client: DCM

Creative Firm: BELYEA - SEATTLE, WA
Creative Team: PATRICIA BELYEA, RON LARS HANSEN, AARON CLIFFORD
Client: COLORGRAPHICS

Creative Firm: **CHEN DESIGN ASSOCIATES - SAN FRANCISCO, CA**
Creative Team: **JOSHUA CHEN, MAX SPECTOR**
Client: **STANFORD LIVELY ARTS**

Creative Firm: **HORNALL ANDERSON DESIGN WORKS - SEATTLE, WA**
Creative Team: **LISA CERVENY, JANA NISHI, MICHAEL CONNORS,**
ANDREW WICKLUND, BELINDA BOWLING, HANS KREBS
Client: **HORNALL ANDERSON DESIGN**

Creative Firm: **ELLEN BRUSS DESIGN - DENVER, CO**
Creative Team: **ELLEN BRUSS, CHARLES CARPENTER**
Client: **BROWN AND TEDSTROM**

Creative Firm: **WINSPER INC. - BOSTON, MA**
Creative Team: **STEVE BAUTISTA, BRIAN FANDETTI, KEVIN CIMO, KAITY MALONEY,**
GEORGE PETRAKIS, PATSY BURKE
Client: **EVERYTHING BUT THE DOG**

Creative Firm: **ZUAN CLUB - TOKYO, JAPAN**
Creative Team: **AKIHIKO TSUKAMOTO**
Client: **NADIFF / TARO NASU GALLERY**

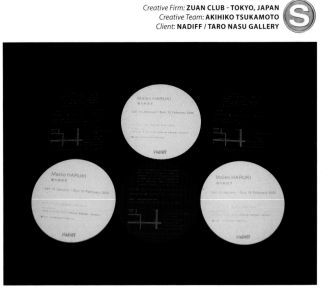

The challenge

was to restore relevance to a formerly iconic brand that, during the 80s, had slipped into retail private label status.

The solution was to re-launch the Perry Ellis brand by appealing to American men who wanted to dress as adults without becoming overly metro-sexual.

To do so, New York creative firm MFP, created stories that accurately reflected the lives of the target market. Executed without photography, the engaging stories were told in non-fashion magazines, newspapers and outdoor locations.

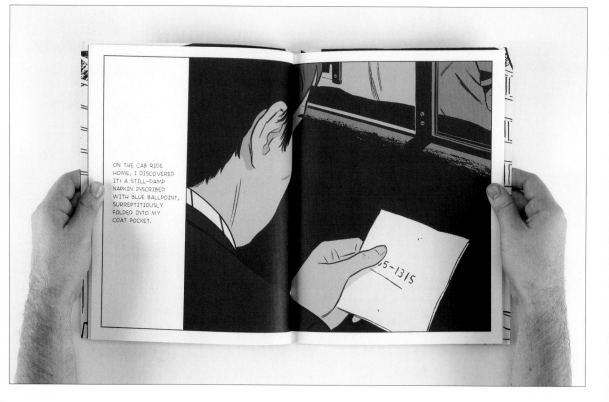

Creative Firm: **MFP - NEW YORK, NY**
Creative Team: **NEIL POWELL, JOSH ROGERS, MARK SLOAN**
Client: **PERRY ELLIS**

Creative Firm: **DARLING DESIGN - NEW YORK, NY**
Creative Team: **COURTNEY DARLING, SARAH SKAPIK**
Client: **HINT WATER**

Creative Firm: **THE COLLEGE OF SAINT ROSE - ALBANY, NY**
Creative Team: **MARK HAMILTON, BERMUDA CHRIS PARODY,**
LISA HALEY THOMSON, JOHN BACKMAN,
GREGORY CHERIN, GARY GOLD
Client: **THE COLLEGE OF SAINT ROSE**
WWW.STROSE.EDU/VIEWBOOK

Creative Firm: **DIALOG ABC LTD - LONDON, ENGLAND**
Creative Team: **DAVID LOCK, MERVYN RAND,**
MARCEL FEIGEL, JENNIFER GREEN
Client: **NORTEL**

Dior
The New Look

Creative Firm: **SGDP - CHICAGO, IL**
Creative Team: **ALBENA IVANOVA**
Client: **CHICAGO HISTORY MUSEUM**
WWW.SGDP.COM

Creative Firm: **WE ARE GIGANTIC - NEW YORK, NY**
Creative Team: **NEIL POWELL, JOSH ROGERS, BRAD DIXON, KRISTOFER DELANEY, MARY WILLIAMS**
Client: **MIKE'S HARD LEMONADE**

Creative Firm: **EMERSON, WAJDOWICZ STUDIOS - NEW YORK, NY**
Creative Team: **JUREK WAJDOWICZ, LISA LAROCHELLE, YOKO YOSHIDA, MANNY MENDEZ**
Client: **JULIUS BLUM & CO. INC.**

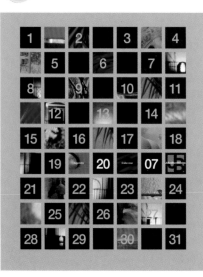

Creative Firm: **RULE29 - GENEVA, IL**
Creative Team: **JUSTIN AHRENS, KERRI LIU, JOSH JENSEN**
Client: **AMERICAN RED CROSS**

Creative Firm: **DEVON ENERGY - OKLAHOMA CITY, OK**
Creative Team: **TIM LANGENBERG, CHIP MINTY,
ALESHA LEEMASTER**
Client: **DEVON ENERGY CORPORATION**

Creative Firm: **RUDER FINN - NEW YORK, NY**
Creative Team: **MICHAEL SCHUBERT, LISA GABBAY, KEI CHAN, DIANA YEO,
EMILY KORSMO, MARYANN CAMMARATA**
Client: **NOVARTIS**

Creative Firm: **KISSCHASEY - MELBOURNE, AUSTRALIA**
Creative Team: **DEAN PARROTT, CAMERON BEST**
Client: **PPG**

Creative Firm: **M/C/C - DALLAS, TX**
Creative Team: **GREG HANSEN, TODD BRASHEAR,
HILLARY BOULDEN, AMANDA MYERS**
Client: **BCCK**

Creative Firm: **SKIDMORE - ROYAL OAK, MI**
Creative Team: **LAURA LYBEER-HILPERT**
Client: **EPRIZE**

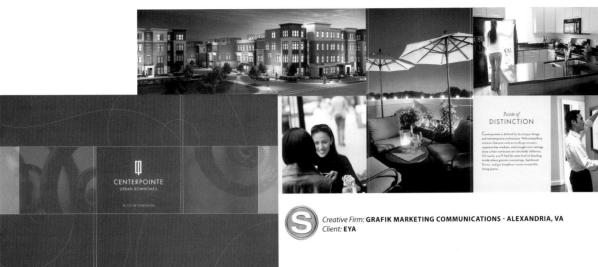

United (States), made easy.

UNITED

A STAR ALLIANCE MEMBER

San Diego
California

The sky is open, and so are the possibilities. Bright, mild weather, long beaches and exquisite natural beauty are just a small part of what makes San Diego so amazing. A comfy flight is the perfect way to begin and end the ideal vacation to sunny Southern California. Which is why so many people travel with United.

Where the wild things are
One of the best in the world, the renowned San Diego Zoo is home to some of the most rare and exotic animals in the world, including giant pandas, apes, polar bears and rainforest birds.

Delightful diversions
Shop in glamorous La Jolla, party in Pacific Beach and soak up the sun in Ocean Beach. In the winter, take a cruise out into the Pacific to see whales at play.

Entertainment for everyone
Fifteen museums, lush gardens, family-friendly exhibits and theaters make up the city's famous Balboa Park. As America's largest cultural urban park, this is definitely a must-see attraction.

Diamonds are forever
Since 1876, beautiful Kapi'olani Park has delighted visitors who hike around the magnificent Diamond Head crater, watch the famous Kodak Hula Show and enjoy the park's 100-year old trees.

Honolulu
Hawaii

Dream under the palms on bright white beaches, trek through tropical rainforests, and experience one of the friendliest places on Earth. "Aloha," Hawaii's capital city welcomes you. United can take you there.

A tribute at sea
Located literally on the water in Pearl Harbor, the breathtaking, historic World War II USS Arizona Memorial commemorates a somber moment in American history.

Fun in the sun, sand and surf
Waikiki Beach is a two-mile stretch of crystal shore world-renowned as a surfing, snorkeling, canoeing and sunbathing paradise. Deluxe hotels and restaurants face the exquisite turquoise water.

Portland
Oregon

Welcome to America's "Green City." Portland's known for friendly people, open spaces and a relaxed way of life. United invites you to take it easy and take it in. This is the perfect balance of man and nature, a thriving city within a flourishing wilderness.

The jewel of the city
With numerous sidewalk cafes and restaurants, charming art galleries and unique boutiques all in one place, the historic industrial Pearl District is a prime feature of the city.

Into the woods
Kids will love experiencing the Pacific Northwest forests in the World Forestry Center's newly renovated Discovery Museum. Visitors can crawl through a nurse log, melt the woods and learn how to plant a tree.

Seattle
Washington

Soothe your senses. It starts the moment you step aboard any United flight and continues amidst the grandeur of the Pacific Northwest—a destination truly in a class by itself. Experience first-hand Seattle's breathtaking natural scenery, Northwestern culture and myriad outdoor activities.

Start fresh
Explore Pike Place Market, America's oldest continually operating farmers' market, featuring more than 300 shops and restaurants, 100 farmers, 150 craftspeople and 80 street performers.

Stop and smell the roses
One of the largest and oldest gardens of its kind, the International Rose Test Garden provides more than a glorious array of the most romantic of flowers. It also offers brilliant scenic views of the skyline.

Go skyscraping
Take a ride to the top of the Space Needle. Built for the 1962 World Expo, this distinctive tower rises high above the city and offers 360-degree views of downtown Seattle, Mount Rainier and Elliott Bay.

On the waterfront
See the city surrounded by water from the deck of a fabulous harbor cruise. Or take a close-up look at Northwest marine life at Seattle's highly acclaimed Aquarium.

For more information visit seeamerica.org

10

We can take you there.

Dream big. The great States await, and one airline is dedicated to making your journey simply unforgettable. Which is why, as a member of the Star Alliance® network, reaching over 800 destinations in 152 countries, United proudly offers unparalleled access around the globe. So no matter where you're starting from, when you're headed to the U.S., United is, above and beyond, the best way to fly. Once you're here, we can take you from state to state and coast to coast with routes to hundreds of destinations nationwide.

Experience what makes America one of the best destinations on the planet. This United Destinations Guide features some of the best places to go and things to do throughout the country. Discover even more at SeeAmerica.org, the U.S. travel industry's official website, including information about festivals, attractions, hotels, restaurants and shopping. Plus, find a wealth of planning tools, from maps to suggested itineraries to weather reports at your fingertips. Visit SeeAmerica.org today.

West region Pages 3—8
Mountain region Pages 11—16
Central region Pages 17—22
East region Pages 23—31
United products and services Pages 29—32

Creative Firm: **SGDP – CHICAGO, IL**
Creative Team: **ALBENA IVANOVA, STEVE BATTERSON**
Client: **UNITED AIRLINES**
WWW.SGDP.COM

Creative Firm: **GRAFIK MARKETING COMMUNICATIONS - ALEXANDRIA, VA**
Client: **EYA**

Creative Firm: **FONA INTERNATIONAL INC. - GENEVA, IL**
Creative Team: **SHEILA BERNAL RAY, CARA NEWKIRK, BARB PUGESEK, TRACY CESARIO**
Client: **FONA INTERNATIONAL**

FLAVOR TRENDS
FONA INTERNATIONAL

Icons Plus

In the world of flavors, there are several icons—the untouchable favorites.

These include flavors such as chocolate, vanilla, orange, cherry, lime, and strawberry. Transcending the classics, however, is an ensemble of varietals or preparations that offer consumers a familiar but fascinating experience.

Examples of these Icons Plus include a range of flavors from the familiar French vanilla flavored ingredients, such as Belgian cinnamon.

The proliferation of these flavors is fueled by the increased flavor complexity and variety demanded by the premiumization of the food and beverage market, the increased competition among food and beverage companies to distinguish their products in the market, and the increased influence of culinary arts on mainstream consumer attitudes.

Premium Trends

It's time to trade up!

However, we don't need an expensive car or an exotic vacation to experience luxury, when we can have a taste of luxury every day with the growing variety of premium food and beverage products available.

The growth of the premium food and beverage markets is sharp, and estimated to continue. Datamonitor has projected the value of the specialty food and drinks market in the United States and Europe to reach USD 119 billion by 2009. This trend is catching on in Asia

as well, as the number of premium product introductions has increased by 124% since 2003, according to new products tracked in Datamonitor ProductScan Online.

So where is all this coming from? First, consider the fascination with the culinary arts. Chefs are celebrities, and everyone has a favorite. These personalities have brought new ingredients into our kitchens and a new enthusiasm for taste sophistication. Next, the proliferation of specialty retail has created even more experiences for consumers to trade up to higher-quality fare, often with a fresh, artisan, exotic or organic presentation.

Our increasing fascination with fine cuisine and specialty retail has prompted mainstream dining and retail channels

to raise the bar on propositions. For example, in recent years store brands have gone beyond bold and simply packaged knockoffs. Now many mainstream food retailers have added a new tier with an exclusive store brand of premium goods. These changes have brought premium to a mass-market scale and we can expect consumers to keep eating it up.

The following flavors encompass the premiumization of food and drinks with flavors that are either popular in premium products or inspired by a premium taste experience.

FONA INTERNATIONAL

Creative Firm: **SGDP - CHICAGO, IL**
Creative Team: **JILL WINDOW, KEVIN KLEBER**
Client: **UNITED AIRLINES**
WWW.SGDP.COM

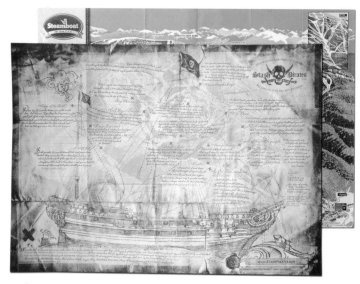

Creative Firm: **RASSMAN DESIGN - DENVER, CO**
Creative Team: **JONATHAN WHEELER, JOHN RASSMAN, ANDY SCHNEIDER**
Client: **STASH PIRATES**

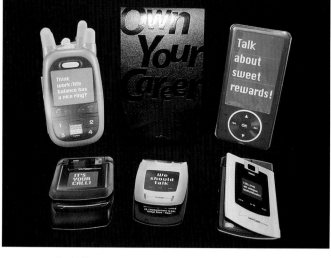

Creative Firm: **NAS RECRUITMENT COMMUNICATIONS - CLEVELAND, OH**
Creative Team: **JAMES HERRINGSHAW, JENNIFER DOOP,**
CHARLES KAPEC, DAVID FIRESTONE
Client: **VERIZON WIRELESS**

Creative Firm: **BELYEA - SEATTLE, WA**
Creative Team: **PATRICIA BELYEA, RON LARS HANSEN,**
AARON CLIFFORD
Client: **WEYERHAEUSER**

Creative Firm: **ADDISON - NEW YORK, NY**
Creative Team: **CHRISTINA ANTONOPOULOS,**
RICHARD COLBOURNE, DARIEN BIRKS
Client: **ISTAR FINANCIAL**
WWW.ISTARFINANCIAL.COM

iStar Financial is a finance company specializing in the commercial real estate industry.

This client asked Addison to create a concept that would work for both iStar's annual report and their print advertising. The new tagline "Return on Ideas" needed to be incorporated within both.

The result was a series of "visual returns" that served as a flag for key growth strategies in the annual report and key benefits in iStar's advertising.

By creating a luxurious and innovative feel, the campaign helped iStar establish a unique brand position within the REIT marketplace.

The (P) *symbol designates a Platinum Award Winner, our Best in Category.*

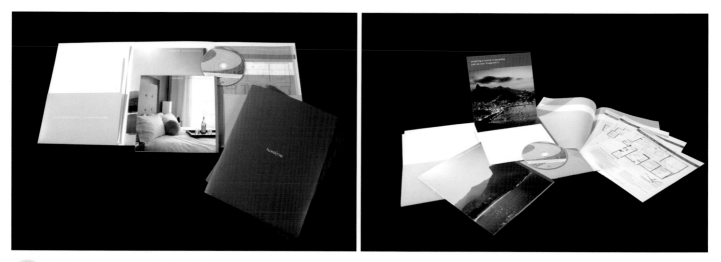

Creative Firm: **DARLING DESIGN - NEW YORK, NY**
Creative Team: **COURTNEY DARLING, SARAH SKAPIK**
Client: **LUXO|RIO CONDOMINIUMS**

Creative Firm: **TIME - NEW YORK, NY**
Creative Team: **LIZA GREENE, RAY RUALO**
Client: **TIME MAGAZINE**

Creative Firm: **PARADOWSKI CREATIVE - ST. LOUIS, MO**
Creative Team: **JOY MARCUS, MATTHEW EVANS**
Client: **MISSOURI BOTANICAL GARDEN**

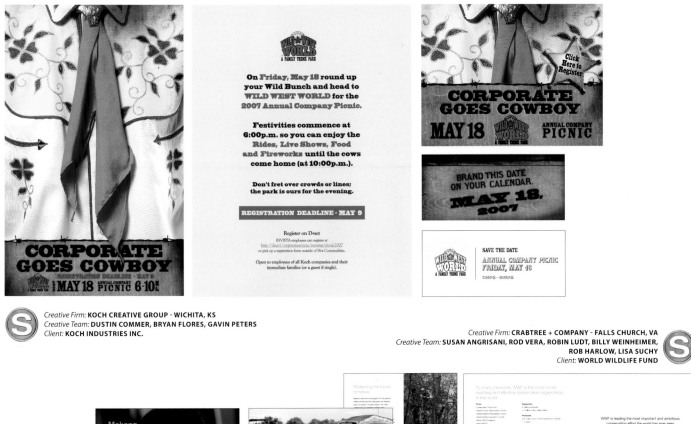

Creative Firm: **KOCH CREATIVE GROUP - WICHITA, KS**
Creative Team: **DUSTIN COMMER, BRYAN FLORES, GAVIN PETERS**
Client: **KOCH INDUSTRIES INC.**

Creative Firm: **CRABTREE + COMPANY - FALLS CHURCH, VA**
Creative Team: **SUSAN ANGRISANI, ROD VERA, ROBIN LUDT, BILLY WEINHEIMER, ROB HARLOW, LISA SUCHY**
Client: **WORLD WILDLIFE FUND**

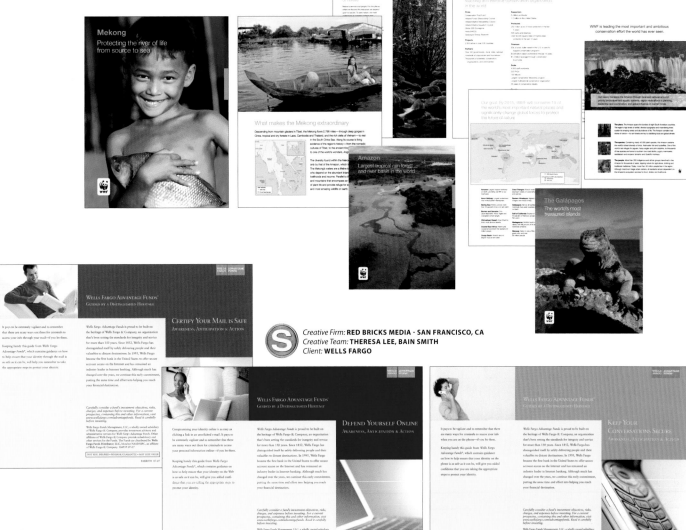

Creative Firm: **RED BRICKS MEDIA - SAN FRANCISCO, CA**
Creative Team: **THERESA LEE, BAIN SMITH**
Client: **WELLS FARGO**

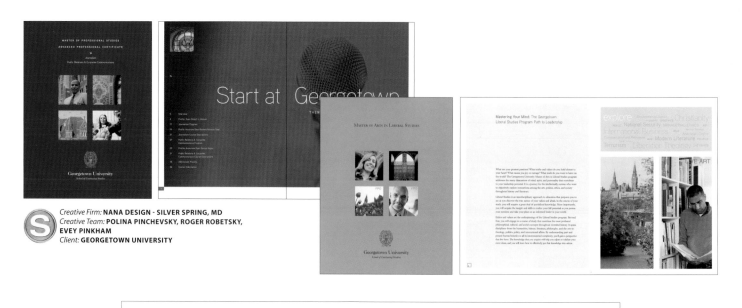

Creative Firm: **NANA DESIGN - SILVER SPRING, MD**
Creative Team: **POLINA PINCHEVSKY, ROGER ROBETSKY, EVEY PINKHAM**
Client: **GEORGETOWN UNIVERSITY**

Creative Firm: **G2 BRANDING AND DESIGN - NEW YORK, NY**
Creative Team: **VICTOR MAZZEO, PHIL KOUTSIS, MEGAN TRINIDAD, RAY MARRERO, ELINOR ZACH**
Client: **RAMADA**

Creative Firm: **SILVER COMMUNICATIONS INC - NEW YORK, NY**
Creative Team: **GREGG SIBERT, CHRISTINA WEISSMAN, NELIA VISHNEVSKY, CORIE WALLACE**
Client: **LOEB & TROPER LLP**

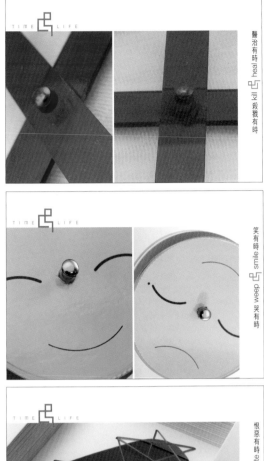

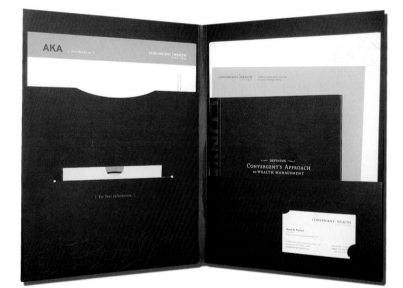

Creative Firm: **ZERO GRAVITY DESIGN GROUP - SMITHTOWN, NY**
Creative Team: **ZERO GRAVITY DESIGN GROUP**
Client: **DIRECT ACCESS PARTNERS**

Creative Firm: **AMEBA DESIGN LTD. - HONG KONG**
Creative Team: **GIDEON LAI**
Client: **6 SAID SHOW**

Creative Firm: **GRAFIK MARKETING COMMUNICATIONS - ALEXANDRIA, VA**
Creative Team: **JUDY KIRPICH, KRISTIN MOORE, MICHAEL MATEOS, CHRIS HONG**
Client: **CONVERGENT WEALTH ADVISORS**

Creative Firm: **FRANKE+FIORELLA - MINNEAPOLIS, MN**
Creative Team: **LESLIE MCDOUGALL, CRAIG FRANKE**
Client: **CHILDRENS CANCER RESEARCH FUND**

Novartis Brand Toolkit

When the Novartis Brand Identity was rolled out in March 2006, the brand ambassadors needed an instructional tool to both teach and implement the Novartis personality.

Ruder Finn Design created a comprehensive toolkit that was both highly instructional and allowed for consistent and compelling brand communications.

The boxed toolkit included a brand personality wheel, brand checklist, posters, a pen, brochures, a quick reference guide and a color palette booklet.

A series of three booklets showcasing the "Novartis Purpose, Aspiration and Strategy" was designed to slip into the front section of the toolkit after distribution.

A global mailing of 1,000 brand toolkits helped create and build support for the Novartis Brand Identity.

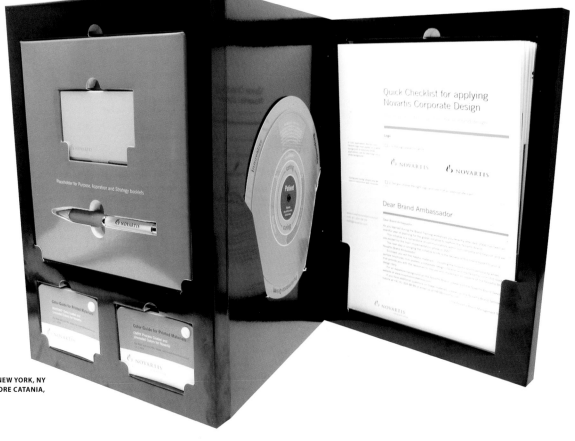

Creative Firm: **RUDER FINN DESIGN - NEW YORK, NY**
Creative Team: **LISA GABBAY, SALVATORE CATANIA, LAURA VINCHESI, DIANA YEO**
Client: **NOVARTIS**

The (P) *symbol designates a Platinum Award Winner, our Best in Category.*

Creative Firm: **KARACTERS DESIGN GROUP - VANCOUVER, BC**
Creative Team: **MARIA KENNEDY, JAMES BATEMAN, TIM HOFFPAUIR**
Client: **VANOC**

SIGNS, *SINGLE UNIT*

Creative Firm: **KARACTERS DESIGN GROUP - VANCOUVER, BC**
Creative Team: **JAMES BATEMAN, DAN O'LEARY**
Client: **VANOC AND OMEGA**

Live Well. Play Well. Dream Well.

Honolulu's first true luxury boutique hotel has arrived

hotel renew
129 Paoakalani Avenue
Waikiki Beach, Hawaii 96815
Tel: + 808.687.7715
www.hotelrenew.com

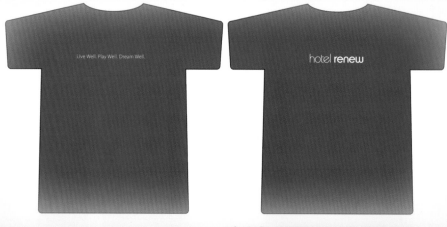

In response to a total renovation of Hotel Renew, John Wingard Design developed a complete brand package, repositioning the hotel as the premier boutique hotel in Waikiki. The brand packaging incorporated logo design, collateral, Web site, signage, apparel brand standards, stationery, in-room communication and marketing literature into a seamless experience for hotel guests.

Live Well. Play Well. Dream Well.

hotel renew

Creative Firm: **JOHN WINGARD DESIGN - HONOLULU, HI**
Creative Team: **JOHN WINGARD, BUD MUTH, SHEILA HODGES**
Client: **HOTEL RENEW**

Inspired by the hotel's modern interior design and rich colors, a full corporate identity package and brand overhaul was created. With the knowledge that the hotel guests are younger and more affluent business travelers, an identity based on contemporary design elements was conceived (no florals or rainbows).

The fresh solution reflects Hawaii's sense of place in a subtle, elegant manner while communicating an urban, cosmopolitan look and feel that's in keeping with the guest expectations and lifestyle.

The (P) *symbol designates a Platinum Award Winner, our Best in Category.*

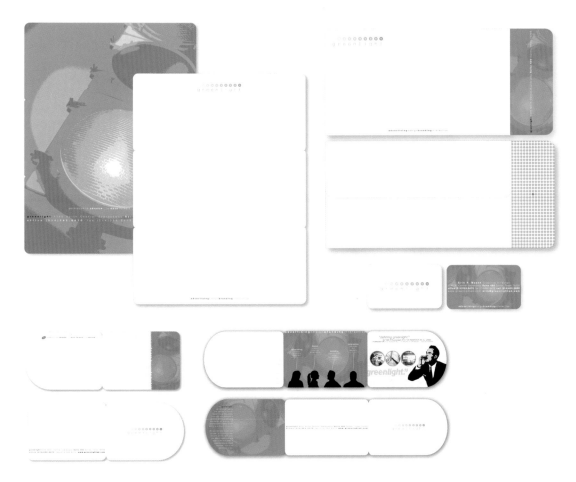

Creative Firm: **GREENLIGHT ADVERTISING - DALLAS, TX**
Creative Team: **ERIN RADICE MASON**
Client: **GREENLIGHT**
WWW.GREENLIGHTAD.COM

Creative Firm: **WINSPER INC. - BOSTON, MA**
Creative Team: **STEVE BAUTISTA, BRIAN FANDETTI, KEVIN CIMO, KAITY MALONEY,**
GEORGE PETRAKIS, PATSY BURKE
Client: **EVERYTHING BUT THE DOG**
WWW.EVERYTHINGBUTTHEDOG.NET

 Creative Firm: **KARACTERS DESIGN GROUP - VANCOUVER, BC**
Creative Team: **JAMES BATEMAN, TIM HOFFPAUIR, MARSHA LARKIN**
Client: **CANADIAN TOURISM COMMISSION**

Creative Firm: **FUTUREBRAND - NEW YORK, NY**
Creative Team: **PAUL GARDNER, REBECCA COBB,**
SCOTT WILLIAMS, ISABELLA OSSOTT
Client: **INTEL**

 Creative Firm: **CREATIVE COMPANY - MCMINNVILLE, OR**
Creative Team: **STEVE DONATELLI, JENNIFER LARSEN MORROW, RANDY THAEMERT, MIKE PEMBERTON**
Client: **CREATIVE COMPANY**

Creative Firm: **ADDISON - NEW YORK, NY**
Creative Team: **DAVID KOHLER, RICK SLUSHER, AIDAN GIUTTARI**
Client: **AES**
WWW.AES.COM

Creative Firm: **PURPLE CIRCLE - NOTTINGHAM, UNITED KINGDOM**
Creative Team: **SIMON HARRISON, JOHN LYLE, ABI JACKSON**
Client: **BEWILDERWOOD**

Creative Firm: **G2 BRANDING AND DESIGN - NEW YORK, NY**
Creative Team: **VICTOR MAZZEO, JASON BORZOUYEH**
Client: **BLUE STAR JETS**

Creative Firm: **TANGRAM STRATEGIC DESIGN/BARBERO DESIGN - NOVARO, ITALY**
Creative Team: **ENRICO SEMPI, ANTONELLA TREVISAN, FABRIZIO BARBERO**
Client: **HOTMAN**

Creative Firm: **LOOPMEDIA INC - TORONTO, ON** *Creative Team:* **AARON WHITE**
Client: **ROOSTER**

Creative Firm: **LEMLEY DESIGN COMPANY - SEATTLE, WA**
Creative Team: **DAVID LEMLEY, ENSI MOFASSER, COVENTRY JANKOWSKI**
Client: **SUR LA TABLE**

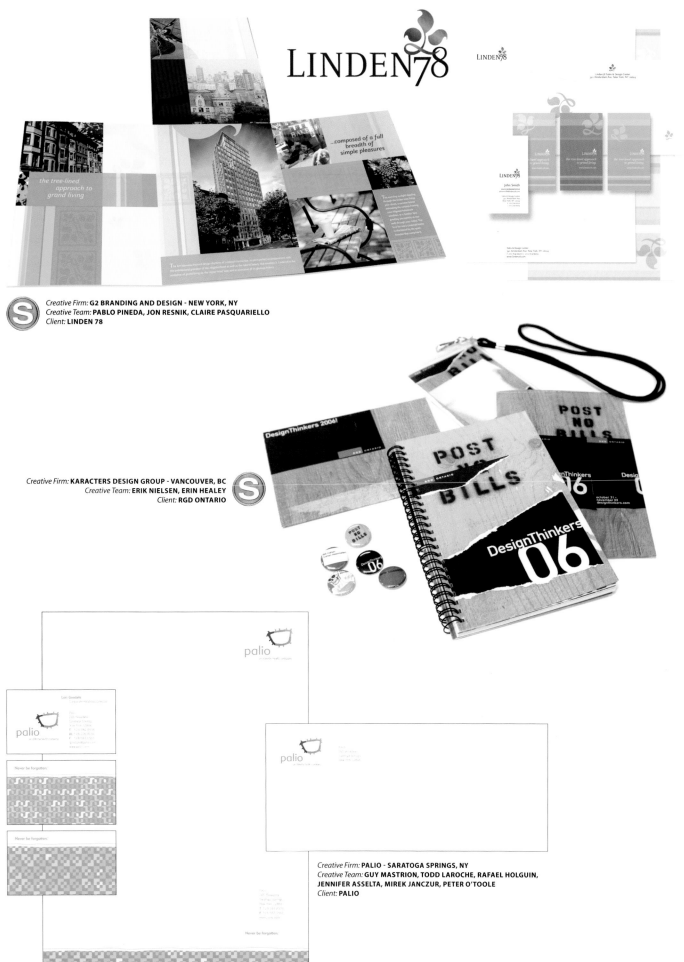

Creative Firm: **G2 BRANDING AND DESIGN - NEW YORK, NY**
Creative Team: **PABLO PINEDA, JON RESNIK, CLAIRE PASQUARIELLO**
Client: **LINDEN 78**

Creative Firm: **KARACTERS DESIGN GROUP - VANCOUVER, BC**
Creative Team: **ERIK NIELSEN, ERIN HEALEY**
Client: **RGD ONTARIO**

Creative Firm: **PALIO - SARATOGA SPRINGS, NY**
Creative Team: **GUY MASTRION, TODD LAROCHE, RAFAEL HOLGUIN,
JENNIFER ASSELTA, MIREK JANCZUR, PETER O'TOOLE**
Client: **PALIO**

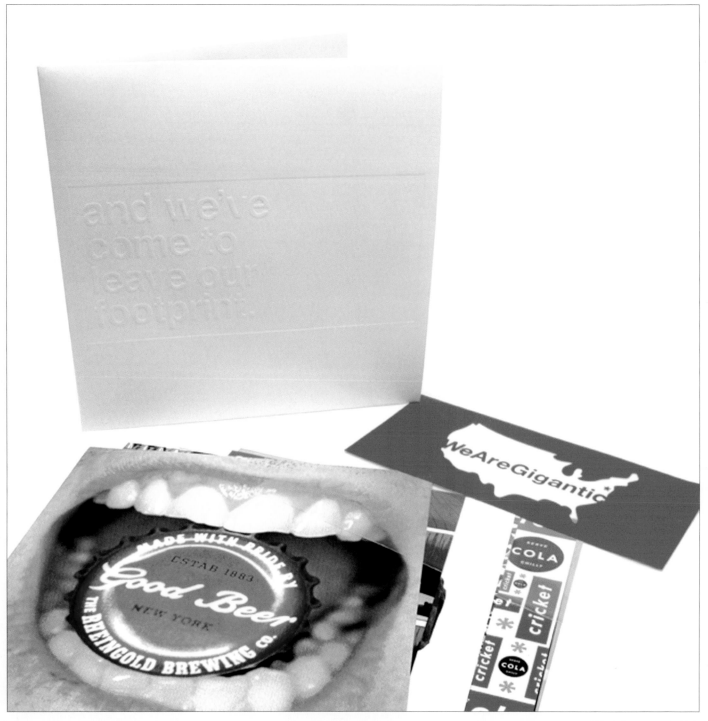

Creative Firm: **WEAREGIGANTIC - NEW YORK, NY**
Creative Team: **NEIL POWELL, JOSH ROGERS**
Client: **WEAREGIGANTIC**

Creative firm We Are Gigantic admits they are more of a 'musical band of outsiders' than an advertising agency. That's why creating their new business materials in the form of an LP, complete with full liner notes, was an obvious, yet still very creative choice.

The (P) *symbol designates a Platinum Award Winner, our Best in Category.*

Creative Firm: **PEGGY LAURITSEN DESIGN GROUP - MINNEAPOLIS, MN**
Creative Team: **BRIAN DANAHER, LAURA DOKKEN, JOHN HAINES, ANESSA MATTHEWS**
Client: **PEGGY LAURITSEN DESIGN GROUP**

Creative Firm: **GRAPHICULTURE - MINNEAPOLIS, MN**
Creative Team: **JANICE STANFORD, LINDSAY GICE, CHERYL WATSON, SELINA LARSEN**
Client: **GRAPHICULTURE**

Creative Firm: **ERIC CAI DESIGN CO. - BEIJING, CHINA**
Creative Team: **CAI SHI WEI, ERIC, TAN YAN, ESTHER**
Client: **ERIC CAI DESIGN CO.**

Creative Firm: **SKIDMORE - ROYAL OAK, MI**
Creative Team: **LIBBY COLE**
Client: **SKIDMORE**

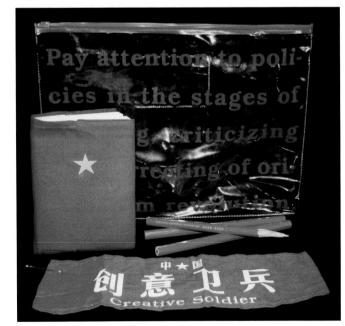

Saran Wrap

It's a Wrap!

Bubble Wrap

Creative Firm: **PARADOWSKI CREATIVE - ST. LOUIS, MO**
Creative Team: **ALEX PARADOWSKI, MATTHEW EVANS**
Client: **PARADOWSKI CREATIVE**

Creative Firm: **KOR GROUP - BOSTON, MA**
Creative Team: **JIM GIBSON, JAMES GRADY, DAN PERRERA, KJERSTIN WESTGAARD OH, RACHEL JOHNSON**
Client: **KOR GROUP**

Creative Firm: **MYTTON WILLIAMS - BATH, UNITED KINGDOM**
Creative Team: **BOB MYTTON, CHRIS ROBERTS**
Client: **MYTTON WILLIAMS**

Creative Firm: **BRAND NEW WORLD - NEW YORK, NY**
Creative Team: **MARK RISIS, ALAN SCHULMAN, MICHAEL MEIKSON, BRENT ALMOND**
Client: **THE NATURE CONSERVANCY**

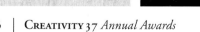

 Creative Firm: **VELOCITY DESIGN WORKS - WINNIPEG, MB**
Creative Team: **LASHA ORZECHOWSKI, LEIGH MCKENZIE**
Client: **VELOCITY DESIGN WORKS**

Creative Firm: **BBK STUDIO - GRAND RAPIDS, MI**
Creative Team: **YANG KIM, TIM CALKINS**
Client: **BBK STUDIO**

Creative Firm: **PENSARÉ DESIGN GROUP - WASHINGTON, DC**
Creative Team: **MARY ELLEN VEHLOW, AMY E. BILLINGHAM**
Client: **PENSARÉ DESIGN GROUP**

Creative Firm: **LAUNCH CREATIVE MARKETING - CHICAGO, IL**
Client: **LAUNCH CREATIVE MARKETING**

Creative Firm: **RED MEAT DESIGN - VENICE, CA**
Client: **RED MEAT DESIGN**

Creative Firm: **NASSAR DESIGN - BROOKLINE, MA**
Creative Team: **NELIDA NASSAR, GABRIELE ANGEVINE**
Client: **LEERS WEINZAPFEL ARCHITECTS**

Creative Firm: **JONI RAE AND ASSOCIATES - ENCINO, CA**
Creative Team: **JONI RAE RUSSELL, BEVERLY TRENGOVE**
Client: **JONI RAE AND ASSOCIATES**

Creative Firm: **HBO OFF-AIR CREATIVE SERVICES - NEW YORK CITY, NY**
Creative Team: **VENUS DENNISON, IVY CALAHORRANO, KATERINA TSIOROS**
Client: **HBO CREATIVE SERVICES**

Creative Firm: **CRABTREE + COMPANY - FALLS CHURCH, VA**
Creative Team: **SUSAN ANGRISANI, ROD VERA, LISA SUCHY**
Client: **CRABTREE+COMPANY**
WWW.CRABTREECOMPANY.COM

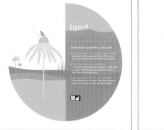

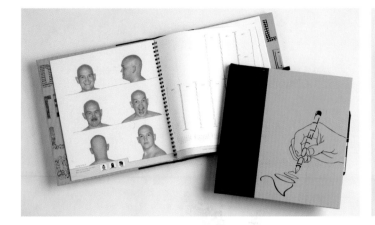

Creative Firm: **RULE29 - GENEVA, IL**
Creative Team: **JUSTIN AHRENS, KERRI LIU, JOSH JENSEN, KARA MERRICK**
Client: **RULE29**

Creative Firm: **BCN COMMUNICATIONS - CHICAGO, IL**
Creative Team: **JIM PITROSKI, ROB SQUIRE**
Client: **BCN COMMUNICATIONS**

Creative Firm: ELLEN BRUSS DESIGN - DENVER, CO
Creative Team: **ELLEN BRUSS, CHARLES CARPENTER**
Client: **ELLEN BRUSS DESIGN**
WWW.EBD.COM

Creative Firm: **Q - WIESBADEN, GERMANY**
Creative Team: **THILO VON DEBSCHITZ, MATTHIAS FREY, LAURENZ NIELBOCK,**
CHRISTOPH DAHINTEN, MARCEL KUMMERER, UTE DERSCH
Client: **Q**

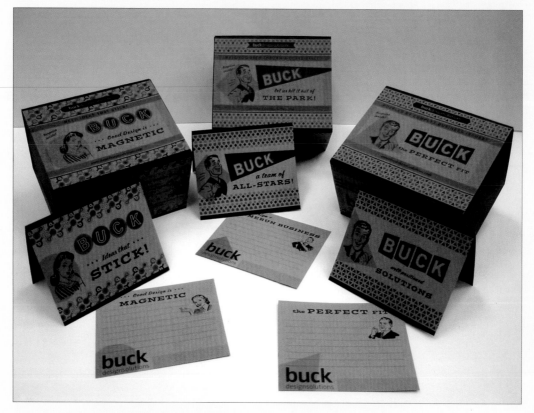

Creative Firm: **BUCK CONSULTANTS, AN ACS COMPANY - ST. LOUIS, MO**
Creative Team: **JENNIFER WHITLOW, STAN SAMS, MELISSA KRAMPER, DEBBIE ROBERTS, MARGARET CIARLEGLIO, BRADY MILLER (I DREAM SOLUTIONS), JACKIE STEWART (STEWART'S INCENTIVES)**
Client: **BUCK CONSULTANTS, AN ACS COMPANY**

Buck Consultants is a consulting firm specializing in human resources management, employee benefits, compensation and communications. Several of the firm's designers have a background in corporate communications, and Buck wanted to capitalize on that experience. To do so, Buck needed to position its design team as an entity in and of itself.

The intended audience for this direct mail campaign was a group of 2,000 client prospects, specifically senior-level marketing communications managers. The project was intended to be a fun, creative way to launch Buck Consultants into the design agency marketplace, and to differentiate the firm from other agencies. The objective was to be both whimsical and strategic.

The solution was a series of collectible toys (a magnetic acrobat, a puzzle, a customized baseball) featuring whimsical, retro design and smart, punchy copy that linked each toy to specific services. Inside each box, the toy was accompanied by a personalized note card and mini-brochure.

The firm originally intended to mail six boxes/toys but needed to scale back to three due to budget constraints. This did not hurt the campaign's effectiveness, however, as the pieces served as a foot in the door with several prospects and helped the sales force secure face-to-face meetings.

The **P** *symbol designates a Platinum Award Winner, our Best in Category.*

Creative Firm: **HAFENBRACK MARKETING - DAYTON, OH**
Creative Team: **JON BROOKS, DERICK MEYERS**
Client: **HAFENBRACK MARKETING**

Creative Firm: **30SIXTY ADVERTISING+DESIGN, INC. - STUDIO CITY, CA**
Creative Team: **HENRY VIZCARRA, PÄR LARSSON, DAVID FUSCELLARO, KASEY CHATILA, ERIC PEREZ, TUYET VONG**
Client: **30SIXTY ADVERTISING+DESIGN, INC.**

Creative Firm: **TORRE LAZUR MCCANN - PARSIPPANY, NJ**
Creative Team: **CHRISTOPHER BEAN, MARK OPPICI, JENNIFER ALAMPI, MARCIA GODDARD**
Client: **TORRE LAZUR MCCANN**

Creative Firm: **KINDRED DESIGN STUDIO, INC. - HINESBURG, VT**
Creative Team: **STEVE REDMOND**
Client: **KINDRED DESIGN STUDIO**

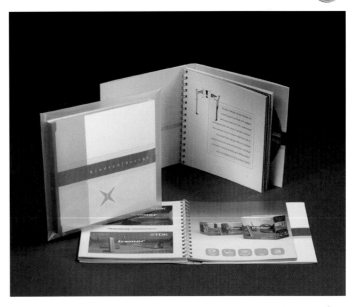

 Creative Firm: **NEALEDESIGN - WELLINGTON, NEW ZEALAND**
Creative Team: **DEBBIE NEALE**
Client: **NWT PUBLIC HEALTH**

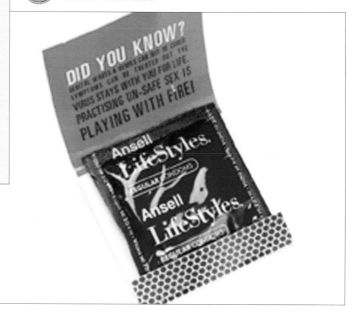

Creative Firm: **JACK NADEL INTERNATIONAL - LOS ANGELES, CA**
Creative Team: **JOSH EBRAHEMI**
Client: **MTV NETWORK**

Creative Firm: **SCHOOL OF VISUAL ARTS - NEW YORK, NY**
Creative Team: **RICHARD WILDE, CHRIS AUSTOPCHUK,**
YELENA DEYNEKO, ADAM WAHLER
Client: **SCHOOL OF VISUAL ARTS**

The Senior Library 2006 is a collection of the best work created by seniors in the Advertising and Graphic Design department at the School of Visual Arts in New York.

In portfolio classes, students work with established professionals to develop concepts that are uniquely their own. The editor of the annual Senior Library selects from a wide variety of portfolios to create the book. It is mailed to members as well as current and prospective students.

This edition was designed by Christopher Austopchuck, a senior portfolio instructor, and includes work in several disciplines, including advertising, graphic design, typography, 3D design and motion graphics.

The ⓟ symbol designates a Platinum Award Winner, our Best in Category.

Creative Firm: **ZEESMAN COMMUNICATIONS, INC. - BEVERLY HILLS, CA**
Creative Team: **AMBER PODRATZ, NANCY WINEBARGER**
Client: **W. M. KECK FOUNDATION**

Creative Firm: **PEGGY LAURITSEN DESIGN GROUP - MINNEAPOLIS, MN**
Creative Team: **BRIAN DANAHER**
Client: **PLATO LEARNING**

Creative Firm: **MEDIA CONSULTANTS - LYNDHURST, NJ**
Creative Team: **HARVEY HIRSCH, FILIPE VALENTE, BARRY GOULD**
Client: **DIGITAL DIMENSIONS3, INC.**

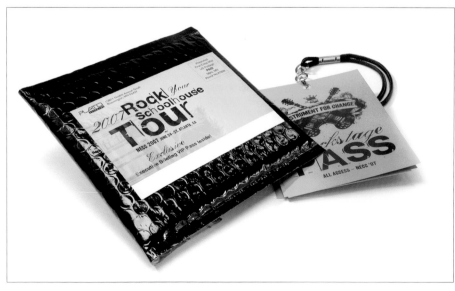

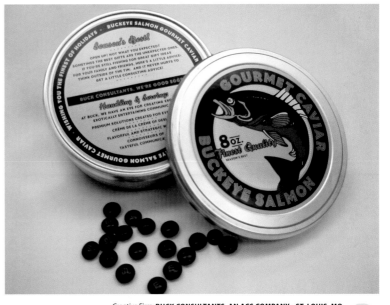

Creative Firm: **BUCK CONSULTANTS, AN ACS COMPANY - ST. LOUIS, MO**
Creative Team: **MELISSA KRAMPER, ELIZABETH LOHMEYER, DEBBIE ROBERTS, JAN BRIDGES, EBB WATSON (BENDER PRINTING)**
Client: **BUCK CONSULTANTS, AN ACS COMPANY**

Creative Firm: **GREENFIELD/BELSER LTD. - WASHINGTON, DC**
Creative Team: **BURKEY BELSER, MARGO HOWARD, JAIME CHIRINOS, DREW MAGARY**
Client: **GREENFIELD/BELSER, LTD.**

Creative Firm: **RAPP COLLINS CANADA - TORONTO, ON**
Creative Team: **SHELLEY SUTHERLAND, MARK PORTER, JAKE RITTER, ANDREA COOK, STEPHANIE BARBIERI, SUSAN POWELL**
Client: **UNILEVER CANADA**

This is an action for abandoned dogs rescuing.

The leaflet is pushed under the door.
When people come home they see a cute
puppy reminding them he could wait for them
anytime if they pick him up from the Association
for protection of abondoned dogs...

"Hi! My name is Max.
If you need someone to welcome you when
you come home, come to the Association for
protection of abandoned dogs Second
chance at 1. Stara Peščenica
Tel: 091 582 0073

And pick me up!"

Creative Firm: **BRUKETA & ZINIC OM - ZAGREB, CROATIA**
Creative Team: **DANIEL VUKOVIC, GOGA GOLIK**
Client: **DRUGA PRILIKA**

Creative Firm: **SPLASH PRODUCTIONS PTE LTD - SINGAPORE**
Creative Team: **NORMAN LAI, SERENE SEE**
Client: **SURBANA INTERNATIONAL CONSULTANTS PTE LTD**

Creative Firm: **TV LAND - NEW YORK, NY**
Client: **TV LAND**

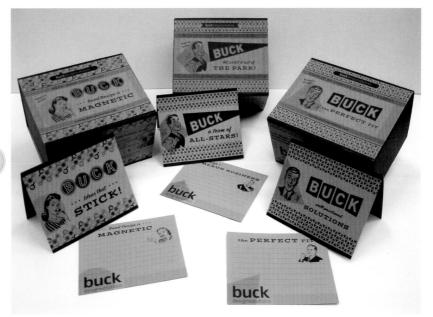

Creative Firm: **BUCK CONSULTANTS, AN ACS COMPANY - ST. LOUIS, MO**
Creative Team: **JENNIFER WHITLOW, STAN SAMS, MELISSA KRAMPER,**
DEBBIE ROBERTS, MARGARET CIARLEGLIO,
BRADY MILLER (I DREAM SOLUTIONS),
JACKIE STEWART (STEWART'S INCENTIVES)
Client: **BUCK CONSULTANTS, AN ACS COMPANY**

Creative Firm: **INTERROBANG DESIGN COLLABORATIVE, INC. - RICHMOND, VT**
Creative Team: **MARK SYLVESTER, ROBERT PACKERT, SHARON WHITE**
Client: **WHITE-PACKERT PHOTOGRAPHY**

Creative Firm: **MTV NETWORKS CREATIVE SERVICES - NEW YORK, NY**
Creative Team: **SCOTT WADLER, CHERYL FAMILY, ANDREW LOPEZ, CASEY STOCK, ROBERTA MINTZ,**
JOSEPH FIORDIMONDO, KEN SAJI, DAVID LANFAIR
Client: **MTV NETWORKS**

Creative Firm: **BRUKETA & ZINIC OM - ZAGREB, CROATIA**
Creative Team: **SLAVICA OLUJIC KLAPCIC, KRESIMIR TADIJA KAPULICA, DAVOR BRUKETA, NIKOLA ZINIC, MARCO ZANUSO**
Client: **PODRAVKA**

The food company Podravka is famous for its soup. For the company's annual party, creative firm Bruketa & Zinic decided to hold the event within a museum. They chose the location for one key reason: The museum is a circular-shaped building—a perfect fit for their plans.

They added extensions to make the building look like a cooking pot. Strategic lighting and overhead "steam" completed the effect. In nearby fountains, they placed giant spoons to mimic bowls of soup. The party itself was focused around different ingredients and food commonly used for making soup.

The biggest challenge was creating the 'handles' of the cooking pot on each side of the round building, since the museum building was extremely large. The technical and logistical aspect of creating and placing the extensions was an extensive and detailed project, but the results were spectacular.

The (P) *symbol designates a Platinum Award Winner, our Best in Category.*

Creative Firm: **BERRY DESIGN INC - ALPHARETTA, GA**
Creative Team: **BOB BERRY, CHIP WALLER**
Client: **POPEYES LOUISIANA KITCHEN**

Creative Firm: **STEPHEN LONGO DESIGN ASSOCIATES - WEST ORANGE, NJ**
Creative Team: **STEPHEN LONGO**
Client: **EKKO RESTAURANT**

Timberland Outdoor Performance

represents the extreme edge of the overall Timberland brand personality as it relates to the consumer, activities and its vigilance for environmental things. This 3,000 square foot exhibit was created by Michigan design firm JGA for the Outdoor Retailer Winter Market Tradeshow.

The exhibit conveyed its eco-friendly message through repurposed industrial objects and natural and recycled materials. Among the most visible components, shipping containers were repurposed to be used for ongoing shipping and storage, as well as for the booth's physical selling rooms. Significant use was made of "found," repurposed, recycled and reprocessed elements and materials. The outside of the booth features a 3-D "nutrition label," a signature element that is part of the Outdoor Performance packaging and is translated into a large panel element, highlighting the various materials and an environmental "scorecard" for full transparency and accountability.

The booth was constructed of 98% Earth-conscious materials, and 88% of the booth can be recycled at the end of its use.

Creative Firm: **JGA - SOUTHFIELD, MI**
Creative Team: **KEN NISCH, GORDON EASON**
Client: **THE TIMBERLAND COMPANY**

The ⓟ *symbol designates a Platinum Award Winner, our Best in Category.*

Creative Firm: **KIKU OBATA & COMPANY - ST. LOUIS, MO**
Creative Team: **KIKU OBATA, PAUL SCHERFLING, RUSSELL BUCHANAN, JR.,**
FARRAH KATZER, CARLA CRUZ, CAROLE JEROME, ITALY
Client: **BAKERS FOOTWEAR GROUP**

Creative Firm: **HORNALL ANDERSON DESIGN WORKS - SEATTLE, WA**
Creative Team: **JAMES TEE, MARK POPICH, ANDREW WELL, JON GRAEFF,**
ETHAN KELLER, JAVAS LEHN AND KALANI GREGOIRE
Client: **T-MOBILE**

Creative Firm: **JGA - SOUTHFIELD, MI**
Creative Team: **KEN NISCH, MIKE CURTIS, GEORGE VOJNOVSKI**
Client: **THE NORTH FACE**

Creative Firm: **HORNALL ANDERSON DESIGN WORKS - SEATTLE, WA**
Creative Team: **JAMIE AND CHRIS MONBERG, NATHAN YOUNG, JOSEPH KING, HANS KREBS, ADRIEN LO, COREY PAGANUCCI**
Client: **SPACE NEEDLE**

Creative Firm: **MTV NETWORKS - NEW YORK, NY**
Creative Team: **RICHARD BROWD, JIM DEBARROS**
Client: **MTV OFF-AIR CREATIVE**

Creative Firm: **JGA - SOUTHFIELD, MI**
Creative Team: **KEN NISCH, KATHI MCWILLIAMS, GEORGE VOJNOVSKI**
Client: **LENOX**

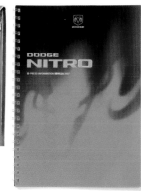

Creative Firm: **DESIGN HOCH DREI - STUTTGART, GERMANY**
Creative Team: **TOBIAS KOLLMANN, IOANNIS KARANASIOS, SANDY MANIG**
Client: **DAIMLERCHRYSLER**

Creative Firm: **M/C/C - DALLAS, TX**
Creative Team: **GREG HANSEN, TODD BRASHEAR, HILLARY BOULDEN, AMANDA MYERS**
Client: **GOALTENDER DEVELOPMENT INSTITUTE (GDI)**

Creative Firm: **PCBC® AND CHAMPION NATIONWIDE - SACRAMENTO, CA**
Creative Team: **CHRIS YOUNG, RÉMY FRANK, SUSAN BURCH**
Client: **PCBC® THE PREMIER BUILDING SHOW**

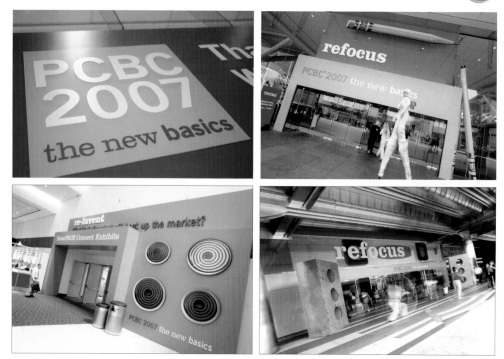

Creative Firm: **KOCH CREATIVE GROUP - WICHITA, KS**
Creative Team: **DUSTIN COMMER, PAUL CHAUNCEY**
Client: **KOCH INDUSTRIES, INC.**

Creative Firm: **FATHOM CREATIVE - WASHINGTON, DC**
Creative Team: **SHERI GRANT, CRAIG HILL, DREW MITCHELL, SHIKHA SAVDAS**
Client: **HISTORIC DUPONT CIRCLE**

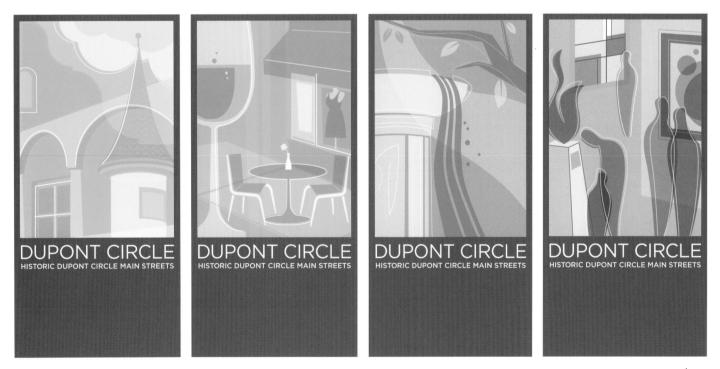

Creative Firm: **SAYLES GRAPHIC DESIGN - DES MOINES, IA**
Creative Team: **JOHN SAYLES**
Client: **CAMPBELL'S NUTRITION**

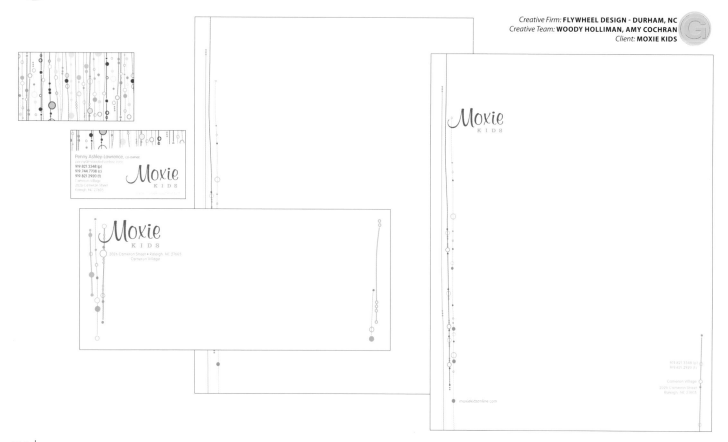

Creative Firm: **FLYWHEEL DESIGN - DURHAM, NC**
Creative Team: **WOODY HOLLIMAN, AMY COCHRAN**
Client: **MOXIE KIDS**

Creative Firm: **DESIGN SOURCE - APTOS, CA**
Creative Team: **CARI CLASS, STACEY BOSCOE**
Client: **DESIGN SOURCE**
WWW.DESIGNSOURCE.BIZ

Creative Firm: **HORNALL ANDERSON DESIGN WORKS - SEATTLE, WA**
Creative Team: **JACK ANDERSON, ANDREW WICKLUND, PETER ANDERSON,
ENSI MOFASSER, BELINDA BOWLING, KATHLEEN GIBSON**
Client: **MAJESTIC AMERICA LINE**

VIVENDI IS DERIVED FROM THE LATIN PHRASE FOR "LIVING." OFTEN USED TOGETHER IN ITS COMPOUND FORM AS "MODUS VIVENDI," IT MEANS MODE OF LIVING OR LIFESTYLE.

Creative Firm: **HELENA SEO DESIGN - SUNNYVALE, CA**
Creative Team: **HELENA SEO**
Client: **VIVENDI DEVELOPMENT**

Creative Firm: **KAA DESIGN GROUP, INC. - GRAPHICS STUDIO - LOS ANGELES, CA**
Creative Team: **MELANIE ROBINSON, ANNETTE LEE, LOUIS-PHILIPPE CARRETTA**
Client: **BROCKMEIER CONSULTING ENGINEERS, INC.**

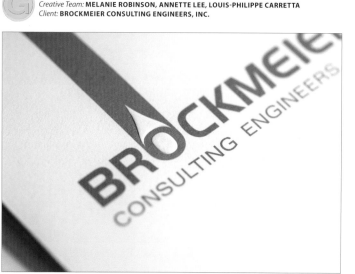

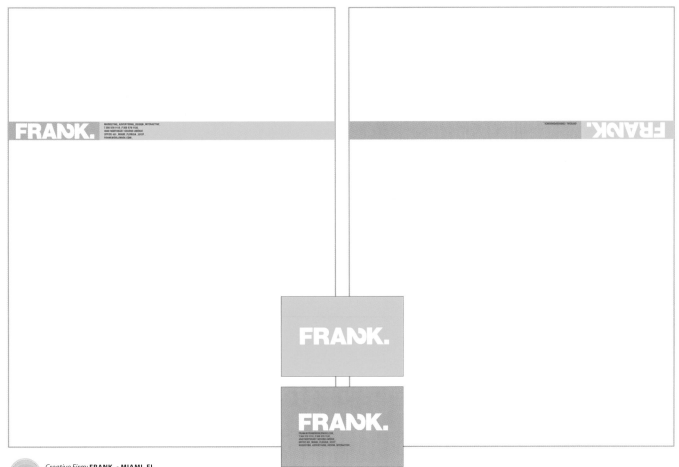

Creative Firm: **FRANK. - MIAMI, FL**
Creative Team: **TODD HOUSER, RAYMOND ADRIAN**
Client: **FRANK.**

Creative Firm: **WINSPER INC. - BOSTON, MA**
Creative Team: **STEVE BAUTISTA, BRIAN FANDETTI, KEVIN CIMO**
Client: **WINSPER INC.**

Creative Firm: **THE UXB - BEVERLY HILLS, CA**
Creative Team: **NJ GOLDSTON, GLENN SAKAMOTO, MYLA ECONOMOUS**
Client: **SWATFAME**

Creative Firm: **DD+A - OMAHA, NE**
Client: **REDIMENSIONS**

Creative Firm: **BBK STUDIO - GRAND RAPIDS, MI**
Creative Team: **SHARON OLENICZAK, BRIAN HAUCH, JASON MURRAY, ADAM RICE**
Client: **GRAND RAPIDS ART MUSEUM (GRAM)**

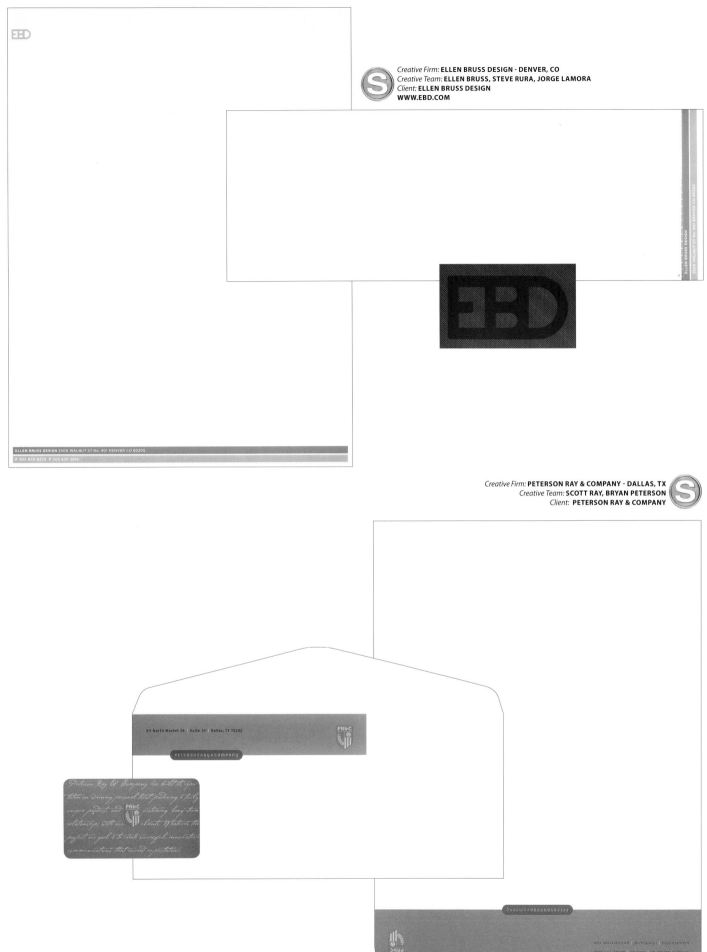

Creative Firm: **ELLEN BRUSS DESIGN - DENVER, CO**
Creative Team: **ELLEN BRUSS, STEVE RURA, JORGE LAMORA**
Client: **ELLEN BRUSS DESIGN**
WWW.EBD.COM

Creative Firm: **PETERSON RAY & COMPANY - DALLAS, TX**
Creative Team: **SCOTT RAY, BRYAN PETERSON**
Client: **PETERSON RAY & COMPANY**

Creative Firm: **AMEBA DESIGN LTD. - HONG KONG**
Creative Team: **GIDEON LAI**
Client: **BY MOEA, TAIWAN**

This design was inspired by the Chinese proverb, "A hundred cases of tolerance can turn into gold."

The designer used 99 Chinese characters for "tolerance" to form the background of the poster. The 100th character of "tolerance" is formed using lines and curves that are seemingly scratched on top of another Chinese character meaning "gold."

The symbolic message is this: hardship endured during moments of tolerance can produce valuable consequences.

The Chinese character meaning "gold," was painted in traditional calligraphy to resemble a pine tree. The design firm selected a pine tree as the final image because within Chinese culture it is known for it's endurance and ability to tolerate a variety of harsh conditions.

The ⓟ symbol designates a Platinum Award Winner. This piece tied for Best in Category in "Posters, Single."

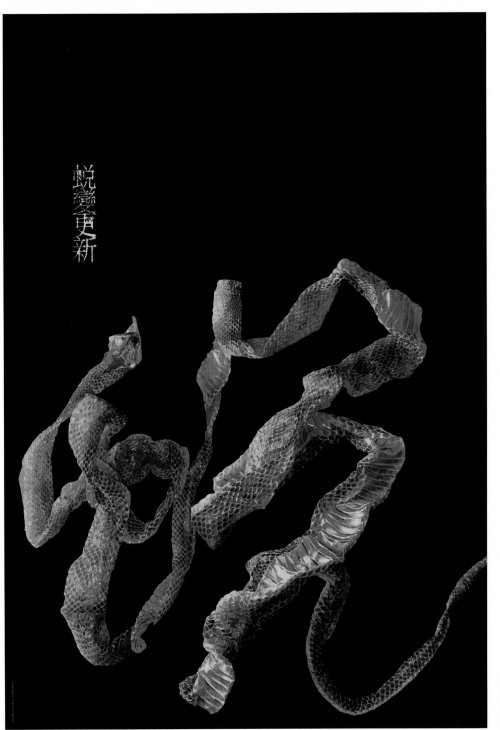

Creative Firm: **AMEBA DESIGN LTD. - HONG KONG**
Creative Team: **GIDEON LAI**
Client: **SOUL ENVIRONMENTAL PROTECTION**

There is a lot of symbolism within this poster for Soul Environmental Protection Agency, which has an underlying theme of "Transformation and renewal."

The design team was inspired by nature, specifically that changes in the natural world often demonstrate that relinquishing can lead to renewal. The discarded skin of a snake proved to be an ideal image to convey this message.

The designer used Chinese characters to illustrate the "Transformation and Renewal" theme. The shed skin of a snake is formed into the Chinese character for "transformation." It is then placed within a broken cage to symbolize that the snake has not only relinquished its old skin, but has also broken free from its restraint.

The ⓟ symbol designates a Platinum Award Winner. This piece tied for Best in Category in "Posters, Single."

Just how will Johnny come marching home again?

This is a simple graphic reminder of the dangers and plight of the American soldier. Do you realize over 20,000 of our soldiers have been wounded in battle in Iraq and Afghanistan? Many suffering severe life altering injuries such as amputations and head traumas. Regardless of your political affiliation or feelings towards the war, the very least we all can do is treat our soldiers, home and abroad, with the respect and support they deserve. Remember, it's a pretty safe bet that most of us will never have what it takes to walk in their shoes.

Creative Firm: **SUNSPOTS CREATIVE - FRANKLIN LAKES, NJ**
Creative Team: **RICK BONELLI, DEENA HARTLEY, AB SESAY**
Client: **SUNSPOTS CREATIVE**
WWW.SUNSPOTSCREATIVE.COM

Creative Firm: **CHEMI MONTES DESIGN - FALLS CHURCH, VA**
Creative Team: **CHEMI MONTES**
Client: **AMERICAN UNIVERSITY**

Creative Firm: **GREENLIGHT DESIGNS - N. HOLLYWOOD, CA**
Creative Team: **TAMI SHELLY, DARRYL SHELLY, MELISSA IRWIN, SHAUN WOOD, ROGER MOTTI**
Client: **SUBTERRANEAN NETWORK**

Creative Firm: **HBO OFF-AIR CREATIVE SERVICES - NEW YORK CITY, NY**
Creative Team: **VENUS DENNISON, ANA RACELIS**
Client: **HBO DOCUMENTARY FILMS**

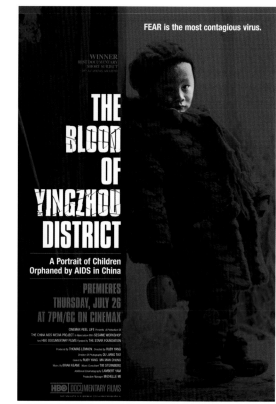

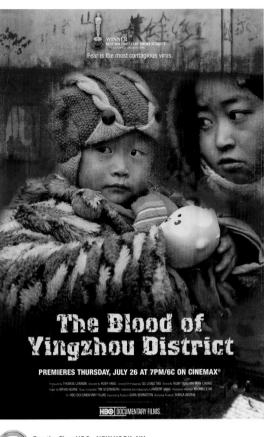

Creative Firm: **HBO - NEW YORK, NY**
Creative Team: **SETH LUTSKY, ANA RACELIS, VENUS DENNISON**
Client: **HBO**

Creative Firm: **FRY HAMMOND BARR - ORLANDO, FL**
Creative Team: **TIM FISHER, SEAN BRUNSON**
Client: **MAC PAPERS**

Creative Firm: **AMEBA DESIGN LTD. - HONG KONG**
Creative Team: **GIDEON LAI**
Client: **CO1**

Creative Firm: **HBO OFF-AIR CREATIVE SERVICES - NEW YORK CITY, NY**
Creative Team: **VENUS DENNISON, CHRISTIAN MARTILLO, MARIA MARCIAL**
Client: **HBO DOCUMENTARY FILMS**

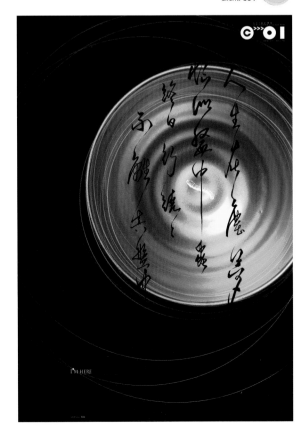

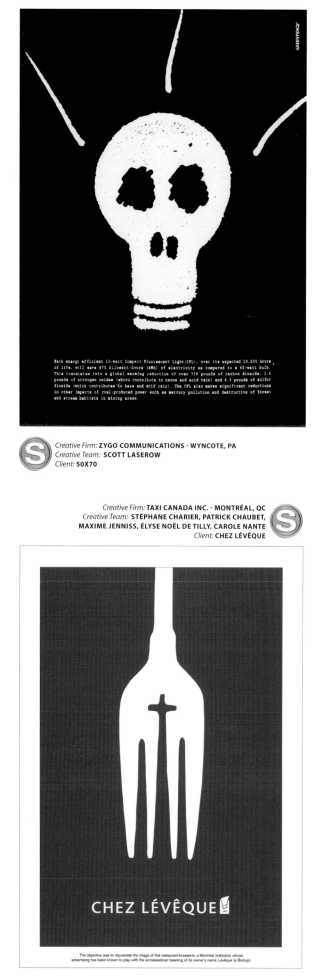

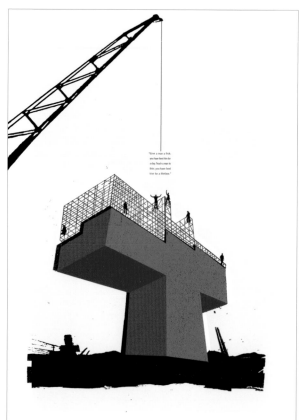

Creative Firm: **ZYGO COMMUNICATIONS - WYNCOTE, PA**
Creative Team: **SCOTT LASEROW**
Client: **50X70**

Creative Firm: **ZYGO COMMUNICATIONS - WYNCOTE, PA**
Creative Team: **SCOTT LASEROW**
Client: **ANTIAIDS UKRAINE**

Creative Firm: **TAXI CANADA INC. - MONTRÉAL, QC**
Creative Team: **STÉPHANE CHARIER, PATRICK CHAUBET,**
MAXIME JENNISS, ÉLYSE NOËL DE TILLY, CAROLE NANTE
Client: **CHEZ LÉVÊQUE**

Creative Firm: **ZYGO COMMUNICATIONS - WYNCOTE, PA**
Creative Team: **SCOTT LASEROW**
Client: **RED CROSS**

You could come back to Fantasia 2008 as a robot, but it would be much cooler returning as a VIP. Go to Zip.tv to tell the world why you love your film, and you could win...

zip.tv

Creative Firm: **CYAN CONCEPT INC. - JONQUIÈRE, QC**
Creative Team: **VALÉRIE JESSICA LAPORTE**
Client: **ALLARD HERVIEU COMMUNICATION**

HACKING DEMOCRACY

87% of America's votes are counted on electronic voting machines
But, there's a glitch in the system

Premieres Thursday, November 2 at 9PM/8c

Executive Producers EARL KATZ SARAH TEALE SIAN EDWARDS Directed by SIMON ARDIZZONE RUSSELL MICHAELS
Produced by SIMON ARDIZZONE ROBERT CARRILLO COHEN RUSSELL MICHAELS Edited by SASHA OLSWANG
For HBO Supervising Producer JOHN HOFFMAN Executive Producer SHEILA NEVINS

HBO

Creative Firm: **HBO OFF-AIR CREATIVE SERVICES - NEW YORK CITY, NY**
Creative Team: **VENUS DENNISON, ANA RACELIS**
Client: **HBO DOCUMENTARY FILMS**

 Creative Firm: **LUNA\TBWA - BELGRADE, YUGOSLAVIA**
Creative Team: **DEJAN PAROSKI**
Client: **NISSAN SERBIA**

VERAN DO KRAJA

NISSAN
SHIFT_future

FAITHFUL FOREVER

NISSAN
SHIFT_future

Creative Firm: JWT - DUBAI
Creative Team: CHAFIC HADDAD, NIZAR SWAILEM, ASH CHAGLA, LAYAN AZIZ, DANA AL-KUTOBI
Client: UNILEVER BERTOLLI OIL

Creative Firm: ID + ASSOCIATES - LAWRENCE, KS
Creative Team: J. GRUBER
Client: SOUTHWEST BAPTIST UNIVERSITY

Creative Firm: DAVIS DESIGN PARTNERS - HOLLAND, OH
Creative Team: MATT DAVIS
Client: BGSU SCHOOL OF ART

Creative Firm: MAD DOG GRAPHX - ANCHORAGE, AK
Creative Team: KRIS RYAN-CLARKE
Client: NORDIC SKIING ASSOCIATION OF ANCHORAGE

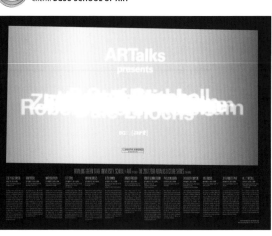

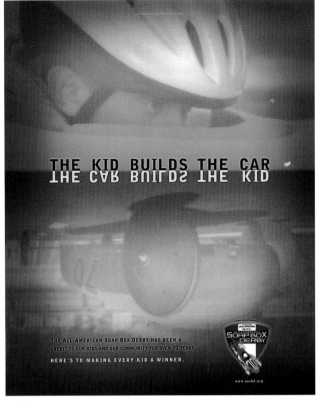

Creative Firm: **STUDIO INTERNATIONAL - ZAGREB, CROATIA**
Creative Team: **BORIS LJUBICIC, DARKO BAVOLJAK**
Client: **STUDIO INTERNATIONAL**

 Creative Firm: **HITCHCOCK FLEMING & ASSOCIATES INC. - AKRON, OH**
Creative Team: **NICK BETRO, MIKE MICKLEY, GREG PFIFFNER**
Client: **ALL-AMERICAN SOAP BOX DERBY**

 Creative Firm: **BERNARD CHIA - SINGAPORE**
Creative Team: **BERNARD CHIA**
Client: **KIM SENG COMMUNITY CENTRE**

Creative Firm: **HBO OFF-AIR CREATIVE SERVICES - NEW YORK CITY, NY**
Creative Team: **VENUS DENNISON, IVY CALAHORRANO, ANTHONY VIOLA**
Client: **HBO DOCUMENTARY FILMS**

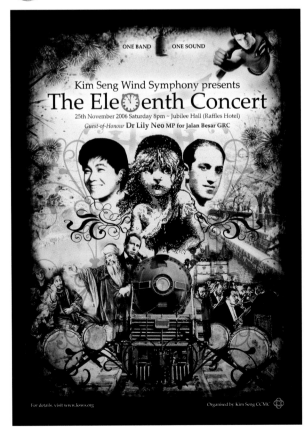

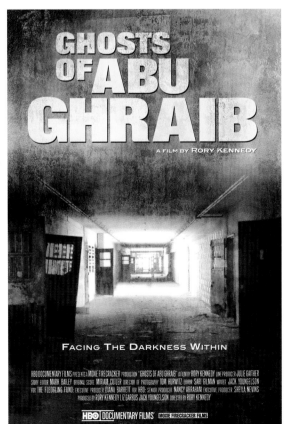

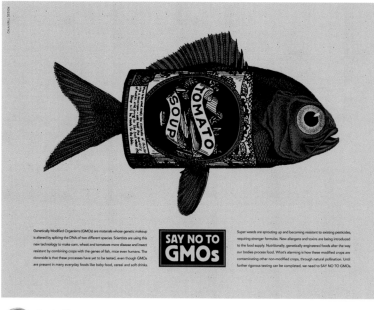

SAY NO TO GMOs

Genetically Modified Organisms (GMOs) are materials whose genetic makeup is altered by splicing the DNA of two different species. Scientists are using this new technology to make corn, wheat and tomatoes more disease and insect resistant by combining crops with the genes of fish, mice even humans. The downside is that these processes have yet to be tested, even though GMOs are present in many everyday foods like baby food, cereal and soft drinks.

Super weeds are sprouting up and becoming resistant to existing pesticides, requiring stronger formulas. New allergens and toxins are being introduced to the food supply. Nutritionally, genetically engineered foods alter the way our bodies process food. What's alarming is how these modified crops are contaminating other non-modified crops, through natural pollination. Until further rigorous testing can be completed, we need to SAY NO TO GMOs.

 Creative Firm: **CALA/KRILL DESIGN - CLAYMONT, DE**
Creative Team: **RON CALA, ALYSSA KRILL**
Client: **CALA/KRILL DESIGN**

RECYCLED LIFE
A STORY OF SURVIVAL AND THE HUMAN SPIRIT
PREMIERES THURSDAY, AUGUST 16, 7PM/6C ON CINEMAX

Creative Firm: **HBO - NEW YORK, NY**
Creative Team: **SETH LUTSKY, ANA RACELIS, VENUS DENNISON**
Client: **HBO**

Creative Firm: **DAVIS DESIGN PARTNERS - HOLLAND, OH**
Creative Team: **MATT DAVIS**
Client: **BGSU SCHOOL OF ART, DIVISION OF GRAPHIC DESIGN**
HTTP://CLIENTS2.SERVERSIDE.NET/ASDS/

Creative Firm: **LIGHTHOUSE COMMUNICATIONS - PUNE, INDIA**
Creative Team: **RAMESHWAR JAWANJAL, UDAYENDU LAHIRI**
Client: **OPULENT AUTO CAR CARE PVT. LTD.**

Creative Firm: **CHEMI MONTES DESIGN - FALLS CHURCH, VA**
Creative Team: **CHEMI MONTES**
Client: **AMERICAN UNIVERSITY**

Creative Firm: **GUNNAR SWANSON DESIGN OFFICE - GREENVILLE, NC**
Creative Team: **GUNNAR SWANSON, MATT EGAN, TYLER PHILIPS, MICHAEL EHLBECK, CRAIG MALMROSE, LISA BETH ROBINSON**
Client: **EAST CAROLINA UNIVERSITY**

Creative Firm: **RASSMAN DESIGN - DENVER, CO**
Creative Team: **LYN D'AMATO, JOHN RASSMAN**
Client: **DENVER BOTANIC GARDENS**

Creative Firm: **MTV NETWORKS - NEW YORK, NY**
Creative Team: **JAMES HITCHCOCK, MICHAEL ENGLEMAN, JASON SKINNER, CATHERINE JAYCOX, ERICA MYERS, NORA GAFFNEY**
Client: **CMT**

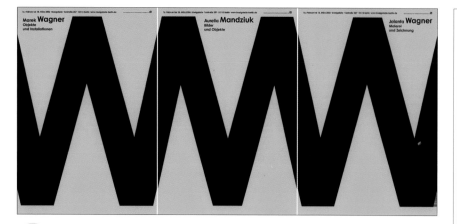

 Creative Firm: **MICHAL KACPERCZYK - LODZ, POLAND**
Creative Team: **JMICHAL KACPERCZYK**
Client: **INSELGALERIE, BERLIN**

Creative Firm: **MARCUS THOMAS LLC - CLEVELAND, OH**
Creative Team: **JAMIE VENORSKY, ROGER FRANK,**
JOANNE KIM, LITTLE JACKET
Client: **REACHING HEIGHTS**

 Creative Firm: **KIKU OBATA & COMPANY - ST. LOUIS, MO**
Creative Team: **RICH NELSON**
Client: **THE SHAKESPEARE FESTIVAL OF ST. LOUIS**

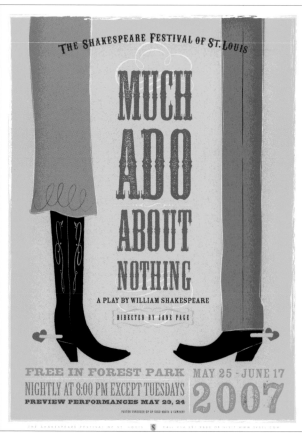

Creative Firm: **MTV NETWORKS - NEW YORK, NY**
Creative Team: **JAMES HITCHCOCK, MICHAEL ENGLEMAN, JASON SKINNER,**
CATHERINE JAYCOX, ANDREW VASTAGH
Client: **CMT**

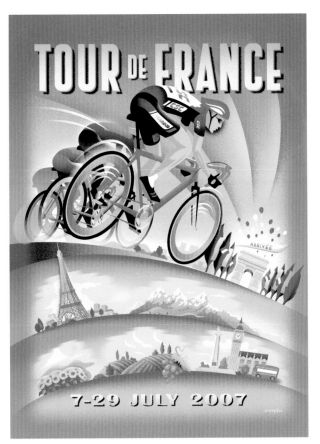

 Creative Firm: **CSC'S P2 COMMUNICATIONS SERVICES - FALLS CHURCH, VA**
Creative Team: **TERRY WILSON, JENNIFER VOLTAGGIO, MICHAEL CRAMPTON**
Client: **CSC CORPORATE**

Creative Firm: **GOLD - PONTE VEDRA BEACH, FL**
Creative Team: **KEITH GOLD, BRIAN GOLD, PETER BUTCAVAGE, JAN HANAK**
Client: **SYNCHRONICITYLIVE.COM**

Creative Firm: **CALAGRAPHIC DESIGN - ELKINS PARK, PA**
Creative Team: **RONALD J. CALA II, JOE SCORSONE**
Client: **ART MAKING MACHINE STUDIOS**

Creative Firm: **FATHOM CREATIVE - WASHINGTON, DC**
Creative Team: **ANJEANETTE AGRO, SHERI GRANT, CRAIG HILL, SHIKHA SAVDAS**
Client: **AARP**

Creative Firm: **CALAGRAPHIC DESIGN - ELKINS PARK, PA**
Creative Team: **RONALD J. CALA II**
Client: **ART MAKING MACHINE STUDIOS**

Creative Firm: **SAYLES GRAPHIC DESIGN - DES MOINES, IA**
Creative Team: **JOHN SAYLES**
Client: **SAYLES GRAPHIC DESIGN/DES MOINES PLAYHOUSE**

Creative Firm: **CUNNING COMMUNICATIONS - NEW YORK, NY**
Creative Team: **MARK VOYSEY, FLOYD HAYES, ANNETTE DUNCAN, MARISSA SHRUM**
Client: **NBC: SCI FI CHANNEL**

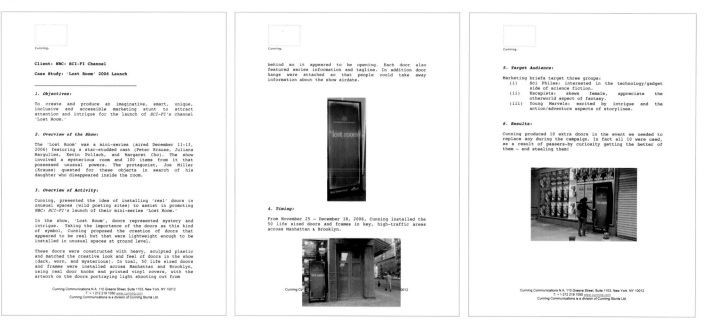

Creative Firm: **VH1 - NEW YORK, NY**
Client: **VH1**

Each year, "VH1 Hip Hop Honors" is an annual awards show—that pays tribute to the pioneers of hip hop. This poster series was a promotional giveaway at the Hip Hop Honors event in 2006.

That year's theme celebrated the concept of "representing" in the culture of hip hop. The honorees were photographed in a location that was significant to them and their journey as artists.

The line, "They represent. We recognize." brought it all together.

The (P) *symbol designates a Platinum Award Winner, our Best in Category.*

 Creative Firm: **BERRY DESIGN - ALPHARETTA, GA**
Creative Team: **BOB BERRY, CHIP WALLER**
Client: **POPEYES LOUISIANA KITCHEN**

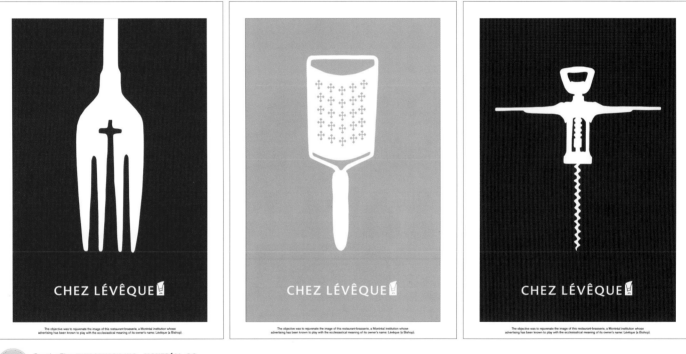

Creative Firm: **TAXI CANADA INC. - MONTRÉAL, QC**
Creative Team: **STÉPHANE CHARIER, PATRICK CHAUBET, MAXIME JENNISS, ÉLYSE NOËL DE TILLY, CAROLE NANTEL**
Client: **CHEZ LÉVÊQUE**

Creative Firm: **AMEBA DESIGN LTD. - HONG KONG**
Creative Team: **GIDEON LAI**
Client: **6 SAID SHOW**

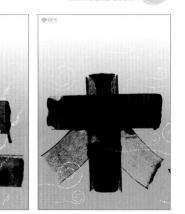

Creative Firm: **MCCANN ERICKSON KOREA - SEOUL, SOUTH KOREA**
Creative Team: **JUNG HYUN SHON, YONG BEOM SHIN, BYUNG HO AHN, GUNWOO KIM, WON KUK KIM**
Client: **DIAGEO KOREA**

Creative Firm: **NELSON SCHMIDT - MILWAUKEE, WI**
Creative Team: **JANE KRAMER, RICK LAGAN, JEFF SALZER, GINA FERRISE**
Client: **MILWAUKEE ART MUSEUM**

Creative Firm: **EMERSON, WAJDOWICZ STUDIOS - NEW YORK, NY**
Creative Team: **JUREK WAJDOWICZ, LISA LAROCHELLE, MANNY MENDEZ, YOKO YOSHIDA, HANS JURGEN BURKARD, PAOLO PELLEGRIN, SEBASTIAO SALGADO, FRANCESCO ZIZOLA**
Client: **MEDECINS SANS FRONTIERES/DOCTORS WITHOUT BORDERS**

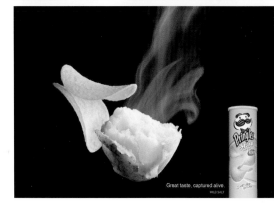

Creative Firm: **GREY WORLDWIDE INC. - SHIBUYA-KU, JAPAN**
Creative Team: **YOICHIRO SERIZAWA, MASANORI TAGAYA, KOUJIRO KAWADA, YOSHIHITO SAITO**
Client: **P&G**

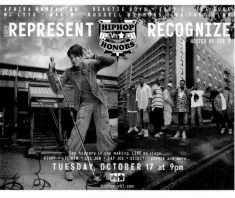

Creative Firm: **PG CREATIVE - MIAMI, FL**
Creative Team: **MARITZA PENSADO, YVI GARCIA**
Client: **DRUG FREE CHARLOTTE COUNTY**

Creative Firm: **VH1 - NEW YORK, NY**
Client: **VH1**

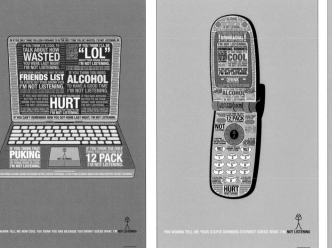

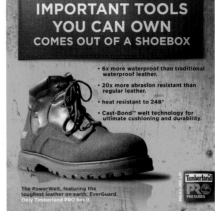

Creative Firm: **WINSPER INC. - BOSTON, MA**
Creative Team: **STEVE BAUTISTA, BRIAN FANDETTI,**
KEVIN CIMO, KAITY MALONEY,
CAROLINE BISHOP, BOB CLINTON
Client: **TIMBERLAND PRO**

Creative Firm: **MFP - NEW YORK, NY**
Creative Team: **NEIL POWELL, JOSH ROGERS,**
MARY WILLIAMS, ADAM KENNEDY, BRANDON
Client: **GRINCH**

Creative Firm: **FRY HAMMOND BARR - ORLANDO, FL**
Creative Team: **TIM FISHER, SEAN BRUNSON, SANDRA LAWTON, STEPHANIE RUELKE, JOHN DEEB**
Client: **ORLANDO SCIENCE CENTER**

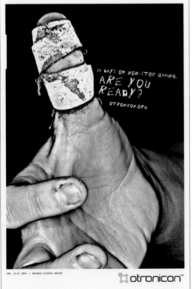

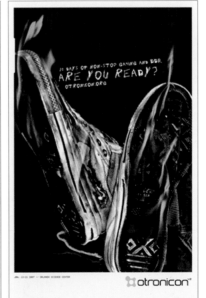

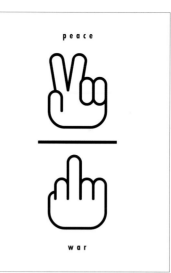

Creative Firm: **CALAGRAPHIC DESIGN - ELKINS PARK, PA**
Creative Team: **RONALD J. CALA II, JOE SCORSONE**
Client: **TYLER SCHOOL OF ART, TEMPLE UNIVERSITY**

Creative Firm: **FRY HAMMOND BARR - ORLANDO, FL**
Creative Team: **TIM FISHER, SANDRA LAWTON, SEAN BRUNSON, CATHERINE HAYES**
Client: **ORLANDO SCIENCE CENTER**

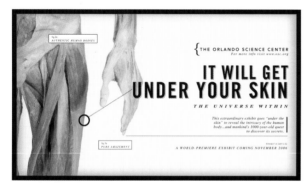

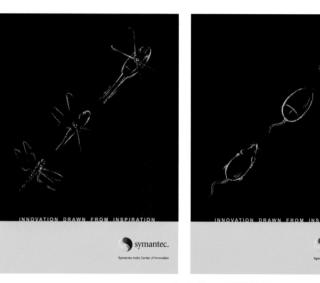

Creative Firm: **LIGHTHOUSE COMMUNICATIONS - PUNE, INDIA**
Creative Team: **RAMESHWAR JAWANJAL, UDAYENDU LAHIRI**
Client: **SYMANTEC CORPORATION**

Creative Firm: **MCCANN ERICKSON KOREA - SEOUL, SOUTH KOREA**
Creative Team: **JUNG HYUN SHON, YONG BEOM SHIN, BYUNG HO AHN, GUNWOO KIM, WON KUK KIM**
Client: **DIAGEO KOREA**

Creative Firm: **PEGGY LAURITSEN DESIGN GROUP - MINNEAPOLIS, MN**
Creative Team: **BRIAN DANAHER**
Client: **PLATO LEARNING**

TRADE SHOW DISPLAY GRAPHICS

Creative Firm: **BETH SINGER DESIGN - ARLINGTON, VA**
Creative Team: **BETH SINGER, SUCHA SNIDVONGS, SUHEUN YU**
Client: **AMERICAN ISRAEL PUBLIC AFFAIRS COMMITTEE (AIPAC)**

"FREAK SHOW", an animated program on Comedy Central television, was highly anticipated within the comedy and comic book communities due to the success of previous projects by the show's creators. The absurd nature of the show and its characters is what led the creativity of these outdoor postings.

Focus was placed on the unique and humorous main characters of the show—carnival workers that moonlight as secret government agents. The outrageous nature of the show presented some challenges, mainly with presenting the work in an outdoor, public environment. Visuals needed to be adjusted to meet community standards and push creative and comedy boundaries to attract the core audience of young men.

The postings were designed in the vein of classic circus/carnival posters, with vintage fonts, muted colors and worn edges. This look helped the postings stand out against their modern city environments and resulted in images and content that is uniquely Comedy Central.

Creative Firm: **COMEDY CENTRAL OFF-AIR CREATIVE - NEW YORK, NY**
Creative Team: **ROLYN BARTHELMAN, ANGELINA BATTISTA**
Client: **COMEDY CENTRAL**

The ℗ *symbol designates a Platinum Award Winner, our Best in Category.*

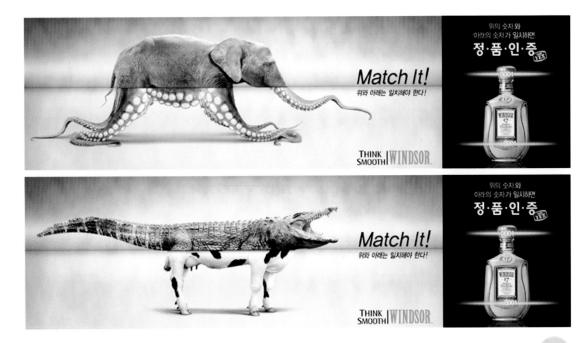

Match It!
위와 아래는 일치해야 한다!

THINK SMOOTH | WINDSOR.

위의 숫자와
아래의 숫자가 일치하면
정·품·인·증 YES

Match It!
위와 아래는 일치해야 한다!

THINK SMOOTH | WINDSOR.

위의 숫자와
아래의 숫자가 일치하면
정·품·인·증 YES

Creative Firm: **MCCANN ERICKSON KOREA - SEOUL, SOUTH KOREA**
Creative Team: **JUNG HYUN SHON, YONG BEOM SHIN, BYUNG HO AHN, GUNWOO KIM, WON KUK KIM**
Client: **DIAGEO KOREA**

Creative Firm: **GREY WORLDWIDE INC. - SHIBUYA-KU, JAPAN**
Creative Team: **MASAYOSHI SOEDA, KEI OKI, TAKESHI IWAMOTO, REIKO KIOWAI, MASAHARU NOJIMA, NIPPON COLOR ENGINEERS CO., LTD.**
Client: **SUSHI RESTAURANT JUN**

Creative Firm: **WINSPER INC. - BOSTON, MA**
Creative Team: **STEVE BAUTISTA, BRIAN FANDETTI, KEVIN CIMO, KAITY MALONEY, CAROLINE BISHOP, BOB CLINTON**
Client: **TIMBERLAND PRO**

EVER-GUARD.
IT'S LEATHER.
IT'S TOUGH. IT BREATHES.

Creative Firm: **WEAREGIGANTIC - NEW YORK, NY**
Creative Team: **NEIL POWELL, JOSH ROGERS, BRAD DIXON, KRISTOFER DELANEY, MARY WILLIAMS**
Client: **MIKE'S HARD LEMONADE**

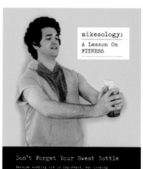

 Creative Firm: **GREY WORLDWIDE INC. - SHIBUYA-KU, JAPAN**
Creative Team: **YOICHIRO SERIZAWA, MASANORI TAGAYA,**
KOUJIRO KAWADA, YOSHIHITO SAITO
Client: **P&G**

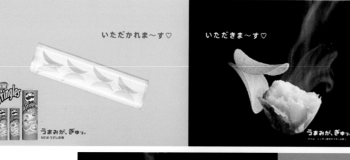

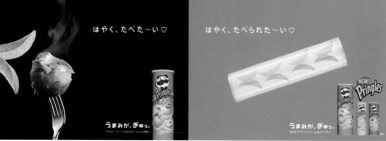

Goldfish have a memory span of 3 seconds.

They can't even see the past, much less the future.
But you can. With proven business intelligence and analytic software from SAS.

www.sas.com/goldfish

Hamsters spend their lives running in place.

They'll never get where they want to be.
But you can. With proven performance management software from SAS.

www.sas.com/hamsters

Giraffes get dropped 6 feet to the ground at birth.

They can't avoid rude awakenings.
But you can. With proven performance management software from SAS.

www.sas.com/giraffes

Gophers burrow through life without seeing the havoc they create.

They can't help having tunnel vision.
But you can. With proven business intelligence and analytic software from SAS.

www.sas.com/gophers

Creative Firm: **SAS MARKETING CREATIVE - CARY, NC**
Creative Team: **STEVE BENFIELD, GRAY HEFFNER, ANNETTE MARETT, AMANDA GADD, BETH HEINIG, BRIAN LLOYD**
Client: **SAS**

Creative Firm: **GREY WORLDWIDE INC. - SHIBUYA-KU, JAPAN**
Creative Team: **MASAYOSHI SOEDA, KEI OKI, TAKESHI IWAMOTO, REIKO KIOWAL, MARINE PRESS JAPAN CO., LTD., NIPPON COLOR ENGINEERS CO., LTD.**
Client: **SUSHI RESTAURANT JUN**

Creative Firm: **MTV NETWORKS - NEW YORK, NY**
Creative Team: **RICHARD BROWD, CHIE ARAKI, JAMES BLADGEN**
Client: **MTV OFF-AIR CREATIVE**

Creative Firm: **HEYE & PARTNER GMBH - UNTERHACHING, GERMANY**
Creative Team: **NORBERT HEROLD, VOLKER HEUER**
Client: **THEATER MAINFRANKEN**

Team CDM/CDMi

HOW'S MY RUNNING?
Please Call: 1.212.907.4300

Creative Firm: **CLINE DAVIS & MANN/CDMI CONNECT - NEW YORK, NY**
Creative Team: **KIERAN ALLING, RON LEWIS, MICHAEL FOSTER**
Client: **CDM/CDMI (INTERNAL)**

Creative Firm: **BBK STUDIO - GRAND RAPIDS, MI**
Creative Team: **MICHELE CHARTIER**
Client: **SPOUT**

Creative Firm: **ROSSLYN SNITRAK DESIGN - SEATTLE, WA**
Creative Team: **ROSSLYN SNITRAK**
Client: **ROSY RINGS**

Creative Firm: **FRANK. - MIAMI, FL**
Creative Team: **RAYMOND ADRIAN**
Client: **FUNKSHION LOUNGE**

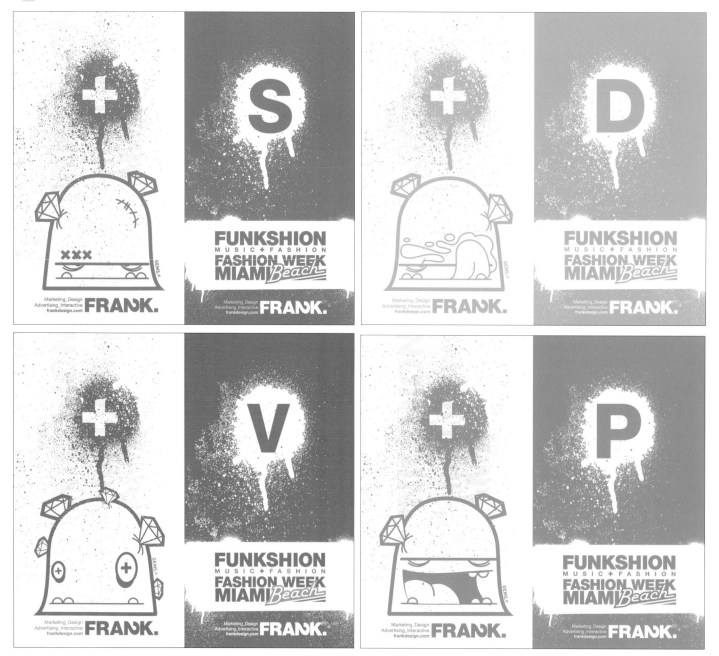

Boomsday was the premier title of the new publishing imprint TWELVE, which publishes only one book per month. The company's goal is to focus on quality and sales, not on quantity of titles.

The twelve covers for that year needed to radiate sophistication and commercial appeal. The mantra for the TWELVE covers was that they be bold, beautiful, smart, modern and uniquely appropriate for each book.

Having become bored with dust jackets, the designer chose to focus on a four-color paper-laminated case. From day one, he envisioned a balloon die cut around the title. The balloon was later inverted to a 'burst' to avoid tearing around the diecut during handling.

All departments—art and production, as well as the printer and binder—embraced the project. Adjustments and supervision were needed on press in order for everything to line up perfectly, but in the end, even the financial department agreed it was worth the cost and effort.

Creative Firm: **HACHETTE BOOK GROUP - NEW YORK, NY**
Creative Team: **ANNE TWOMEY, WILL STAEHLE**
Client: **TWELVE, HACHETTE BOOK GROUP**

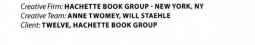 *The* (P) *symbol designates a Platinum Award Winner, our Best in Category.*

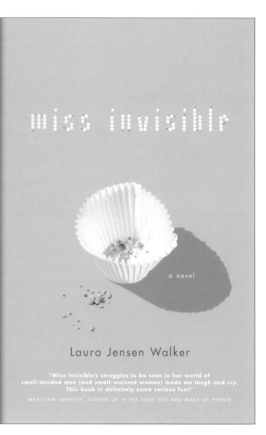

Creative Firm: **MIRACLE PUBLISHING - MANAMA, BAHRAIN**
Creative Team: **KHALID JUMAN, GEIR ERDAL, RIPUNJAY BHAGAWATI**
Client: **MIRACLE PUBLISHING**

Creative Firm: **RED CANOE - DEER LODGE, TN**
Creative Team: **DEB KOCH, MARK ROSS, CAROLINE KAVANAGH, PETE MCARTHUR, LAURA JENSEN WALKER**
Client: **THOMAS NELSON PUBLISHERS**

Creative Firm: **CORCHIAWOLINERRHODA - NEW YORK, NY**
Creative Team: **CHRIS TOWERY, BRANDON ANTOL**
Client: **TODD RHODA**

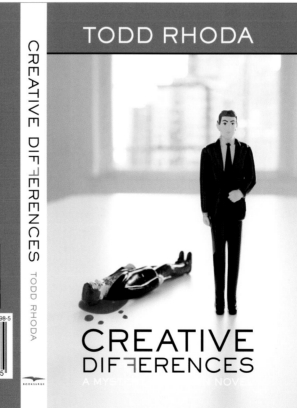

Creative Firm: **HACHETTE BOOK GROUP - NEW YORK, NY**
Creative Team: **ANNE TWOMEY, DANIEL PELAVIN**
Client: **HACHETTE BOOK GROUP**

Creative Firm: **DREAMEDIA STUDIOS - LITTLE ROCK, AR**
Creative Team: **KYLE HOLMES, MAX DELSON**
Client: **PEARLDIVER - A SUBSIDIARY OF RRY PUBLICATIONS**

Creative Firm: **CHRIS CORNEAL - EAST LANSING, MI**
Creative Team: **CHRIS CORNEAL**
Client: **RUTGERS UNIVERSITY PRESS**

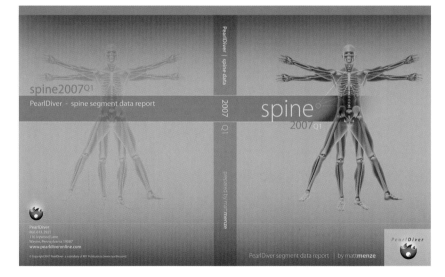

Creative Firm: **DISTURBANCE - JOHANNESBURG, SOUTH AFRICA**
Creative Team: **RICHARD HART, GARETH PAUL, MICHELLE CAVÉ**
Client: **SUB URBAN**

Creative Firm: **VITA-MIX CORP. - CLEVELAND, OH**
Creative Team: **ELIZABETH SCHINDELAR, TOM POJE, JON SAKOLA, ANDREW WICK,
DANIEL ROSS, ANNE MENDENHALL**
Client: **VITA-MIX CORP.**

Creative Firm: **DREAMEDIA STUDIOS - LITTLE ROCK, AR**
Creative Team: **KYLE HOLMES**
Client: **GREGORY HALL - AUTHOR**

Creative Firm: **RED CANOE - DEER LODGE, TN**
Creative Team: **DEB KOCH, BELINDA BASS, CAROLINE KAVANAGH, SEAN JUSTICE,
DR. JOSEPH MERCOLA, DR. BEN LERNER**
Client: **THOMAS NELSON PUBLISHERS**

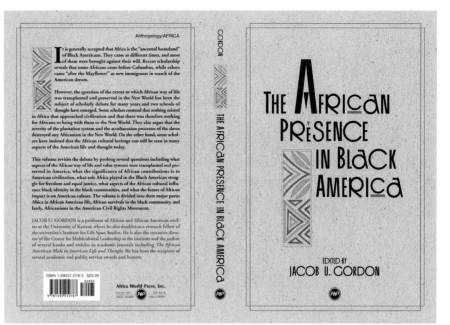

Creative Firm: **RED CANOE - DEER LODGE, TN**
Creative Team: **DEB KOCH, MARK ROSS, CAROLINE KAVANAGH, MASTERFILE ROYALTY FREE, MEGUMI TAKAMURA, LISA SAMSON**
Client: **THOMAS NELSON PUBLISHERS**

Creative Firm: **RDORMANN DESIGN - MILLTOWN, NJ**
Creative Team: **ROGER DORMANN**
Client: **AFRICA WORLD PRESS, TRENTON, NJ**

Creative Firm: **LAU DESIGN LLC - NORWALK, CT**
Creative Team: **JEFFREY LAU**
Client: **GREENWOOD PUBLISHING GROUP**

Creative Firm: **RED CANOE - DEER LODGE, TN**
Creative Team: **DEB KOCH, MARK ROSS, CAROLINE KAVANAGH, ARTEMI KYRIACOU, DENISE HILDRETH**
Client: **THOMAS NELSON PUBLISHERS**

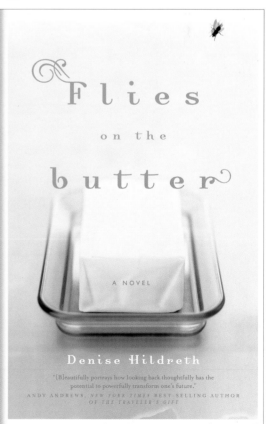

143

Creative Firm: **MARSHALL CAVENDISH - CALIFON, NJ**
Creative Team: **ANAHID HAMPARIAN, LISA FALKENSTERN**
Client: **MARSHALL CAVENDISH**

Creative Firm: **HACHETTE BOOK GROUP - NEW YORK, NY**
Creative Team: **ANNE TWOMEY, ELIZABETH WATT**
Client: **HACHETTE BOOK GROUP**

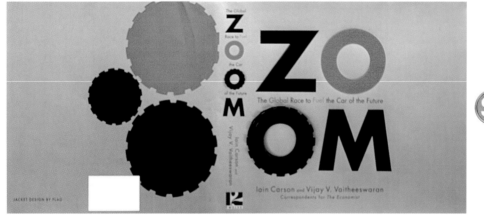

Creative Firm: **HACHETTE BOOK GROUP - NEW YORK, NY**
Creative Team: **ANNE TWOMEY, FLAG TONUZIL**
Client: **HACHETTE BOOK GROUP**

Creative Firm: **HACHETTE BOOK GROUP - NEW YORK, NY**
Creative Team: **ANNE TWOMEY**
Client: **HACHETTE BOOK GROUP**

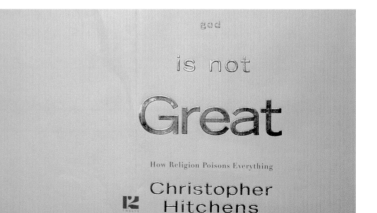

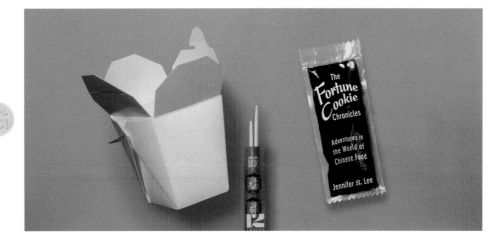

Creative Firm: **HACHETTE BOOK GROUP - NEW YORK, NY**
Creative Team: **ANNE TWOMEY**
Client: **HACHETTE BOOK GROUP**

Creative Firm: **HACHETTE BOOK GROUP - NEW YORK, NY**
Creative Team: **ANNE TWOMEY**
Client: **HACHETTE BOOK GROUP**

Creative Firm: **HACHETTE BOOK GROUP - NEW YORK, NY**
Creative Team: **ANNE TWOMEY, ANDREW ECCLES, ELLEN BERKENBLIT, TODD OLDHAM**
Client: **HACHETTE BOOK GROUP**

Creative Firm: **HACHETTE BOOK GROUP - NEW YORK, NY**
Creative Team: **ANNE TWOMEY**
Client: **HACHETTE BOOK GROUP**

145

Creative Firm: **FUTURA DDB - LJUBLANA, SLOVENIA**
Creative Team: **ZARE KERIN, MATEVZ KMET, JANEZ PUKSIC**
Client: **CUBO**

 The idea of creating a book about the desserts at Cubo's restaurant occurred during a conversation between master chef Bostjan Trstenjak, dessert master Matevz Kmet and photographer Janez Puksic. The goal was to capture the unique spirit of the restaurant, which is one of contemporary, yet subtle cuisine in a comfortable, friendly atmosphere.

Great emphasis was placed, of course, on the photography. The text is more subtly organized. The book was designed to serve a dual purpose: to be read as a cookbook with useful recipes and to be leafed through with a focus on the strong images.

The ℗ *symbol designates a Platinum Award Winner, our Best in Category.*

Creative Firm: **WILDE DESIGN - NEW YORK, NY**
Creative Team: **RICHARD WILDE, JUDITH WILDE, OLGA MEZHIBOVSKAYA**
Client: **JUDITH/RICHARD WILDE**

Creative Firm: **KEVIN SPRAGUE PHOTOGRAPHY - LENOX, MA**
Creative Team: **KEVIN SPRAGUE**
Client: **KEVIN SPRAGUE PHOTOGRAPHY**

Creative Firm: **HAMES DESIGN - MOHEGAN LAKE, NY**
Creative Team: **KATHERINE HAMES**
Client: **AMERICAN HUNGARIAN FOUNDATION**

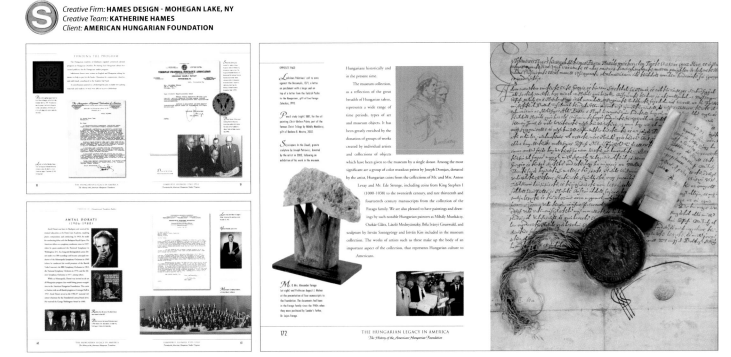

Creative Firm: **VOLUME INC. - SAN FRANCISCO, CA**
Creative Team: **ADAM BRODSLEY, ERIC HEIMAN, AMBER REED**
Client: **CHRONICLE BOOKS**

Creative Firm: **MIRACLE PUBLISHING - MANAMA, BAHRAIN**
Creative Team: **KHALID JUMAN, GEIR ERDAL,**
RIPUNJAY BHAGAWATI
Client: **MIRACLE**

Creative Firm: **RIVANNA FOUNDATION - EARLYSVILLE, VA**
Creative Team: **MICHAEL FITTS, AVERY CHENOWETH, ROBERT LLEWELLYN**
Client: **RIVANNA FOUNDATION**

Creative Firm: **TOM FOWLER, INC. - NORWALK, CT**
Creative Team: **BRIEN O'REILLY, ELIZABETH P. BALL**
Client: **TOM FOWLER, INC.**

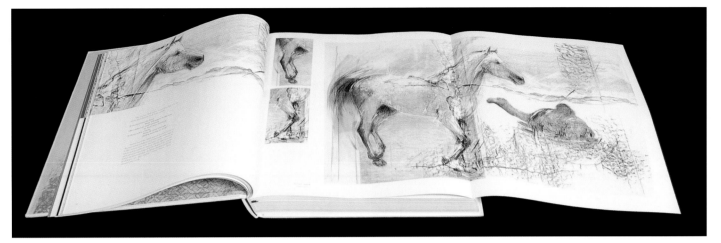

Creative Firm: **MIRACLE PUBLISHING - MANAMA, BAHRAIN**
Creative Team: **KHALID JUMAN, GEIR ERDAL, RIPUNJAY BHAGAWATI**
Client: **HH SHAIKHA SABEEKA BINT EBRAHIM AL KHALIFA**

Creative Firm: **ADVANTAGE LTD - HAMILTON, BERMUDA**
Creative Team: **SHEILA SEMOS**
Client: **BELCO - BERMUDA ELECTRIC LIGHT COMPANY**

Creative Firm: **SCHOOL OF VISUAL ARTS - NEW YORK, NY**
Creative Team: **GENEVIEVE WILLIAMS, JULIAN GONZALEZ,**
JIYOON LEE, JAMIE BARTOLACCI, TOMOMI FUJIMARU
Client: **SCHOOL OF VISUAL ARTS**

Creative Firm: **HAASE & KNELS - BREMEN, GERMANY**
Creative Team: **EVELYN FRISINGER, SIBYLLE HAASE, FRITZ HAASE,**
JENS LEHMKÜHLER DANIELA GODE, ANSELM DWORAK, ALLEGRA SCHNEIDER
Client: **EVELYNS SHOWROOM**

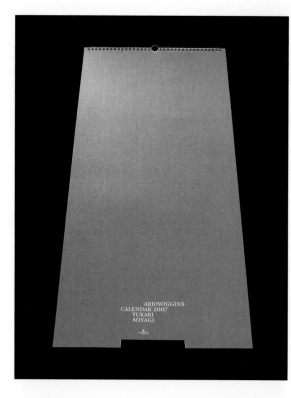

 ArjoWiggins is a paper company with a company strategy of "Innovative for customers." To showcase their products, and coincide with their strategy, the design firm Zuan Club decided to create an abstract calendar in the shape of the client's initial—A. To keep the focus on the paper, simple illustrations and minimal two-color printing were used.

Creative Firm: **ZUAN CLUB - TOKYO, JAPAN**
Creative Team: **AKIHIKO TSUKAMOTO, MASAMI OUCHI, YUKARI MIYAGI**
Client: **ARJOWIGGINS K.K.**

The Ⓟ *symbol designates a Platinum Award Winner, our Best in Category.*

Creative Firm: **CROWE DESIGN - ORINDA, CA**
Creative Team: **NANCY CROWE, DON CROWE**
Client: **HEARTSENT ADOPTIONS**

 Creative Firm: **MISSOURI BOTANICAL GARDEN - BRENTWOOD, MO**
Creative Team: **JUSTIN VISNESKY**
Client: **MISSOURI BOTANICAL GARDEN**

Creative Firm: **RIORDON DESIGN - OAKVILLE, ON**
Creative Team: **RIC RIORDON, SHIRLEY RIORDON**
Client: **RIORDON DESIGN**

Creative Firm: **FUTURA DDB - LJUBLANA, SLOVENIA**
Creative Team: **ZARE KERIN, ANDRAZ FILAC**
Client: **PIVK DRY CLEANERS**

Creative Firm: **JOHN WINGARD DESIGN - HONOLULU, HI**
Creative Team: **JOHN WINGARD, PAUL CHESLEY, KEITH LORENZ**
Client: **CORINNE CHING**

Creative Firm: **ALL NITE GRAPHICS - MIDVALE, UT**
Creative Team: **RANEE STAM, ANONYMOUS**
Client: **INTERMOUNTAIN THERAPY CALENDAR**

Creative Firm: **LEON MONTANA GRAPHIC DESIGN - BROOKLYN, NY**
Client: **PARAGON IMAGING GROUP**

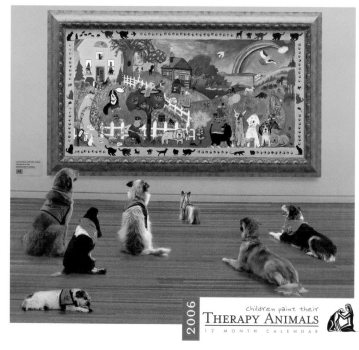

Creative Firm: **RUDER FINN DESIGN - NEW YORK, NY**
Creative Team: **LISA GABBAY, EMILY KORSMO, DAVID FINN**
Client: **RUDER FINN**

Creative Firm: **PRX COMMUNICATION STRATEGISTS - SAN JOSE, CA**
Creative Team: **EVA ZENO, STEVE MANGOLD,**
SUSAN BRAUSS, JOY ALEXIOU
Client: **VALLEY HEALTH PLAN**

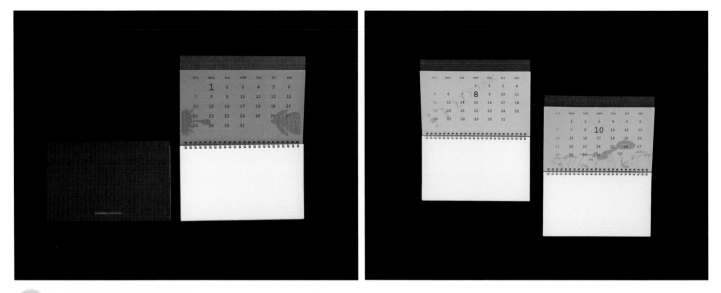

Creative Firm: **ZUAN CLUB - TOKYO, JAPAN**
Creative Team: **AKIHIKO TSUKAMOTO, MASAMI OUCHI, YUKARI MIYAGI**
Client: **ARJOWIGGINS K.K.**

Creative Firm: **THE HUMANE SOCIETY OF THE UNITED STATES -
WASHINGTON, DC**
Creative Team: **PAULA JAWORSKI, ELIZABETH MCNULTY**
Client: **THE HUMANE SOCIETY OF THE UNITED STATES**

Green Tree Frog *(Hyla cinerea)*

Creative Firm: **PREMIA SRL - ROME, ITALY**
Creative Team: **DEBORA ARGOMENTI**
Client: **NBC UNIVERSAL GLOBAL NETWORKS ITALIA SRL**
WWW.STUDIOUNIVERSAL.IT

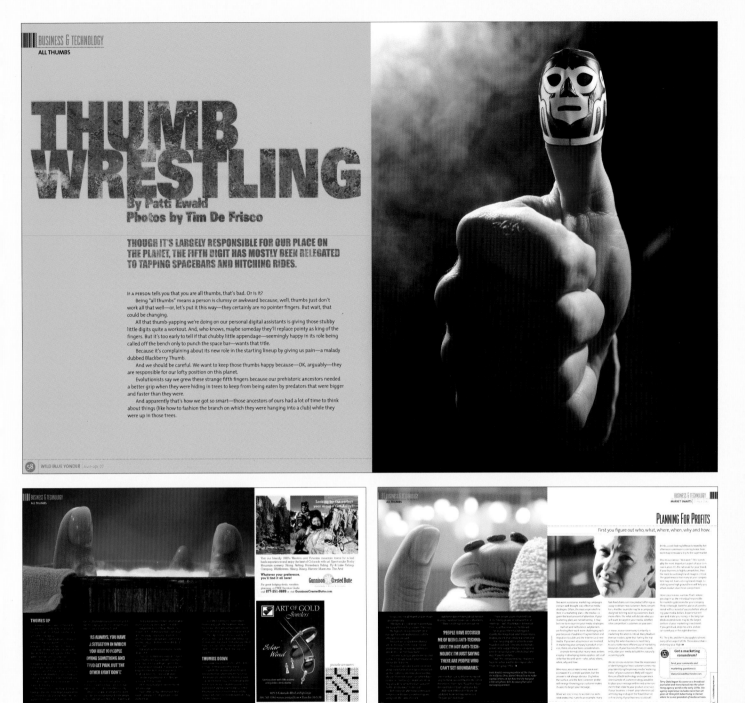

Creative Firm: **HENRYGILL ADVERTISING - DENVER, CO**
Creative Team: **BRYANT FERNANDEZ**
Client: **FRONTIER AIRLINES**

The Editorial Design category had two platinum winning entries, both created by HenryGill Advertising, and both for client Frontier Airlines.

The colors and typography for this design came from the designer's memories of trips to Tijuana, where one finds "an abundance of wrestling and bull fighting posters, usually worn out and sun-bleached, but still bold and in your face."

That inspiration resulted in an overall look that managed to enhance the wrestling motif of this article, and give it a bit more attitude.

The ⓟ *symbol designates a Platinum Award Winner. This piece tied for Best in Category in "Editorial Design, Single."*

Creative Firm: **HENRYGILL ADVERTISING - DENVER, CO**
Creative Team: **BRYANT FERNANDEZ**
Client: **FRONTIER AIRLINES**

This story, which appeared in Frontier Airlines magazine, had an audience of primarily business travelers. Appealing to the target market's nostalgic side was a fun assignment for HenryGill Advertising. The only challenge was finding material that authentically represented "'60s retro".

The firm wanted the overall look to have a Technicolor feel but slightly aged, which is why the colors are not true primary colors. They are slightly "off" to communicate "no longer brand new."

The fonts are all from that period and were chosen for their style and playfulness.

The Ⓟ *symbol designates a Platinum Award Winner. This piece tied for Best in Category in "Editorial Design, Single."*

CRUISING THE COAST

Creative Firm: **INK PUBLISHING - BROOKLYN, NY**
Creative Team: **SHANE LUITJENS, SAM POLCER, ORION RAY-JONES, BROOKE PORTER**
Client: **ATA AIRLINES**

GROWING PAINS

While Am Law 100
firms keep adding more
lawyers, converting
those bodies into
revenue can pose a
challenge. It turns out,
big isn't always better.

By Alison Frankel

Creative Firm: **AMERICAN LAWYER MEDIA - NEW YORK, NY**
Creative Team: **JOAN FERRELL, BEPPE GIACOBBE**
Client: **THE AMERICAN LAWYER**

Creative Firm: **ENERGY TIMES MAGAZINE - MELVILLE, NY**
Creative Team: **DONNA CASOLA**
Client: **ENERGY TIMES MAGAZINE**

IN SEARCH OF SALT SUBSTITUTES

By Lisa James

Creative Firm: **AMERICAN LAWYER MEDIA - NEW YORK, NY**
Creative Team: **JOAN FERRELL, ELIZABETH WILLIAMS, PAUL GODWIN**
Client: **THE AMERICAN LAWYER**

Creative Firm: **AMERICAN LAWYER MEDIA - NEW YORK, NY**
Creative Team: **JOAN FERRELL, ELIZABETH WILLIAMS, PAUL GODWIN**
Client: **THE AMERICAN LAWYER**

Creative Firm: **INK PUBLISHING - BROOKLYN, NY**
Creative Team: **SHANE LUITJENS, ALEXANDRA P. KARPLUS, ORION RAY-JONES,**
GERONNA LEWIS-LYTE, BROOKE PORTER
Client: **AIRTRAN AIRWAYS**

Creative Firm: **HENRYGILL ADVERTISING - DENVER, CO**
Creative Team: **DANA BARAK**
Client: **FRONTIER AIRLINES**

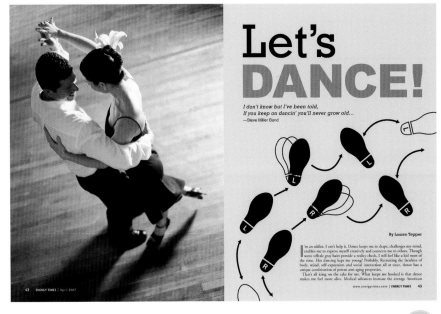

Creative Firm: **EMPHASIS MEDIA LIMITED - HONG KONG**
Creative Team: **VINCENT YUN**
Client: **THAI AIRWAYS**

Creative Firm: **ENERGY TIMES MAGAZINE - MELVILLE, NY**
Creative Team: **DONNA CASOLA, CHAD RENFROE**
Client: **ENERGY TIMES MAGAZINE**

Creative Firm: **MEDIASCOPE PUBLICITAS - MUMBAI, INDIA, INDIA**
Creative Team: **FARUQUI JAAN, LAKSHMINARAYANAN, MARIA SHAMSI**
Client: **JET LITE**

IMMERSE YOURSELF IN PITTSBURGH'S STRIP DISTRICT,

The Hip Strip District

WHERE OLD WORLD CHARM MEETS TRUE MODERN STYLE.

• KATHRYN HAWKINS • • DAVID MCLAIN •

THIS SCENE SOUNDS A LOT LIKE NEW YORK CITY, OR MAYBE LONDON

An eclectic mix of shops and restaurants that blend Old World European charm with modern sophistication can also be found in the heart of Pittsburgh, in a half-mile area known as the Strip District.

The city is a diverse and exciting metropolitan center: all year long, crowds swarm the Strip for delicious food, great shopping and a taste of the area's unique vitality. There are only a few hundred people who actually live in the district.

PENNSYLVANIA MACARONI CO. 1902

specialties—thick pancakes fresh from the griddle, smothered in ice cream, whipped cream and cherries. Rather stick with coffee? Stop by **La Prima Espresso**, a small Italian café that's frothed up the city's best cappuccinos for almost 20 years.

Back in time
HISTORY OF THE STRIP

The future Strip District is a Native American village called **Shannopin's Town**. Thanks to a convenient location between the Allegheny and Susquehanna rivers, the town hosts many traders, speculators and military officials—including a pre-presidential **George Washington**.

1929

The area, now known as "Bayardstown," is officially made a borough of Pittsburgh. By the following year, **more than 2,000 people live here.**

During the Civil War, the **Strip District's Fort Pitt Cannon Foundry** produces 15 pieces of the Union army's artillery, including the legendary Rodman cannons. Weighing 50 tons each, they were larger than any weapon produced in the past.

The Strip serves as Pittsburgh's Shantytown during the Great Depression, with more than 200 men camping on the streets for three years. **Father James Cox of Old St. Patrick's Church**, the "mayor of Shantytown," makes headlines across the country by leading 25,000 unemployed men to Washington, D.C., to petition for government relief.

There are **71 wholesale produce suppliers** in the Strip District. The fresh fruits and vegetables are brought in on trains and often sold straight out of the boxcars.

The Strip's cultural revival begins with the opening of now-defunct dance club called **Metropol**. More clubs, shops, bars and restaurants soon follow.

for her 9,000-square-foot restaurant, **Lidia's**, because of the area's ambiance and proximity to fresh meats and produce. Design features include a 17-foot-wide fireplace and beautiful hand-blown glass chandeliers, while the menu specializes in Italian-Slavic "border" cuisine.

A newer arrival, **Eleven** serves contemporary American cuisine in a uniquely beautiful space. Located in a former warehouse, the dining room features original wood floors and steel beams, and an open kitchen, allowing diners to watch the chef prepare specialties like the veal and lobster entrée—a succulent combination of sautéed veal medallions and butter-poached lobster tail.

The Strip is also home to dozens of grocers and ethnic markets. Step up to the cheese counter at **Pennsylvania Macaroni Company** (known to locals as "Penn Mac"), a wholesale grocer that sells thousands of traditional Italian products. Carole Pascuzzi will call you "dear heart" and help you find the perfect cheese to go with your pinot noir out of the hundred-odd wheels on display. Another specialty shop, **Parma Sausage** sells authentic sopressata, proscuitto, and other delicacies cured and seasoned in their own hanging room. There's also Mexican and Asian, and everything in between.

But the Strip District isn't just about food. At boutiques like **Collage**, discerning shoppers can find a selection of artisan crafts and jewelry, including dragon-shaped weathervanes, copper candlesticks and wall hangings made from antique Indian saris. **Eide's Entertainment** is one of the oldest and best comic stores in the U.S.; the three-level shop also sells a wealth of collectible records, books and videos. Endless sidewalk stalls carry remaindered books, Steelers shirts, hand puppets and more. "Everything you buy, you can come home with the story behind it," says Becky Rodgers, executive director of the nonprofit group Neighbors in the Strip.

You can't do Pittsburgh right without tasting a world-famous **Primanti Brothers** sandwich. First created for dock workers in the '30s, it includes french fries and coleslaw inside the bread, along with your choice of meat. As legend has it, the invention was born of necessity; the workers didn't have time to sit down to eat, so they needed a meal they could wolf down with one hand. Primanti Brothers came to the rescue, stuffing the side dishes right into the sandwich. Though there are many locations in Pittsburgh, the Strip location is the original shop. Even better, it's open 24 hours a day.

If you prefer a more upscale meal, you can't go wrong in this neck of the woods either. In 2000, celebrity chef Lidia Bastianich chose the Strip

To learn more about Pittsburgh, visit the **Heinz History Center** to see images and relics from the city's smoky past. Grab a stool at the Heinz 57 exhibit's soda counter to hear about the humble beginnings of the world's most famous ketchup. Steelers fans can step into the **Western Pennsylvania Sports Museum** located in the same building; the hands-on exhibits will give you a chance to hit your own home run, and the theater shows highlights of Pittsburgh's legendary sports history.

If you're still awake after a long day strolling through the Strip, have no fear. Though most of Pittsburgh shuts down after dark, the Strip leaves the lights on all night. Traveling with teens? Send them to **Club Zoo**, Pittsburgh's only underage nightclub, while you head to **Mullaney's Harp & Fiddle**, a traditional Irish pub.

For a more sophisticated night on the town, **DejaVu Live** has a comfortable lounge area, an abundant bar and a spacious dance floor. Later, if you want to keep on moving to the music, head over to **Altar Bar**, a nightclub based in a beautiful converted church.

A nightclub/church might seem strange to some, but in the Strip District, it fits right in. The neighborhood effortlessly melds tradition with innovation; you see it in the warehouses-cum-gourmet restaurants and in the grocery shops, where octogenarians stand in line behind 20-year-olds for sopressata and fresh-baked bread.

All through the Strip District, the old and new come together in surprising forms. The neighborhood has changed from a long block of industrial warehouses and wholesale stores into a vibrant, eclectic mix of shops, restaurants, galleries and clubs. It's a by-the-locals, for-the-locals kind of place, but the Strip District will welcome you with open arms, no matter where you're coming from. ▪

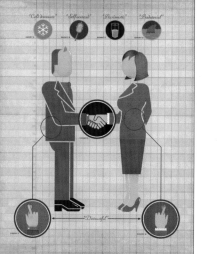

Creative Firm: **INK PUBLISHING - BROOKLYN, NY**
Creative Team: **SHANE LUITJENS, KELLY BARBIERI, ORION RAY-JONES, MARIXSA RODRIGUEZ, BROOKE PORTER**
Client: **MIDWEST AIRLINES**

TRADITIONAL JAPAN

An Invitation to Noh

The highly-polished performances and on-stage tension created by Noh plays have enthralled audiences since the 14th century. In 2001, Noh was officially designated by UNESCO as a "masterpiece of the oral and intangible heritage of humanity."

Creative Firm: **KF DESIGN - TAKASAKI, JAPAN**
Creative Team: **KEVIN FOLEY, KEIZO OKUBO, HISASHI KONDO**
Client: **JIJI GAHO SHA, INC.**

Creative Firm: **MEDIASCOPE PUBLICITAS - MUMBAI, INDIA**
Creative Team: **FARUQUI JAAN, LAKSHMINARAYANAN, MARIA SHAMSI**
Client: **CITIBANK**

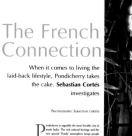

■ FOOTPRINTS

The French Connection

When it comes to living the laid-back lifestyle, Pondicherry takes the cake. **Sebastian Cortés** investigates

PHOTOGRAPHS: SEBASTIAN CORTÉS

Pondicherry is arguably the most livable city in south India. The rich cultural heritage and the very special 'Pondy' atmosphere keeps people coming back, often for long periods of time.

Creative Firm: **AMERICAN LAWYER MEDIA - NEW YORK, NY**
Creative Team: **JOAN FERRELL, HEADCASE DESIGN**
Client: **THE AMERICAN LAWYER**

The qualities that propel lawyers to success can also make forging a cohesive law firm nearly impossible. Can people who are trained to be skeptical and detached put the mistrust aside when dealing with their own partners?

By *David Marster*

The Trouble with Lawyers

AFTER SPENDING 25 YEARS SAYING THAT ALL PROFESSIONALS are similar and can learn from each other, I'm now ready to make a concession: Law firms are different. The ways of thinking and behaving that help lawyers excel in their profession may be the very things that limit what they can achieve as firms. For firm managers, challenges occur not in spite of lawyers' intelligence and training, but because of it.

ILLUSTRATIONS BY HEADCASE DESIGN

APRIL 2000 97

Creative Firm: **DEVER DESIGNS - LAUREL, MD**
Creative Team: **JEFFREY L. DEVER, KRISTIN DEUEL DUFFY, JACK GALLAGHER**
Client: **APICS MAGAZINE**

Creative Firm: **KF DESIGN - TAKASAKI, JAPAN**
Creative Team: **KEVIN FOLEY, TADASHI OKOCHI, SHINICHI OKADA, HISASHI KONDO**
Client: **JIJI GAHO SHA, INC.**

HIROSHI SUGIMOTO

ALCHEMIST OF LIGHT AND DARK

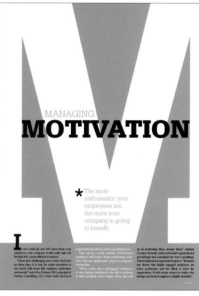

MANAGING
MOTIVATION

Creative Firm: **DEVER DESIGNS - LAUREL, MD**
Creative Team: **JEFFREY L. DEVER, CHARLIE POWELL**
Client: **LIBERTY MAGAZINE**

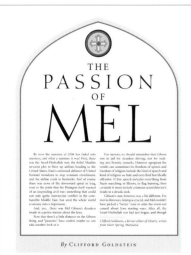

THE PASSION OF MEL

By Clifford Goldstein

Creative Firm: **INK PUBLISHING - BROOKLYN, NY**
Creative Team: **SHANE LUITJENS, ALEXANDRA P. KARPLUS, ORION RAY-JONES, BROOKE PORTER**
Client: **AIRTRAN AIRWAYS**

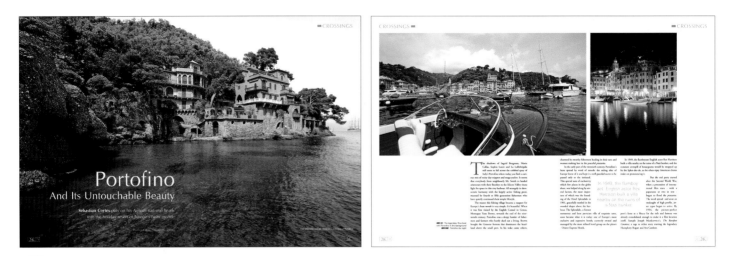

Portofino
And Its Untouchable Beauty

Sebastian Cortes puts on his Armani suit and heads into the holiday resort of Europe's beau monde.

Creative Firm: **MEDIASCOPE PUBLICITAS - MUMBAI, INDIA**
Creative Team: **FARUQUI JAAN, RAJAN SONAWANE, MARIA SHAMSI**
Client: **CITIBANK**

Creative Firm: **AMERICAN LAWYER MEDIA - NEW YORK, NY**
Creative Team: **JOAN FERRELL, DAVID LESH**
Client: **THE AMERICAN LAWYER**

Creative Firm: **CCM - WEST ORANGE, NJ**
Creative Team: **STEPHEN LONGO, CHRISTINE CABRERA, JACIE WOZNICKI, JEFF FLEISCHMANN, KAYA RYBACZEK, SARAH HUGHES**
Client: **PROME, ITALYTHEAN 2007**

Power & glory

By John Hoskin Photography by Philipp Engelhorn

Creative Firm: **AMERICAN LAWYER MEDIA - NEW YORK, NY**
Creative Team: **JOAN FERRELL, PIERRE MORNET**
Client: **THE AMERICAN LAWYER**

Creative Firm: **EMPHASIS MEDIA LIMITED - HONG KONG**
Creative Team: **TERESITA KHAW**
Client: **THAI AIRWAYS**

ASSOCIATES *Survey*

*When it comes to complaints, associates in 2006 sound an
awful lot like their counterparts of two decades ago.
Will a midlevel's lot in life ever change?*

BY ELIZABETH GOLDBERG

Midlevel *Blues*

ILLUSTRATION BY PIERRE MORNET

98 THE AMERICAN LAWYER

Creative Firm: **MEDIASCOPE PUBLICITAS - MUMBAI, INDIA**
Creative Team: **FARUQUI JAAN, LAKSHMINARAYANAN, MARIA SHAMSI**
Client: **JET LITE**

Heritage

The Cultured Thread

Dialogue with gravity

The *Butoh* style of Japanese dance company Sankai Juku has had a major impact on the world of contemporary dance. Artistic director Ushio Amagatsu reveals the secrets of its creations.

Creative Firm: **KF DESIGN - TAKASAKI, JAPAN**
Creative Team: **KEVIN FOLEY, SHINICHI OKADA, KITCHEN MINORU**
Client: **JIJI GAHO SHA, INC.**

Creative Firm: **INK PUBLISHING - LONDON, ENGLAND**
Creative Team: **ANDREW HUMPHREYS, BRENDAN ALTHORPE**
Client: **GULF AIR**

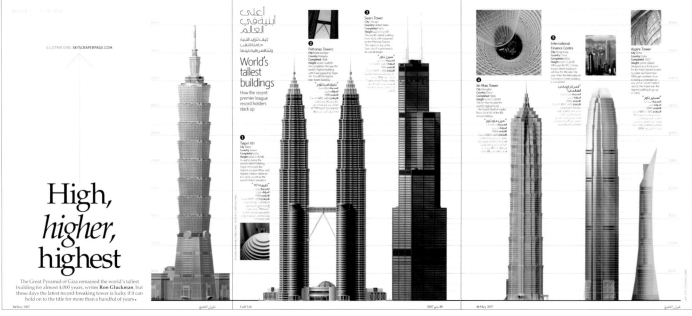

High, *higher,* highest

The Great Pyramid of Giza remained the world's tallest building for almost 4,000 years, writes **Ron Gluckman**, but these days the latest record-breaking tower is lucky if it can hold on to the title for more than a handful of years ▸

Creative Firm: **AMERICAN LAWYER MEDIA - NEW YORK, NY**
Creative Team: **JOAN FERRELL, OWEN SMITH**
Client: **THE AMERICAN LAWYER**

Tort reformers, business interests, and plaintiffs lawyers themselves have helped kill the mass torts bonanza—and it's not coming back.

By Alison Frankel

It's Over

The power of the plaintiffs bar is on the wane in this country, and will be for a long time to come.

Creative Firm: **AMERICAN LAWYER MEDIA - NEW YORK, NY**
Creative Team: **JOAN FERRELL, KRISTA BRAUCKMANN-TOWNS**
Client: **THE AMERICAN LAWYER**

Creative Firm: **AMERICAN LAWYER MEDIA - NEW YORK, NY**
Creative Team: **JOAN FERRELL, CHRISTOPHER SILAS NEAL**
Client: **THE AMERICAN LAWYER**

PRO BONO

Am Law 200 firms took up our challenge to have every lawyer work at least 20 hours of pro bono per year. The result? Not a bad start.

Room to Improve

BY MICHAEL ANEIRO

Creative Firm: **AMERICAN LAWYER MEDIA - NEW YORK, NY**
Creative Team: **JOAN FERRELL, LARA TOMLIN**
Client: **THE AMERICAN LAWYER**

In the almost-forgotten scandal over *Chinese spying,* only one person is going to trial: a junior FBI agent accused of *leaking information* to a family friend. How *mismanagement* by the bureau and personal loyalties placed a once-promising agent on a *path to prison.*

The Deception of Denise Woo

By Alison Frankel

Creative Firm: **DISTURBANCE - JOHANNESBURG, SOUTH AFRICA**
Creative Team: **RICHARD HART, SUSIE HART, CINDENE SHEASBY,**
LINDA NOTELOVITZ GOODALL, MILES GOODALL, MICHELLE CAVÉ
Client: **SUB URBAN**

Located in Johannesburg, South Africa, Sub urban helps other businesses with their film production needs. The company's fun, cheerful culture and knack for delivering imaginative solutions needed to be conveyed in their advertising.

The story told in this magazine advertisement is of a few drops of graffiti paint leaking into a manhole and morphing into a magical, vibrant 'otherworld' where anything is possible. The viewer gets the message that magic can occur right beneath the surface.

The design team wanted the illustration to be something the viewer would enjoy studying closely, even for a long periods of time. And although there are some intended meanings in the 'magical world' illustration, it is mostly meant to be open to the viewer's interpretation.

When viewed as a whole, the illustration clearly forms a face, which helps demonstrate a human side to the brand, but it is the markedly strong contrast between the dreary, gray 'real' world and the bright, friendly 'otherworld' that causes the viewer to stop and pay attention.

The (P) *symbol designates a Platinum Award Winner, our Best in Category.*

3:00pm meeting.
Somehow, you just know you're surrounded
by a different kind of creative team...

we create. 954-574-0810 peakseven.com

Peak Seven
ADVERTISING

Ⓖ **Creative Firm:** PEAK SEVEN ADVERTISING - DEERFIELD BEACH, FL
Creative Team: JONATHAN BERG

Creative Firm: VITA-MIX CORP. - CLEVELAND, OH
Creative Team: ELIZABETH SCHINDELAR, TOM POJE, JON SAKOLA, ANDREW WICK,
DANIEL ROSS, ANNE MENDENHALL
Client: VITA-MIX CORP. Ⓖ

Creative Firm: FOODMIX - WESTMONT, IL Ⓖ
Creative Team: FOODMIX CREATIVE
Client: LACTALIS FOODSERVICE

Ⓢ **Creative Firm:** WINSPER INC. - BOSTON, MA
Creative Team: STEVE BAUTISTA, BRIAN FANDETTI, KEVIN CIMO,
JIM ERICKSON, JOANNE DECARLO, CAROLINE BISHOP
Client: TIMBERLAND PRO

Creative Firm: **Y&R GERMANY - FRANKFURT AM MAIN, GERMANY**
Creative Team: **UWE MARQUARDT, NORBERT HUEBNER, LOTHAR MUELLER, MARION LAKATOS, KAI VAN DER MARE**
Client: **NEUDORFF GMBH KG**

Creative Firm: **TV LAND - NEW YORK, NY**
Client: **TV LAND**

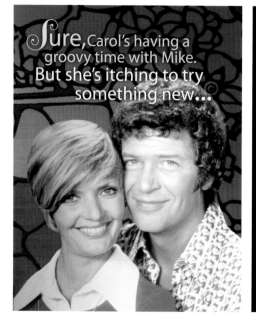

Creative Firm: **WINSPER INC. - BOSTON, MA**
Creative Team: **STEVE BAUTISTA, BRIAN FANDETTI, KEVIN CIMO, JIM ERICKSON, JOANNE DECARLO, CAROLINE BISHOP**
Client: **TIMBERLAND PRO**

Creative Firm: **SILVER COMMUNICATIONS INC - NEW YORK, NY**
Creative Team: **GREGG SIBERT, CHRISTINA WEISSMAN, CORIE WALLACE**
Client: **BNY CONVERGEX GROUP**

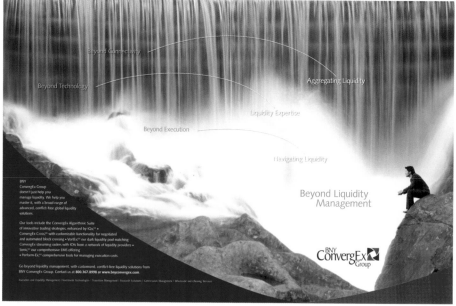

 Creative Firm: **DIESTE HARMEL & PARTNERS - DALLAS, TX**
Creative Team: **ALDO QUEVEDO, JAVIER GUEMES, GABRIEL PUERTO, WALTER BARRAZA, FRANCISCO CARDENAS, KENT GARCIA**
Client: **NATIONWIDE**

Creative Firm: **JONI RAE AND ASSOCIATES - ENCINO, CA**
Creative Team: **JONI RAE RUSSELL, BEVERLY TRENGOVE**
Client: **THERMAFUSE**

Creative Firm: **BRAND NEW WORLD - NEW YORK, NY**
Creative Team: **MARK RISIS, ALAN SCHULMAN, BRIAN BROWN, LINDSAY BOURGET**
Client: **ABOUT.COM**

Creative Firm: **PEAK SEVEN ADVERTISING - DEERFIELD BEACH, FL**
Creative Team: **BRIAN TIPTON, JONATHAN BERG**
Client: **DECKTIGHT ROOFING**

Creative Firm: **LEKASMILLER DESIGN - WALNUT CREEK, CA**
Creative Team: **LANA IP, TINA LEKAS MILLER**
Client: **U.C. BERKELEY, BOALT HALL SCHOOL OF LAW**

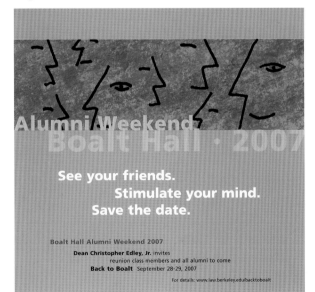

Patience may be a virtue...

...But it's not always an option.

Get immediate access to your deferred contract payments in one lump sum. Peachtree is a leading specialty finance company that purchases high-quality deferred payment obligations. Peachtree has purchased billions of dollars worth of contract payments and has relationships with major financial institutions the world over.

Call our funding specialists at **800.963.6484** for a no-cost, no-obligation proposal or visit www.peachholdings.com.

Creative Firm: **PEAK SEVEN ADVERTISING - DEERFIELD BEACH, FL**
Creative Team: **DARREN SEYS**
Client: **PEACHTREE FUNDING**

atural Gas

N 7 / 14

Nitrogen. Take it out and tap into more reserves today. Without a cost-effective way to remove high levels of nitrogen, you've bypassed would-be opportunities again and again. Now is the time to stop, go back, tap into those reserves and start making more money.

BCCK Engineering will help you remove nitrogen from your gas streams quickly, efficiently and affordably. And with nitrogen out of the picture, all that gas — and all those profits — are there for the taking. Thanks to BCCK, it's time to get both.

For a personal consultation, call BCCK at 888-518-6459, or for more information, go to www.bcck.com.

BCCK ENGINEERING, INC.

Creative Firm: **M/C/C - DALLAS, TX**
Creative Team: **GREG HANSEN, TODD BRASHEAR, HILLARY BOULDEN, AMANDA MYERS**
Client: **BCCK**

Creative Firm: **FOODMIX - WESTMONT, IL**
Creative Team: **FOODMIX CREATIVE**
Client: **LACTALIS FOODSERVICE**

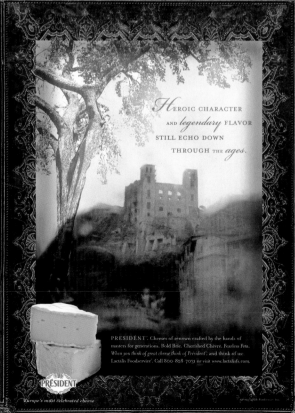

HEROIC CHARACTER AND *legendary* FLAVOR STILL ECHO DOWN THROUGH THE *ages*.

PRESIDENT. Cheeses of renown crafted by the hands of masters for generations. Bold Brie. Cherished Chevre. Fearless Feta. *When you think of great cheese think of President*, and think of us: Lactalis Foodservice. Call 800-828-7031 or visit www.lactalisfs.com.

PRESIDENT
Europe's most celebrated cheese

Creative Firm: **WINSPER INC. - BOSTON, MA**
Creative Team: **STEVE BAUTISTA, BRIAN FANDETTI, KEVIN CIMO, JIM ERICKSON, JOANNE DECARLO, CAROLINE BISHOP**
Client: **TIMBERLAND PRO**

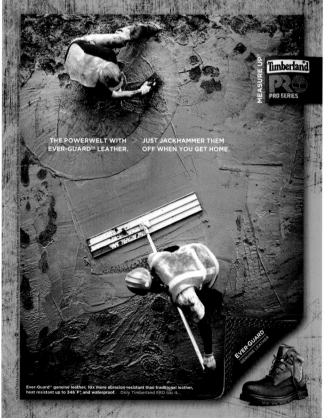

Timberland PRO PRO SERIES MEASURE UP

THE POWERWELT WITH EVER-GUARD™ LEATHER. JUST JACKHAMMER THEM OFF WHEN YOU GET HOME.

EVER-GUARD GENUINE LEATHER

Ever-Guard™ genuine leather; 10x more abrasion resistant than traditional leather, heat resistant up to 346°F*, and waterproof. Only Timberland PRO has it.

Creative Firm: **SAS MARKETING CREATIVE - CARY, NC**
Creative Team: **STEVE BENFIELD, GRAY HEFFNER, ANNETTE MARETT, AMANDA GADD, BETH HEINIG, BRIAN LLOYD**
Client: **SAS**

SAS® software, with advanced analytics, uses complex variables and mathematical equations to render predictive modeling, which gives its users valuable knowledge.

Huh?

Even in business publications, where the copy isn't always titillating, those don't sound like inspiring words. But if you're on the SAS advertising team, they are the facts, and you use them to attract more customers.

A great image might help you, but how can you depict advanced analytics (whatever that means) in a photograph? That's not exactly the kind of thing you find at stock photo houses.

To tackle these challenges, the SAS team took a clever approach, observing that even serious people in business suits have a warm, fuzzy side and a sense of humor.

Who would expect to find a close-up of a hamster nibbling on a seed or a toucan perched in a lush jungle in a business journal? No one. That's why they did it. Amidst a sea of computer images, pie charts and stock photo faces, rodents and colorful birds stand out.

And that's how the "You Can" campaign was hatched.

The (P) *symbol designates a Platinum Award Winner, our Best in Category.*

Creative Firm: **PALIO - SARATOGA SPRINGS, NY**
Creative Team: **KEN MESSINGER, JOE ACEE, JASON VERBICK, ALLEN MERCIER, STACEY THOMAS, MARCIA LYON**
Client: **ADHERIS**

Creative Firm: **STELLAR DEBRIS - HADANO-SHI, JAPAN**
Creative Team: **CHRISTOPHER JONES, CHRISTINE GRANT**
Client: **BYTWARE, INC.**

Creative Firm: **RTS RIEGER TEAM WERBEAGENTUR GMBH - LEINFELDEN-ECHTERDINGEN, GERMANY**
Creative Team: **IRINI JOHANN, ANNETTE PIENTKA, FRIEDERIKE APEL, RAINER TRAUB, RALPH OEHL, ACHIM LITSCHKO**
Client: **SCHWEIZER ELECTRONIC AG**

Creative Firm: **NELSON SCHMIDT - MILWAUKEE, WI**
Creative Team: **JANE KRAMER, RICK LAGAN, ROBERT MIZONO**
Client: **CLUB CAR INC.**

Creative Firm: **SILVER CREATIVE GROUP - SOUTH NORWALK, CT**
Creative Team: **SUZANNE PETROW**
Client: **CREATIVE PLACEMENT**

Creative Firm: **WINSPER INC. - BOSTON, MA**
Creative Team: **STEVE BAUTISTA, BRIAN FANDETTI, KEVIN CIMO,**
JIM ERICKSON, JOANNE DECARLO, CAROLINE BISHOP
Client: **TIMBERLAND PRO**

the power of innovation

the power of global reach

Creative Firm: **BTB MARKETING COMMUNICATIONS, INC. - RALEIGH, NC**
Client: **PAXAR**

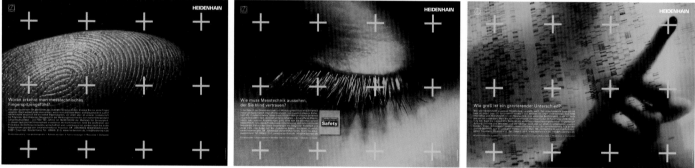

Creative Firm: **RTS RIEGER TEAM WERBEAGENTUR GMBH - LEINFELDEN-ECHTERDINGEN, GERMANY**
Creative Team: **ACHIM LITSCHKO, PHILIPP KEMPF, SIEGFRIED SCHAAL, BORIS POLLIG, CLAUDIA GLÖCKLER**
Client: **DR. JOHANNES HEIDENHAIN GMBH**

Creative Firm: **PCBC® AND GREENHAUS - SACRAMENTO, CA**
Creative Team: **CRAIG FULLER, RÉMY FRANK, SUSAN BURCH**
Client: **PCBC® THE PREMIER BUILDING SHOW**

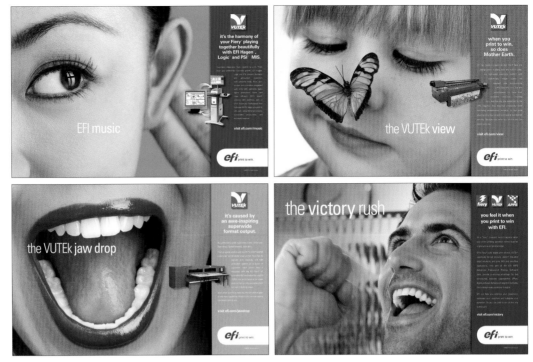

Creative Firm: **CATALYST - PROVIDENCE, RI**
Creative Team: **MICHAEL FRIEND, JENNIE ALLEN, MIKE MAJOR, LAUREN BLAIS, JACK REZNICKI, ELLIOTT LEWIN, JR.**
Client: **EFI**

Creative Firm: **SILVER COMMUNICATIONS INC - NEW YORK, NY**
Creative Team: **GREGG SIBERT, CHRISTINA WEISSMAN, NELIA VISHNEVSKY**
Client: **BNY CONVERGEX GROUP**

Creative Firm: **TMDCREATIVE - SALINAS, CA**
Client: **BELLI ARCHITECTURAL GROUP**

 Creative Firm: **FOODMIX - WESTMONT, IL**
Creative Team: **FOODMIX CREATIVE**
Client: **KOZY SHACK**

Creative Firm: **HITCHCOCK FLEMING & ASSOCIATES INC. - AKRON, OH**
Creative Team: **NICK BETRO, MARK COLLINS, GREG PFIFFNER**
Client: **THERMATRU**

 Creative Firm: **ALONSO & COMPANY - MIAMI, FL**
Creative Team: **JUAN CARLOS ALONSO, MARCO MOURE, CARLOS BAEZ**
Client: **RYDER SYSTEM**

Creative Firm: **ALTERNATIVES - NEW YORK, NY**
Creative Team: **MATT KABEL, JULIE KOCH-BEINKE**
Client: **TIMEX**

 Creative Firm: **BBK STUDIO - GRAND RAPIDS, MI**
Creative Team: **KEVIN BUDELMANN, BRIAN HAUCH, TIM CALKINS, CHUCK SHOTWELL**
Client: **CUMBERLAND FURNITURE**

Creative Firm: **DIESTE HARMEL & PARTNERS - DALLAS, TX**
Creative Team: **ALDO QUEVEDO, CARLOS TOURNE,
RAYMUNDO VALDEZ, PATRICIA MARTINEZ, ALEX TOEDTLI,
KARIN HARGRAVE**
Client: **CLOROX - PINESOL**

 If your target
market is mothers, one thing is certain: they are a busy group. Therefore, it's smart to go with a strong visual and minimal copy. It's even better if you can quickly grab their attention and make them smile.

Dallas creative firm Dieste Harmel & Partners recognized that caring for family is the #1 priority of these women, and having a clean-smelling home instills a sense of pride.

An additional benefit of this advertisement is that the message is clearly conveyed to the growing population of Hispanic-Americans who may not speak fluent English.

The ℗ *symbol designates a Platinum Award Winner, our Best in Category.*

178

Creative Firm: **SILVER CREATIVE GROUP - SOUTH NORWALK, CT**
Creative Team: **SUZANNE PETROW**
Client: **PREFERRED BRANDS**

Creative Firm: **REVOLUCION - NEW YORK, NY**
Creative Team: **ALBERTO RODRIGUEZ, HENRY ALVAREZ, JOEY CRAWFORD**
Client: **PALM BAY INTERNATIONAL**

Creative Firm: **MARTIN RANDAL COMMUNICATIONS - CAMBRIDGE, MA**
Creative Team: **ERIC ROTRAMEL, JACK CRUMBLEY, KELLY NASUTA**
Client: **ISLAND OASIS**

Creative Firm: **SAGON-PHIOR BRAND COMMUNICATIONS - LOS ANGELES, CA**
Creative Team: **PATRICK FEE**
Client: **BENELLI MOTORCYCLES**

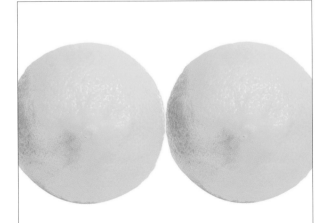

Jovem Pan Radio, 12 years.

Creative Firm: **TV LAND - NEW YORK, NY**
Client: **TV LAND**

Creative Firm: **DC3/UNICOM - BELÉM, BRAZIL**
Creative Team: **ALEXANDRE HELMUT, PAULO SÉRGIO,
GLAUCO LIMA, HAROLDO VALENTE**
Client: **JOVEM PAN BELÉM**

Creative Firm: **LEGO SYSTEMS, INC. - ENFIELD, CT**
Creative Team: **KEITH MALONE, TOBY DUTKIEWICZ**
Client: **LEGO SYSTEMS, INC.**

Creative Firm: **CETRIC LEUNG DESIGN CO - HONG KONG**
Creative Team: **CETRIC LEUNG, DANNY CHAN, PUI HO LEE,
ANTONIUS CHEN, DANIEL ZHENG, PENG YAM LIM**
Client: **Y+ YOGA CENTER**

Creative Firm: **PALIO - SARATOGA SPRINGS, NY**
Creative Team: **GUY MESSINGER, JOE ACEE, MATT DORITY,
CAROLINE BAUMIS, MARCIA LYON**
Client: **MEDICAL MISSIONS FOR CHILDREN**

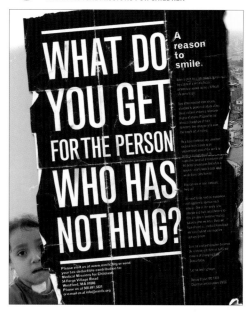

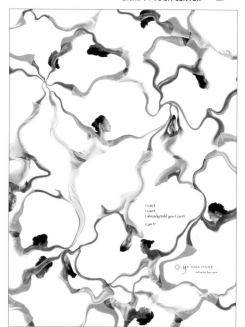

Creative Firm: **MTV NETWORKS - NEW YORK, NY**
Creative Team: **JEFFREY KEYTON, JIM DEBARROS, CHRISTOPHER TRUCH, MELISSA SCOTT, ERHAN ERDEM, KAREN WEISS**
Client: **MTV OFF-AIR CREATIVE**

Creative Firm: **CETRIC LEUNG DESIGN CO - HONG KONG**
Creative Team: **CETRIC LEUNG, DANNY CHAN, PUI HO LEE, ANTONIUS CHEN, DANIEL ZHENG, PENG YAM LIM**
Client: **Y+ YOGA CENTER**

Creative Firm: **JOHN WINGARD DESIGN - HONOLULU, HI**
Creative Team: **JOHN WINGARD, EMI HART**
Client: **FASHIONISTA'S MARKET**

Creative Firm: **REVOLUCION - NEW YORK, NY**
Creative Team: **ALBERTO RODRIGUEZ, HENRY ALVAREZ**
Client: **PALM BAY INTERNATIONAL**

Creative Firm: **HITCHCOCK FLEMING & ASSOCIATES INC. - AKRON, OH**
Creative Team: **NICK BETRO, MIKE MICKLEY, GREG PFIFFNER**
Client: **GOODYEAR TIRE & RUBBER CO.**

Creative Firm: **SAATCHI&SAATCHI SRL - ROME, ITALY**
Creative Team: **LUCA ALBANESE, FRANCESCO TADDEUCCI, CARL JOHAN PAULIN**
Client: **NBC UNIVERSAL GLOBAL NETWORKS ITALIA SRL**
WWW.STUDIOUNIVERSAL.IT

Creative Firm: **VANPELT CREATIVE - GARLAND, TX**
Creative Team: **CHIP VANPELT, TODD BRASHEAR**
Client: **AM APPLIANCE GROUP**

Creative Firm: **COMEDY CENTRAL OFF-AIR CREATIVE - NEW YORK, NY**
Creative Team: **JOHN LEFTERATOS, STEPHEN KAMSLER**
Client: **COMEDY CENTRAL**

Creative Firm: **HEYE&PARTNER GMBH - UNTERHACHING, GERMANY**
Creative Team: **SVEN NAGEL, MARIA SOMMER, NORBERT HEROLD**
Client: **THE AWARD**

The Cleveland International Film Festival is considered one of the most successful independent film festivals in the country. Their 30th annual event showcased more than 120 feature films, and 100 short films from 50 countries.

Marcus Thomas, LLC wanted the promotional pieces to give the audience a sneak peek of a few of the films. Still frames were selected and used as the main visual in each ad. Key elements of the images were obscured with an actual movie ticket, which forced the viewer to speculate about the storyline behind each image. Included in the ads were the title of the movie, shoe dates, and web address.

The message was smart and literal: You can't see it without a ticket.

Because the Marcus Thomas design firm did not design the tickets, incorporating them into the ad was a challenge, as was obtaining actual frame captures and getting the necessary permissions to use them. But the result was successful, with the festival experiencing a 20% increase in attendance from previous years.

Creative Firm: **MARCUS THOMAS LLC - CLEVELAND, OH**
Creative Team: **JAMIE VENORSKY, ROGER FRANK, JOANNE KIM, ACME**
Client: **CLEVELAND FILM SOCIETY**

The Ⓟ *symbol designates a Platinum Award Winner, our Best in Category.*

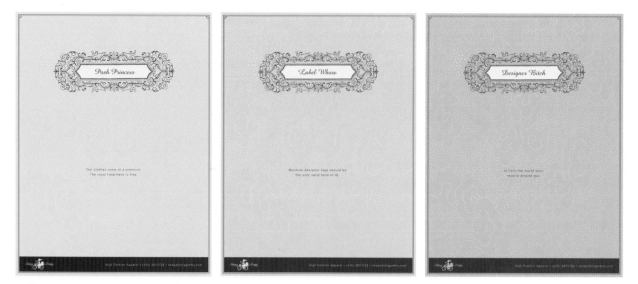

 Creative Firm: **ALCONE MARKETING - IRVINE, CA**
Creative Team: **LUIS CAMANO, CARLOS MUSQUEZ, SHIVONNE MILLER**
Client: **SITTING PRETTY**

Creative Firm: **LITTLE BIRD COMMUNICATIONS - MOBILE, AL**
Creative Team: **DIANE GIBBS**
Client: **BOO RADLEY**

Creative Firm: **Y&R GERMANY - FRANKFURT AM MAIN, GERMANY**
Creative Team: **UWE MARQUARDT, NATALIA RICHEL, KAI-OLIVER SASS,**
MARION LAKATOS, BERTHOLD MEYER, ROLF DZIEDEK
Client: **EURYZA GMBH**

Creative Firm: **MACY'S MERCHANDISING GROUP - NEW YORK, NY**
Creative Team: **ELIZABETH PRINZE, HILDA WONG, FRANCESCA HAYSLETT, ANIK MCGORY, MARYELLEN NEEDHAM, JULIE GANG**
Client: **MACY'S MERCHANDISING GROUP**

Creative Firm: **WINSPER INC. - BOSTON, MA**
Creative Team: **STEVE BAUTISTA, BRIAN FANDETTI, KEVIN CIMO, BOB CLINTON, JD NORMAN, DAVID BEHRENS**
Client: **EXETER HOSPITAL**

Creative Firm: **MACY'S MERCHANDISING GROUP - NEW YORK, NY**
Creative Team: **MARCELLA ACCARDI-SANDERS, CARYLE CRUZ, FRANCESCA HAYSLETT, TESH PATEL, MARYELLEN NEEDHAM**
Client: **MACY'S MERCHANDISING GROUP**

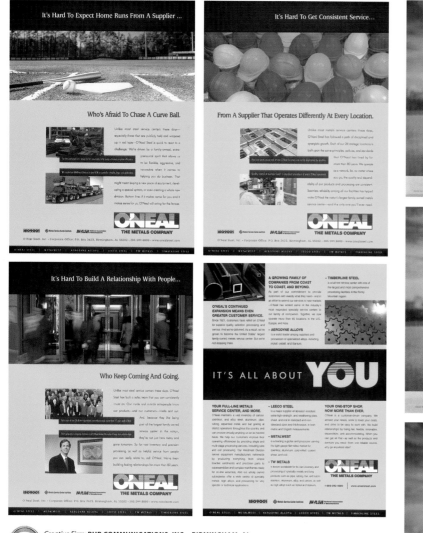

Creative Firm: **PHP COMMUNICATIONS, INC. - BIRMINGHAM, AL**
Creative Team: **BRYAN CHACE, KELLY POIRIER**
Client: **O'NEAL STEEL**

Creative Firm: **D'ADDA, LORENZINI, VIGORELLI, BBDO - ROME, ITALY**
Creative Team: **GIAMPIERO VIGORELLI, LETIZIA ZIACO, NICOLA LAMPUGNANI, ALESSIO GELSINI**
Client: **NBC UNIVERSAL GLOBAL NETWORKS ITALIA SRL**
WWW.STUDIOUNIVERSAL.IT

Creative Firm: **PALIO - SARATOGA SPRINGS, NY**
Creative Team: **KEN MESSINGER, STEPHANIE HOSMER, MICHAEL COSTELLO,
PETER O'TOOLE, NORA KIERNAN, TIFFANY RYAN**
Client: **GLAXOSMITHKLINE**

Creative Firm: MACY'S MERCHANDISING GROUP - NEW YORK, NY
Creative Team: **MARCELLA ACCARDI-SANDERS, CARYLE CRUZ, FRANCESCA HAYSLETT, WALTER CHIN, MARYELLEN NEEDHAM**
Client: **MACY'S MERCHANDISING GROUP**

Creative Firm: **Y&R GERMANY - FRANKFURT AM MAIN, GERMANY**
Creative Team: **CHRISTIAN DAUL, MAJA MILOSEVIC, ANDRES OSSELMANN, JAN HERBOLSHEIMER, MAIKE SCHULENBURG, WOLFGANG KOENIG**
Client: **COLGATE GERMANY**

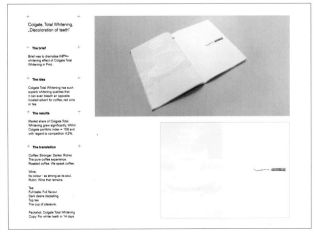

Colgate, Total Whitening,
„Discoloration of teeth"

+ The brief

Brief was to dramatise the
whitening effect of Colgate Total
Whitening in Print.

+ The idea

Colgate Total Whitening has such
superb whitening qualities that
it can even bleach an opposite
located advert for coffee, red wine
or tea.

+ The results

Market share of Colgate Total
Whitening grew significantly. Within
Colgate portfolio index = 158 and
with regard to competition 4.2%.

+ The translation

Coffee: Stronger. Darker. Richer.
The pure coffee experience.
Roasted coffee. We speak coffee.

Wine:
Its colour - as strong as its soul.
Rubin. Wine that remains.

Tea:
Full taste. Full flavour.
Dark desire darjeeling.
Top tea
The cup of pleasure.

Packshot: Colgate Total Whitening
Copy: For whiter teeth in 14 days.

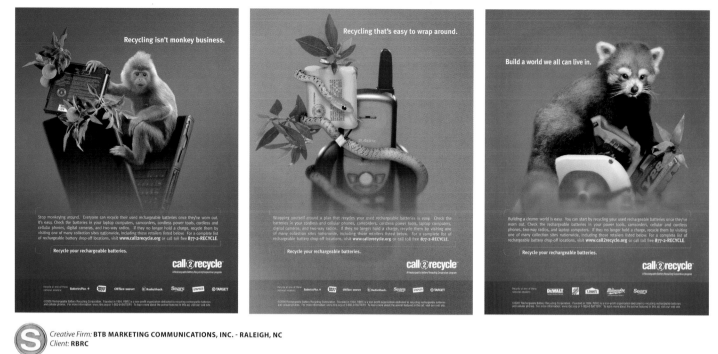

S Creative Firm: **BTB MARKETING COMMUNICATIONS, INC. - RALEIGH, NC**
Client: **RBRC**

Creative Firm: **DESIGN NUT - KENSINGTON, MD**
Creative Team: **BRENT ALMOND, TIMOTHY WORRELL, THOMAS DEMARCO**
Client: **TIMOTHY PAUL CARPETS + TEXTILES**

S Creative Firm: **MACY'S MERCHANDISING GROUP - NEW YORK, NY**
Creative Team: **MARCELLA ACCARDI-SANDERS, VICKI WAN, FRANCESCA HAYSLETT,**
MARK BOTHWICK, MARYELLEN NEEDHAM
Client: **MACY'S MERCHANDISING GROUP**

Creative Firm: **DC3/UNICOM - BELÉM, BRAZIL**
Creative Team: **BRUNO SILVA, ALEXANDRE HELMUT,**
STEVEN DOLZANE, HAROLDO VALENTE, GLAUCO LIMA
Client: **JOVEM PAN BELÉM**

Global conscience advertisements are always challenging. Without strong visual impact, many simply go unnoticed. Others slide quickly into vague-ville and become an ad that almost any non-profit can sign their name to. The design firm DC3/Unicom explains it this way, "The biggest challenge when the creation is developed is to clearly insert the client's characteristics into the work."

The intent of the client, Jovem Pan Radio, was to stress the importance of Worldwide Environment Day. During brainstorming,

DC3/Unicom's aim was to find a common factor between their radio client and the environmental movement. They chose sound.

Music and the environment was the concept used to create the ad, a CD of the "Sounds of Nature," which included a wide variety of beautiful sounds pulled directly from the world around us. The idea was that mankind may try to copy nature but will never match the original.

The simple and direct tagline makes that sentiment very clear: "No copy can substitute the original. Preserve it."

The ⓅP symbol designates a Platinum Award Winner, our Best in Category.

Creative Firm: **SRIJAN ADVERTISING - MADHYA PRADESH, INDIA**
Creative Team: **PRANAV HARIHAR SHARMA, NITIN SARKAR**
Client: **DIVINE GROUP**

Creative Firm: **DC3/UNICOM - BELÉM, BRAZIL**
Creative Team: **ALEXANDRE HELMUT, PAULO SÉRGIO,**
GLAUCO LIMA, HAROLDO VALENTE
Client: **JOVEM PAN BELÉM**

Creative Firm: **THE HUMANE SOCIETY OF THE UNITED STATES - WASHINGTON, DC**
Creative Team: **PAULA JAWORSKI, SUSAN WASHINGTON**
Client: **THE HUMANE SOCIETY OF THE UNITED STATES**

Creative Firm: **SRIJAN ADVERTISING - MADHYA PRADESH, INDIA**
Creative Team: **PRANAV HARIHAR SHARMA, SHAILENDRA AGIWAAL, SHAILENDRA AGIWAAL**
Client: **NAIDUNIA NEWS AND NETWORKS PVT. LTD.**

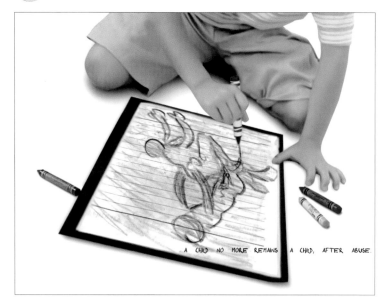

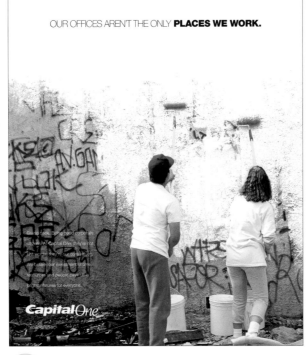

Creative Firm: **JWT SPECIALIZED COMMUNICATIONS - NEW YORK, NY**
Creative Team: **JEFF BOCKMAN, ANANT PANCHAL**
Client: **CAPITAL ONE**

American magazine is the official university magazine for American University. It seeks to build or renew an American University affiliation among alumni, parents, donors, faculty and staff through continuing education, community building and news. It features stories about the significant role AU plays in the larger world; profiles and class notes introducing faculty, students and alumni to one another; and informative, entertaining stories about AU's past, present and future.

Prompted by the increased global awareness of sustainability issues, over 300 colleges and universities have agreed to work toward creating "green" campuses. In Spring 2007, American University joined this group by signing the Tailloires Declaration, a public pledge for colleges and universities to practice environmentally sound policies, create a culture of sustainability and increase environmental literacy. AU's sustainability efforts include the use of biodiesel vehicles, a commitment to recycling, a "green" roof, plans for a "green" design for the new School of International Service building and other initiatives.

All of this was the inspiration for this Platinum award-winning cover. The design was intended to be a lighthearted play on the concept of good things come in brown packages— recycled brown paper packages, that is—to entice the reader into wanting to see what was inside.

AMERICAN

Magazine of American University

Spring 2007

PLEASE RECYCLE THIS MAGAZINE!

Creative Firm: **AMERICAN UNIVERSITY OFFICE OF PUBLICATIONS - WASHINGTON, DC**
Creative Team: **WENDY BECKERMAN, JEFF WATTS**
Client: **AMERICAN UNIVERSITY**
WWW.AMERICAN.EDU/MAGAZINE

The ⓟ *symbol designates a Platinum Award Winner, our Best in Category.*

Creative Firm: **INK PUBLISHING - LONDON, ENGLAND**
Creative Team: **PIERS TOWNLEY, JOSH TAYLOR**
Client: **EASYJET**

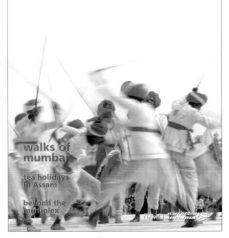

Creative Firm: **MEDIASCOPE PUBLICITAS - MUMBAI, INDIA, INDIA**
Creative Team: **FARUQUI JAAN, UMESH KUTTAN, MARIA SHAMSI**
Client: **AIR INDIA**

 Creative Firm: **THE STANDERD - ORLANDO, FL**
Creative Team: **JAMES KRAWCZYK, JOSH LETCHWORTH, JOEY MEDDOCK**
Client: **THE STANDERD**

Creative Firm: **EMPHASIS MEDIA LIMITED - HONG KONG**
Creative Team: **VINCENT YUN**
Client: **THAI AIRWAYS**

Creative Firm: **AGENCY FISH LTD - LONDON, ENGLAND**
Creative Team: **STEPHEN PEAPLE**
Client: **SRILANKAN AIRLINES**

 Creative Firm: **UNITED STATES POSTAL SERVICE - ARLINGTON, VA**
Client: **UNITED STATES POSTAL SERVICE**

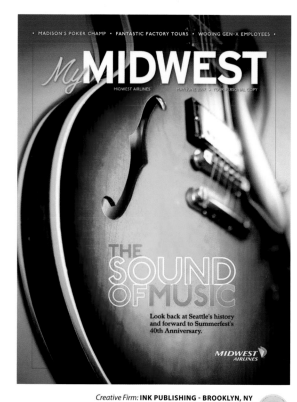

Creative Firm: **INK PUBLISHING - BROOKLYN, NY**
Creative Team: **SHANE LUITJENS, KELLY BARBIERI, ORION RAY-JONES, MARIXSA RODRIGUEZ, BROOKE PORTER**
Client: **MIDWEST AIRLINES**

 Creative Firm: **EMPHASIS MEDIA LIMITED - HONG KONG**
Creative Team: **PERCY CHUNG**
Client: **SINGAPORE AIRLINES**

Creative Firm: **UNITED STATES POSTAL SERVICE - ARLINGTON, VA**
Client: **UNITED STATES POSTAL SERVICE**

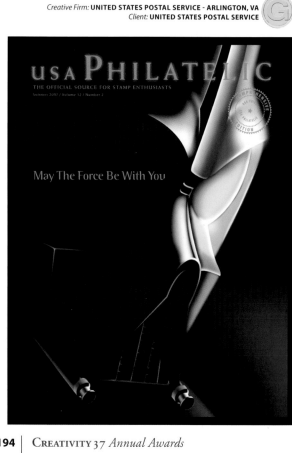

Creative Firm: **EMPHASIS MEDIA LIMITED - HONG KONG**
Creative Team: **LOCKY LAI, MAY LUI**
Client: **CHINA AIRLINES**

Creative Firm: **UNITED STATES POSTAL SERVICE - ARLINGTON, VA**
Client: **UNITED STATES POSTAL SERVICE**

Creative Firm: **MEDIASCOPE PUBLICITAS - MUMBAI, INDIA**
Creative Team: **FARUQUI JAAN, LAKSHMINARAYANAN, MARIA SHAMSI**
Client: **AIR SAHARA (NOW JET LITE)**

Creative Firm: **UNITED STATES POSTAL SERVICE - ARLINGTON, VA**
Client: **UNITED STATES POSTAL SERVICE**

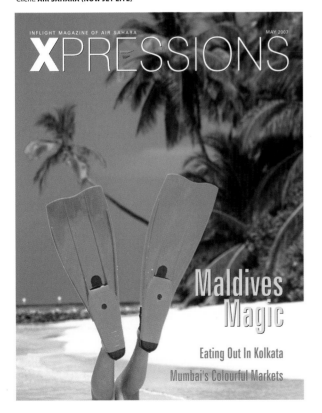

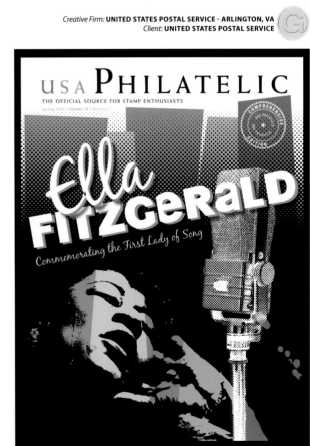

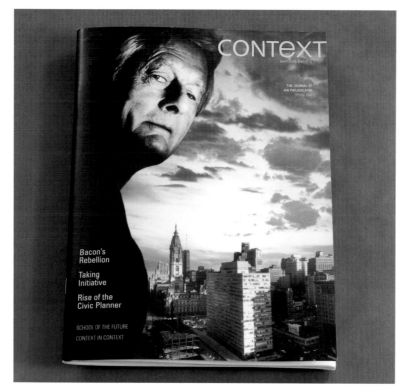

Creative Firm: **DESIGNLORE - PHILADELPHIA, PA**
Creative Team: **LAURIE CHURCHMAN, DAN HUSTED, MICHAEL AHEARN**
Client: **AIA PHILADELPHIA**

Creative Firm: **CHEN DESIGN ASSOCIATES - SAN FRANCISCO, CA**
Creative Team: **JOSHUA CHEN, MAX SPECTOR**
Client: **HOW MAGAZINE**

Creative Firm: **BUCK CONSULTANTS, AN ACS COMPANY - ST. LOUIS, MO**
Creative Team: **ELIZABETH LOHMEYER, MELISSA KRAMPER,
DEBBIE ROBERTS, EBB WATSON (BENDER PRINTING)**
Client: **KELLWOOD COMPANY**

Creative Firm: **AGENCY FISH LTD - LONDON, ENGLAND**
Creative Team: **STEPHEN PEAPLE, GEHAN DE SILVA WIJEYERATNE**
Client: **SRILANKAN AIRLINES**

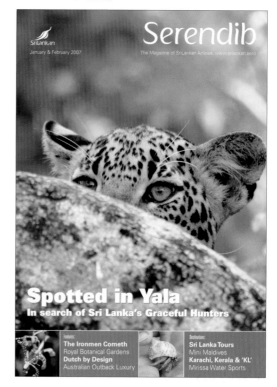

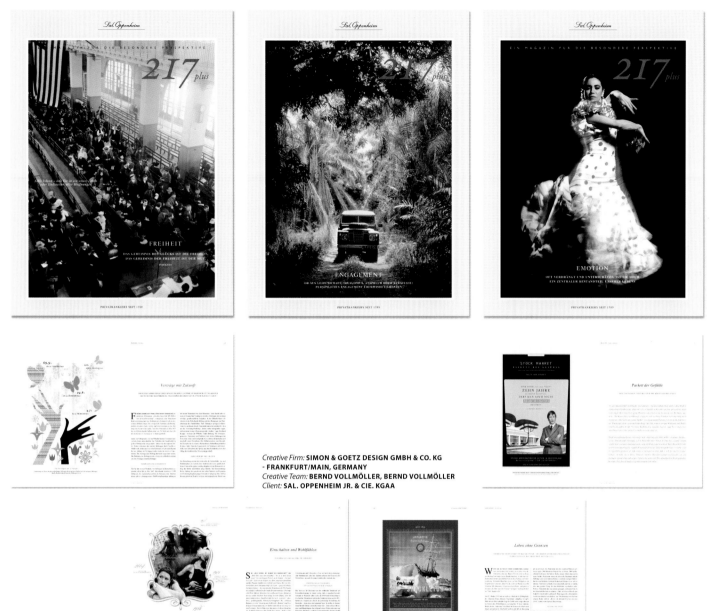

Creative Firm: **SIMON & GOETZ DESIGN GMBH & CO. KG - FRANKFURT/MAIN, GERMANY**
Creative Team: **BERND VOLLMÖLLER, BERND VOLLMÖLLER**
Client: **SAL. OPPENHEIM JR. & CIE. KGAA**

Sal. Oppenheim is one of Europe's leading independent private banks. The focus of their activities is asset management and investment banking for wealthy clients and corporate customers. 217 Plus magazine was created as a public relations tool to provide valuable information to existing and potential clients, as well as employees.

The aim was to make a high-class, attention-grabbing magazine, which corresponds to the ambitious self-image of Sal. Oppenheim. Every issue has an overall topic: engagement, freedom, emotion, etc. The design successfully communicates the traditional values, innovation, exclusiveness and independence of the private bank.

Included in the magazine are topics on economy, society and culture that represent the attitudes of Sal. Oppenheim. The design expresses their open-mindedness to new industrial and economic developments, sensitivity to sociopolitical issues and personal commitment in many fields of art and culture.

The ⓟ symbol designates a Platinum Award Winner, our Best in Category.

Creative Firm: **UIUC SCHOOL OF ART AND DESIGN - CHAMPAIGN, IL**
Creative Team: **JENNIFER GUNJI, JODEE STANLEY**
Client: **UIUC DEPARTMENT OF ENGLISH**
WWW.NINTHLETTER.COM

Creative Firm: **CCM - WEST ORANGE, NJ**
Creative Team: **STEPHEN LONGO, CHRISTINE CABRERA, JACIE WOZNICKI, KAYA RYBACZEK, SARAH HUGHES, JEFF FLEISCHMANN**
Client: **PROME, ITALYTHEAN 2007**

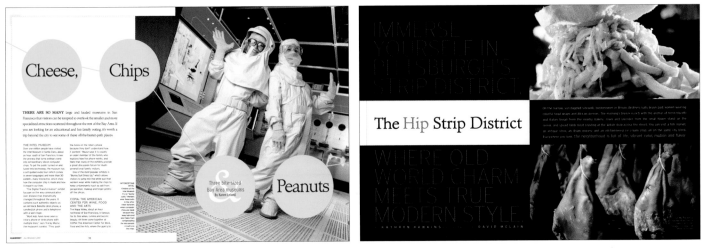

Cheese, Chips & Peanuts

Three bite-sized Bay Area museums
By Karen Leland

THERE ARE SO MANY large and lauded museums in San Francisco that visitors can be tempted to overlook the smaller and more specialized attractions scattered throughout the rest of the Bay Area. If you are looking for an educational and fun family outing, it's worth a trip beyond the city to see some of these off-the-beaten-path places.

The Hip Strip District

IMMERSE YOURSELF IN PITTSBURGH'S STRIP DISTRICT.

WHERE OLD WORLD CHARM MEETS TRUE MODERN STYLE.

Creative Firm: **INK PUBLISHING - BROOKLYN, NY**
Creative Team: **SHANE LUITJENS, KELLY BARBIERI, ORION RAY-JONES, MARIXSA RODRIGUEZ, BROOKE PORTER**
Client: **MIDWEST AIRLINES**

Creative Firm: **SPLASH PRODUCTIONS PTE LTD - SINGAPORE**
Creative Team: **STANLEY YAP, TERRY LEE, EVELYN TENG, NORMAN NG**
Client: **BBA CAREER SERVICE, NUS BUSINESS SCHOOL, NUS**

focus

Staying The Course

"The whole business education in NUS is geared towards starting the students off in the corporate world."

Creative Firm: **THE STANDERD - ORLANDO, FL**
Creative Team: **JAMES KRAWCZYK, JOSH LETCHWORTH, JOEY MEDDOCK**
Client: **THE STANDERD**

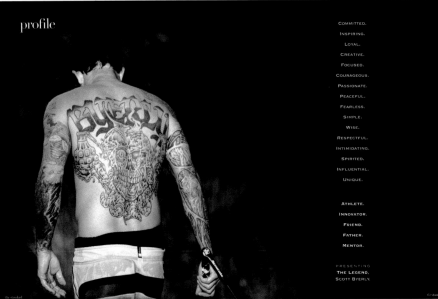

profile

COMMITTED.
INSPIRING.
LOYAL.
CREATIVE.
FOCUSED.
COURAGEOUS.
PASSIONATE.
PEACEFUL.
FEARLESS.
SIMPLE.
WISE.
RESPECTFUL.
INTIMIDATING.
SPIRITED.
INFLUENTIAL.
UNIQUE.

ATHLETE.
INNOVATOR.
FRIEND.
FATHER.
MENTOR.

PRESENTING
THE LEGEND.
SCOTT BYERLY.

Creative Firm: **INK PUBLISHING - BROOKLYN, NY**
Creative Team: **SHANE LUITJENS, SAM POLCER, ORION RAY-JONES, MARIXSA RODRIGUEZ, BROOKE PORTER**
Client: **ATA AIRLINES**

Creative Firm: **INK PUBLISHING - BROOKLYN, NY**
Creative Team: **SHANE LUITJENS, ALEXANDRA P. KARPLUS, ORION RAY-JONES, GERONNA LEWIS-LYTE, BROOKE PORTER**
Client: **AIRTRAN AIRWAYS**

Creative Firm: **SPLASH PRODUCTIONS PTE LTD - SINGAPORE**
Creative Team: **STANLEY YAP, TERRY LEE, NORMAN NG, JOSHUA TAN**
Client: **HOME TEAM ACADEMY**

Creative Firm: **INK PUBLISHING - LONDON, ENGLAND**
Creative Team: **ANDREW HUMPHREYS, BRENDAN ALTHORPE**
Client: **GULF AIR**

Creative Firm: **KF DESIGN - TAKASAKI, JAPAN**
Creative Team: **KEVIN FOLEY, TAKAHIRO SAKUMA, HISASHI KONDO**
Client: **JIJI GAHO SHA, INC.**

Creative Firm: **AGENCY FISH LTD - LONDON, ENGLAND**
Creative Team: **STEPHEN PEAPLE, JULIAN JORDAN**
Client: **SRILANKAN AIRLINES**

Creative Firm: **DESIGN CENTER LTD. - LJUBLJANA, SLOVENIA**
Creative Team: **EDUARD CEHOVIN, FEDJA VUKIC**
Client: **DESIGN CENTER LTD.**

Creative Firm: **INK PUBLISHING - LONDON, ENGLAND**
Creative Team: **ROBINA DAM, SIMON HOUGHTON**
Client: **BMI**

Creative Firm: **DESIGN HOCH DREI - STUTTGART, GERMANY**
Creative Team: **WOLFRAM SCHÄFFER, CHRISTA HEINOLD, TOBIAS TOBIAS KOLLMANN, BÄRBEL JÖRDENS, MAIKE MÄRTZSCHINK, SEPAS MOHAMMADPOUR**
Client: **DAIMLERCHRYSLER**

Creative Firm: **UIUC SCHOOL OF ART AND DESIGN - CHAMPAIGN, IL**
Creative Team: **JENNIFER GUNJI-BALLSRUD, JODEE STANLEY**
Client: **UIUC DEPARTMENT OF ENGLISH**
WWW.NINTHLETTER.COM

Creative Firm: **INK PUBLISHING - LONDON, ENGLAND**
Creative Team: **RICHARD BENCE, JONNY CLARK**
Client: **MAXJET**

Creative Firm: **SKIDMORE - ROYAL OAK, MI**
Creative Team: **LIBBY COLE**
Client: **QUICKEN LOANS**

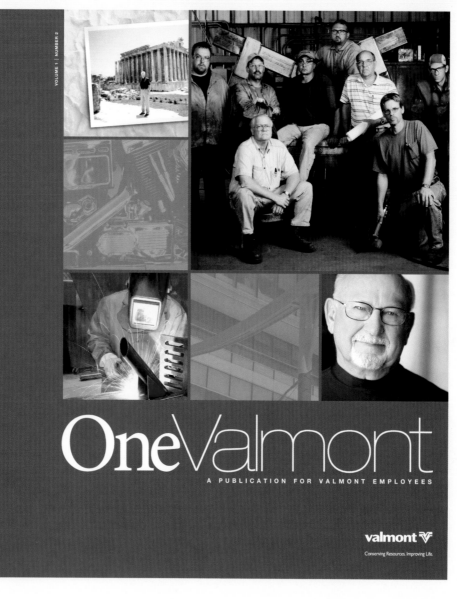

Creative Firm: **DD+A - OMAHA, NE**
Client: **VALMONT INDUSTRIES**

Valmont is a world leader in engineered structures for infrastructure and water management for agriculture, with offices around the world. David Day + Associates was asked to create a semi-annual magazine for Valmont's internal employees, business partners, vendors, and clients. The task was also to inspire, motivate and help close the global distance within the company.

David Day + Associates designed OneValmont, a magazine representing Valmont's family culture and a united Valmont team committed to achieving excellence around the world. The challenge of making it a global communication meant having OneValmont translated and printed in five different languages: English, Spanish, Chinese, French and Portuguese.

David Day + Associates produced a publication that departs from traditional internal publications in format, design and copy. Specifically, OneValmont provides useful content achieved by a team of writers conducting in-depth interviews with Valmont employees to develop engaging and informative stories for the magazine. Local photographers were hired to capture images that complement each article. The magazine features a simple, clean and uncluttered layout. It is distributed to 6,000 Valmont associates around the world.

The Ⓟ *symbol designates a Platinum Award Winner, our Best in Category.*

Creative Firm: **THE BETTER IMAGE COMPANY - SARASOTA, FL**
Client: **CLOCKWORK HOME SERVICES**

Creative Firm: **THE BETTER IMAGE COMPANY - SARASOTA, FL**
Client: **WHITE HAT BRANDS**

Creative Firm: **ELLEN BRUSS DESIGN - DENVER, CO**
Creative Team: **ELLEN BRUSS, JORGE LAMORA**
Client: **THE LABORATORY OF ART AND IDEAS, BELMAR**

The Lab at Belmar is a new institution dedicated to contemporary art and thought, combining elements of an art museum, think tank and public forum. The Lab shows contemporary art's top artists in a way that it is easy for non-artists to digest and understand.

Their creative brief for this project was to create a journal that would provide serious information but in a humorous, somewhat self-deprecating way. The idea was to create a piece beyond the status of a newsletter and design it in a way that people would want to collect them. The Lab wanted Ellen Bruss Design to convey the message that the newsletter was a serious, smart publication by a company that didn't take itself too seriously. The biggest challenge was to go far enough so that the newsletter would be funny, but stay within the line that kept it serious.

The Lab's full name is The Laboratory of Art & Ideas. That sparked the idea to twist the name around and show a Labrador Retriever in a variety of situations. The colors for the newsletter are taken from the interior space of The Lab, which Ellen Bruss Design also picked. The colors where chosen to move away from the traditional art museum black plus primary colors.

The (P) *symbol designates a Platinum Award Winner, our Best in Category.*

Creative Firm: **TMDCREATIVE - SALINAS, CA**
Client: **MONTERRA**

GARDENING

Botany of a Spring Appetizer

Bulbs, Glorious Bulbs

Creative Firm: **MISSOURI BOTANICAL GARDEN - BRENTWOOD, MO**
Creative Team: **ELLEN FLESCH**
Client: **MISSOURI BOTANICAL GARDEN**

MISSOURI
BOTANICAL
GARDEN
bulletin
March/April 2007 Vol. 95 No. 2

KIDSTUFF

spring into learning!

Kids Explore More at the Garden

Discover a Missouri adventure!
open april–october, daily, 9 a.m. to 5 p.m.

Rise and Shine! Children's Garden Wakes up for Spring

Impossible is not our word. Every day we go beyond the ordinary and think beyond the immediate, to discover new challenges. This is what makes us who we are. This is what we call Forward thinking.

Welcome to **Aviva Global Services**, the business process outsourcing arm of Aviva, which is the world's fifth-largest insurance group and the biggest in the UK, with 58,000 employees serving 35 million customers worldwide.

Aviva. Forward thinking

Thinking ahead? So are we.
At Aviva Global Services you could build a career in one of the world's most challenging and fast-moving business environments. We aim to be the **Employer of Choice** wherever we operate.

If you are a forward thinker who wants to be in a workplace that values Teamwork, Integrity, Performance and Progressiveness, write in to us with your resumé at - **careers@avivags.com**

AVIVA
Aviva Global Services

WHO SAYS I CAN'T?

Creative Firm: **LIGHTHOUSE COMMUNICATIONS - PUNE, INDIA**
Creative Team: **RAMESHWAR JAWANJAL, UDAYENDU LAHIRI, SANJAY KAMBLE**
Client: **AVIVA GLOBAL SERVICES**

Aviva Global Services is part of the growing IT/ITES sector in India. The design brief was to position employment at AGS as a career within a fast-growing international insurance industry, and not just another job at any call center.

The message revolved around the company's "Making Impossible Possible" philosophy, and the ad needed to convey the positive, vibrant culture within the company.

The challenge was to find the perfect image to communicate this message. The silhouette of the boy was shot separately and added to a Corbis image. Careful thought was given to the use of corporate colors. Yellow and black were chosen for their high contrast and visual impact within a newspaper format.

The Ⓟ *symbol designates a Platinum Award Winner, our Best in Category.*

MORE **LiVE** THAN REALITY

Go to the **THEATRE**

Visit the Copenhagen theatres. Go to www.ta-i-teatret.dk

Creative Firm: **SCANAD - AARHUS C, DENMARK**
Creative Team: **HENRY RASMUSSEN, JAN MAACK**
Client: **COPENHAGEN THEATERS**

Creative Firm: **M/C/C - DALLAS, TX**
Creative Team: **GREG HANSEN, TODD BRASHEAR, HILLARY BOULDEN, AMANDA MYERS**
Client: **M/C/C**

An image is a
terrible thing to waste.

Don't let this happen to yours.

LIVING THE UNEXPECTED

www.mccom.com   972.480.8383
Advertising Public Relations Internet Marketing Image Interventions

Creative Firm: **ALCONE MARKETING - IRVINE, CA**
Creative Team: **JULIE KIMURA, CARLOS MUSQUEZ,**
LUIS CAMANO
Client: **CALHFA**

When market research showed that Californians within the middle-to-lower-income brackets had lost hope of ever owning a home, the client, California Housing Finance Agency, wanted to correct their misconception.

CalHFA hired Alcone Marketing to create an ad that would efficiently convey the following message: One phone call could put Californians on the path to home ownership.

Because the ad was created to resemble a simple handmade flyer,

it made the message more direct and approachable. It helped convey CalHFA not as a large, intimidating corporation, but as a company you could call anytime for one-on-one assistance. The visual, combined with the simple tagline "We help first-time homebuyers." was all that was needed to get the powerful message across.

The design concept was powerful, and Alcone Marketing developed it rather quickly. In fact, it took them more time to find just the right house to feature in the 'flyer' than it did to create and execute the concept.

The ℗ *symbol designates a Platinum Award Winner, our Best in Category.*

Creative Firm: **MFP - NEW YORK, NY**
Creative Team: **NEIL POWELL, JOSH ROGERS, MARY WILLIAMS, FRANZ HUEBER**
Client: **GRINCH**

Creative Firm: **MENDES PUBLICIDADE - BELÉM, BRAZIL**
Creative Team: **OSWALDO MENDES, MARIA ALICE PENNA**
Client: **UNIMED BELÉM**

Creative Firm: **M/C/C - DALLAS, TX**
Creative Team: **GREG HANSEN, TODD BRASHEAR, HILLARY BOULDEN, AMANDA MYERS**
Client: **GOALTENDER DEVELOPMENT INSTITUTE (GDI)**

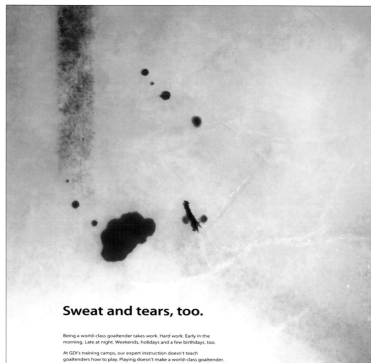

Sweat and tears, too.

Being a world-class goaltender takes work. Hard work. Early in the morning. Late at night. Weekends, holidays and a few birthdays, too.

At GDI's training camps, our expert instruction doesn't teach goaltenders how to play. Playing doesn't make a world-class goaltender. Sure, we teach the physical game. But we do it better. More thoroughly. More technically. At the same time, we teach the mental game. We cultivate and challenge self-discipline. We put young goaltenders to work. And that allows them to be their best.

If you've got the potential to be great — with blood, sweat and tears to spare — there's only one camp for you. GDI. It's no day at the beach. We promise.

For registration details and a camp schedule, go to **gdihockey.com**.

800.667.9044

The Revolution is Now.

Creative Firm: **M/C/C - DALLAS, TX**
Creative Team: **GREG HANSEN, TODD BRASHEAR, HILLARY BOULDEN, AMANDA MYERS**
Client: **GOALTENDER DEVELOPMENT INSTITUTE (GDI)**

Creative Firm: **PURPLE FOCUS PVT. LTD. - INDORE, INDIA**
Creative Team: **MR. VINOD BHARGAV, MR. VALLAN ANTONY, MR. NILESH KULKARNI**
Client: **INDORE LASIK LASER CENTRE**

Indore Lasik Laser Center inaugurates today. And the good news is, you can finally say good bye to your glasses and contact lenses. Brought to you by central India's renowned Ophthalmologists, here's world-class **Laser Vision Correction** at its best.

216-17, DM Tower, 21/1, Race Course Road, Near Janjeerwala Square, Indore. Tel : 91-731 2530303.

Okay, she's just a little farm girl in pigtails, catapulted into the world out of loyalty to her little dog. On one hand she's ready to brave anything, but she's torn, too. She wants both change and familiarity—to see the whole colorful world, but from the safety of her little black-and-white porch. I totally relate to Dorothy. I really do.

spout.com

SP🌕UT™

Creative Firm: **PEOPLE DESIGN - GRAND RAPIDS, MI**
Creative Team: **GEOFFREY MARK, MICHELE CHARTIER, KRISTIN TENNANT**
Client: **SPOUT**

Napoleon Dynamite isn't afraid to really be himself. I'll just say "moon boots" and say no more. I know he isn't a real guy, but he has totally inspired me. I mean, gosh, I think about him every time I'm feeling kinda goofy and self-conscious. He completely changes my perspective.

spout.com

SP🌕UT
We're talkin' movies.

In 2006, People Design created an advertising campaign for Spout.com, a social networking Web site for film and movie enthusiasts. The advertising campaign included television, radio and print ads, and was designed to generate traffic and increase membership to Spout.com—specifically during the 2006 International Film Festival in Telluride, CO.

The ads portray everyday movie fans and the films they love. In fact, the print ads feature People Design and Spout.com employees in a staged "movie addict encounter group."

Both the ad concept and its production employed the grassroots approach of the Spout.com web site, while also accommodating the limited budget and tight turnaround of the project.

Movie addict?
No support group or 12-step program necessary.

spout.com

SP🌕UT
We're talkin' movies.

The ⓟ symbol designates a Platinum Award Winner, our Best in Category.

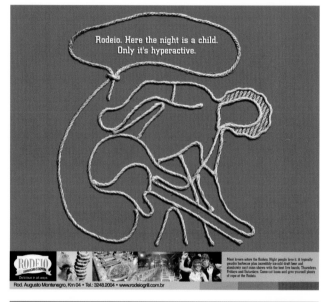

Creative Firm: **REVOLUCION - NEW YORK, NY**
Creative Team: **ALBERTO RODRIGUEZ, ROBERTO ALCAZAR, HENRY ALVAREZ, TRE MILLER**
Client: **PALM BAY INTERNATIONAL**

Creative Firm: **ALL MEDIA PROJECTS LIMITED - PORT OF SPAIN, TRINIDAD & TOBAGO**
Creative Team: **CATHLEEN JONES**
Client: **AMPLE**

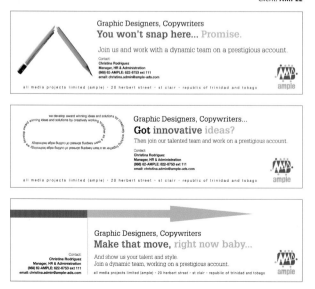

Creative Firm: **DC3/UNICOM - BELÉM, BRAZIL**
Creative Team: **ALEXANDRE HELMUT, GLAUCO LIMA,**
RENATA SEGTOWICK, GLAUCO LIMA, HAROLDO VALENTE
Client: **RODEIO**

Creative Firm: **DC3/UNICOM - BELÉM, BRAZIL**
Creative Team: **ALEXANDRE HELMUT, PAULO SÉRGIO, ANTÔNIO COELHO, HAROLDO VALENTE, GLAUCO LIMA**
Client: **ORM CABO**

S

Creative Firm: **WING CHAN DESIGN, INC. - NEW YORK, NY**
Creative Team: **WING CHAN**
Client: **AMERICAN EXPRESS BANK LTD.**

Creative Firm: **PLANET ADS AND DESIGN P/L - SINGAPORE**
Creative Team: **HAL SUZUKI, RUSTAM MOHAMMED, ERAN HUSNI, YEUNG KIT CHAU, SUZANNE LAURIDSEN, JOCELYN CHENG**
Client: **SUNTEC CITY MALL**

Creative Firm: **CRE8TIVISION - WASHINGTON, DC**
Creative Team: **BARB DICKEY, MEREDITH LIGHT, MYLES MARLOW, GARY WHITE, VERTIS, INC.**
Client: **WATER ADVOCATES**

Newspapers are most often viewed at arm's length and, because of their large size, there is a lot of visual competition on each spread—both from other advertisements and from editorial stories. It's crucial that the design of newspaper ads compels the reader to take notice. Water Advocates looked to the team of Cre8tivision to find solutions to these design dilemmas.

Because the subject matter was serious, Cre8tivision set out to make an immediate emotional connection with the reader. The result is both powerful and intense.

The ad's quick connection with readers helped to raise awareness that clean drinking water is vital to the sustainability of our planet, and that many children go without it each day. The campaign tag line, "Clean Drinking Water. It's The Only Way To Live." helps inspires action.

Because the image shows the young girl receiving clean drinking water, it subtly conveys 'assistance', 'solutions', and 'help'. It implies a happy ending is possible.

More despondent images were available of course, but those would not have communicated the correct message, as the goal of the ad was to 'touch' readers emotionally—not to provoke guilt or shame.

The ℗ *symbol designates a Platinum Award Winner, our Best in Category.*

Creative Firm: **ALL MEDIA PROJECTS LIMITED - PORT OF SPAIN, TRINIDAD**
Creative Team: **CATHLEEN JONES, AISHA PROVOTEAUX, JOSIANE KHAN**
Client: **BPTT**

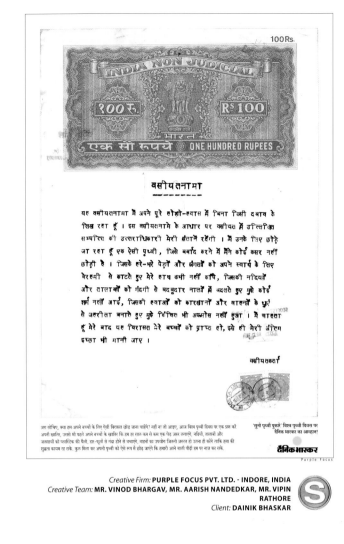

Creative Firm: **PURPLE FOCUS PVT. LTD. - INDORE, INDIA**
Creative Team: **MR. VINOD BHARGAV, MR. AARISH NANDEDKAR, MR. VIPIN RATHORE**
Client: **DAINIK BHASKAR**

Creative Firm: **PURPLE FOCUS PVT. LTD. - MUMBAI, INDIA**
Creative Team: **VINOD BHARGAV, AARISH NANDEDKAR, VIPIN RATHORE, GAURAV DHAKAD, NILESH PARASHAR**
Client: **BHASKAR GROUP**

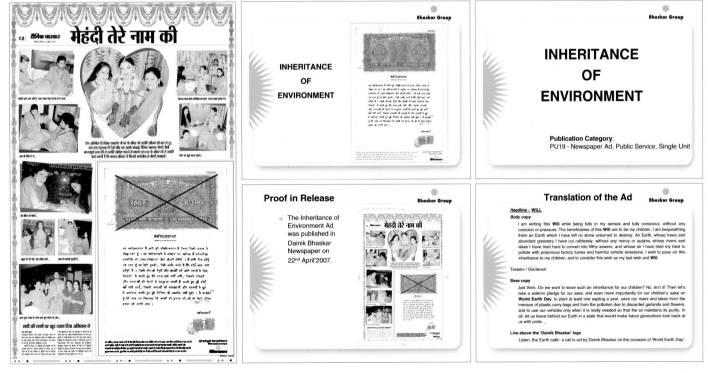

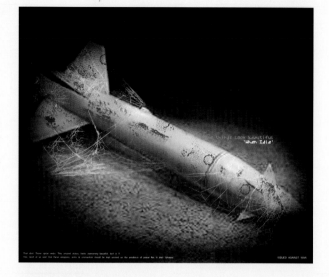

 The instructions were as follows: Find an amazing new way to communicate an age-old message (in this case, "Stop War"), create an entire campaign around it and have it completed by the deadline, which was in two days. To top it off, the design brief was ambiguous and filled with restrictions and vague expectations.

Creative Firm: **SRIJAN ADVERTISING - MADHYA PRADESH, INDIA**
Creative Team: **PRANAV HARIHAR SHARMA, NITIN SARKAR**
Client: **SRIJAN ADVERTISING**

As crazy as it sounds, nearly every designer and copywriter has found themselves in a similarly intense, pressure-filled situation. The next question becomes: How do you handle it?

In this case, the copywriter decided to lie on the couch and watch TV with the design brief lieing across his chest. "The pressure was so much that I started thinking weird things like, 'Maybe if there was no war I wouldn't be in this situation,' and 'Why did I choose this profession?'"

Because of his belief that 'you cannot choose and idea, an idea chooses you', he turned off the TV and remained very still, waiting for the idea to choose him. He told himself to remain idle and the idea would surely arrive. Soon, even more strange thoughts began

to emerge, such as "if I remain this idle for much longer, surely a spider will come build a web on me."

Then he fell asleep. For 2 hours.

When he awoke, his first thought was "Some things look beautiful when idle".

The illustration that would soon accompany this wonderfully subtle, yet strong sentence completed the magic: a bomb covered with dust and spiderwebs.

The *symbol designates a Platinum Award Winner, our Best in Category.*

Creative Firm: **SCANAD - AARHUS C, DENMARK, DENMARK**
Creative Team: **HENRY RASMUSSEN, JAN MAACK**
Client: **COPENHAGEN THEATERS**

PHOTOGRAPHY, *BOOK*

Creative Firm: **EMERSON, WAJDOWICZ STUDIOS - NEW YORK, NY**
Creative Team: **JUREK WAJDOWICZ, LISA LAROCHELLE, MANNY MENDEZ, YOKO YOSHIDA, JONAS BENDIKSEN**
Client: **THE ROCKEFELLER FOUNDATION**

The Rockefeller Foundation 2006 Annual Report

The owner of an online stock photography house, Jim Erickson was inspired by his son Luke to create this 124 page book of photography. The intent of this photography book was to create a promotional catalog for www.Ericksonstock.com that would double as a portfolio for clients and other creatives.

Creative Firm: **ERICKSON PRODUCTIONS, INC. - PETALUMA, CA**
Creative Team: **JIM ERICKSON, CHANNON CEDERNA**
Client: **ERICKSON PRODUCTIONS, INC.**

The concept behind the book is that hidden beauty can be captured in everyday life, and exciting moments don't have to be scripted—they just exist. To convey this, the book is visually narrated the way memories are realized in the brain: The images are not chronological; they have been paired based on loose connections and subliminal cues in tone, color, subject matter and emotion, creating an experience for the viewer, not just a portrait.

The irregularity of the book's shape was used as a cropping mechanism, helping to heighten the intensity and emotion of the image. The square format of the piece makes it more personal and contained.

The ⓟ symbol designates a Platinum Award Winner. This piece tied for Best in Category in "Photography, Book."

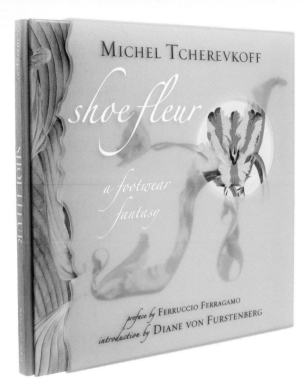

Creative Firm: **TCHREVKOFF STUDIO LTD. / WELCOME BOOKS - NEW YORK, NY**
Creative Team: **MICHEL TCHEREVKOFF, MYRNA KRESH, GREG WAKABAYASHI, KATRINA FRIED**
Client: **WELCOME BOOKS**

Photographer Michel Tcherevkoff's

inspiration for what would eventually become the book, *shoe fleur*, arrived when he looked at one of his photographs from a new perspective.

He'd taken a photograph of a leaf, but it wasn't until the photograph was haphazardly turned upside down on his table that he was able to see it with new eyes. From that perspective, he saw the photo not as a leaf, but as elegant heel of a shoe. That high heel, later named Premiere in the book, would become part of Tcherevkoff's fantasy accessory collection, inspired by the shape of fresh plants and flowers.

He says his biggest challenge was keeping the shoe fleur designs as simple as the flowers themselves. The colors and shapes within shoe fleur have significance to Tcherevkoff, "Every time I went to the flower market in New York, I had to quiet my senses and sharply focus on the shapes, colors, and personalities of each flower. The most stunning blooms were always the most flirtatious, so they demanded my attention and won a place in the final collection," he says.

The publisher's challenge was to turn a collection of shoes, boots and handbags—all with amusing names and stories—into a cohesive book with a design as fresh as the flowered accessories it showcased. The transparent pink slipcase with a simple die-cut center and uniquely curved edges visually communicates there is something very distinctive about the book. Another unique feature is that the front and back case boards are bound on top of the cloth spine, instead of under it. The book and slipcase merge together with a fit that is perfectly snug, a wonderful "coincidence" for a book about shoes.

The ℗ *symbol designates a Platinum Award Winner. This piece tied for Best in Category in "Photography, Book."*

Creative Firm: **STUDIO JMV LLC - MIAMI, FL**
Creative Team: **JOSE MANUEL VIDAURRE, JUAN JOSE POSADA, JOHN FORERO**
Client: **COCACOLA**
HTTP://WWW.JMV-STUDIO.COM

The client wanted the photograph to elicit cravings—a simple design brief, but not as easy as it first appears.

Photographing moving liquids is always challenging. The 'splash' had to look natural and enticing. The flowing liquid needed to remain transparent as well as color-accurate for the product. Studio JMV understood that capturing the exact caramel color was crucial.

Everything had to be done in very slow motion because, as soon as the speed of the liquid increased, it lost its transparency due to the carbonation. By rigging technical devices that allowed them to manipulate the liquid as if it was in a zero-gravity environment, Studio JMV was able to capture the transparent look of the liquid.

The (P) *symbol designates a Platinum Award Winner. This piece tied for Best in Category in "Photography, Commercial."*

222

 During the conceptual phase, Erickson Productions, Inc. knew it was crucial that the photography brought out the essence of the character who was going to appear in each Copenhagen ad. To do this, they specifically chose real people—not models—to capture the honesty and authenticity of each action.

In post-production, the focus was on creating a desaturated tone to enhance the simplicity, grittiness and pure raw emotion of each image. Harsh colors and contrast within the photography would have complicated the moment each image captures, so this was consciously avoided.

Creative Firm: **DOE ANDERSON - PETALUMA, CA**
Creative Team: **JIM ERICKSON, BILL SCHELLING, KATHYRN NASSER**
Client: **COPENHAGEN**

The (P) *symbol designates a Platinum Award Winner. This piece tied for Best in Category in "Photography, Commercial."*

Creative Firm: **MASTRO PHOTOGRAPHY+DESIGN - MOBILE, AL**
Creative Team: **MICHAEL MASTRO**
Client: **WWW.NALL.ORG**

Creative Firm: **STUDIO JMV LLC - MIAMI, FL**
Creative Team: **JOSE MANUEL VIDAURRE, JUAN JOSE POSADA, JOHN FORERO**
Client: **COCACOLA**
HTTP://WWW.JMV-STUDIO.COM

Creative Firm: **STUDIO JMV LLC - MIAMI, FL**
Creative Team: **JOSE VIDAURRE, KEN BAKER, JONATHAN RITCHIE, JULIE HORTON**
Client: **ANHEUSER BUSCH**
HTTP://WWW.JMV-STUDIO.COM

Creative Firm: **BERNSTEIN REIN ADVERTISING - PETALUMA, CA**
Creative Team: **JIM ERICKSON, STEVE SPENCE, DAVID FOX**
Client: **USAA**

Creative Firm: **EMERSON, WAJDOWICZ STUDIOS - NEW YORK, NY**
Creative Team: **JUREK WAJDOWICZ, LISA LAROCHELLE, MANNY MENDEZ, YOKO YOSHIDA**
Client: **JULIUS BLUM & CO. INC.**

 Creative Firm: **MORAD BOUCHAKOUR PHOTOGRAPHY -
AMSTERDAM, THE NETHERLANDS**
Creative Team: **MORAD BOUCHAKOUR**
Client: **ADIDAS**
WWW.MORADPHOTO.COM

Creative Firm: **WINSPER, INC. - PETALUMA, CA**
Creative Team: **JIM ERICKSON, CAROLINE BISHOP, BRIAN FANDETTI**
Client: **TIMBERLAND**

Creative Firm: *TAXI CANADA INC. - MONTRÉAL, QC*
Creative Team: *STÉPHANE CHARIER, PATRICK CHAUBET, MAXIME JENNISS, ÉLYSE NOËL DE TILLY, CAROLE NANTEL*
Client: *CHEZ LÉVÊQUE*

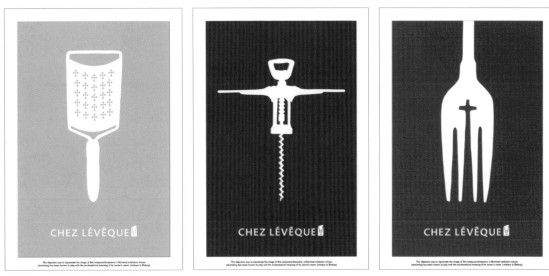

The Standerd is an independently published quarterly photo journal that covers the action, lifestyle and beauty of wakeboarding and wakeskating. Started by acclaimed photographers Joey Meddock and Josh Letchworth and art director James Krawczyk, The Standerd strives to define perfection in action sports publications.

Book 1.1 was the premiere issue, featuring hundreds of exclusive photos. Each book is about 120 pages in length and features less than 20% advertising, creating an uncluttered and seamless reader experience.

All pages are printed using stochastic screens on a sheetfed offset press for ultimate image sharpness and quality. Every image is meticulously checked on press.

Photos are contributed from around the world and are designed to tell a story without words.

the
stand∂rd
WAKE QUARTERLY

book 1.1
BYERLY | ASTERISK² | NO RIGHTS

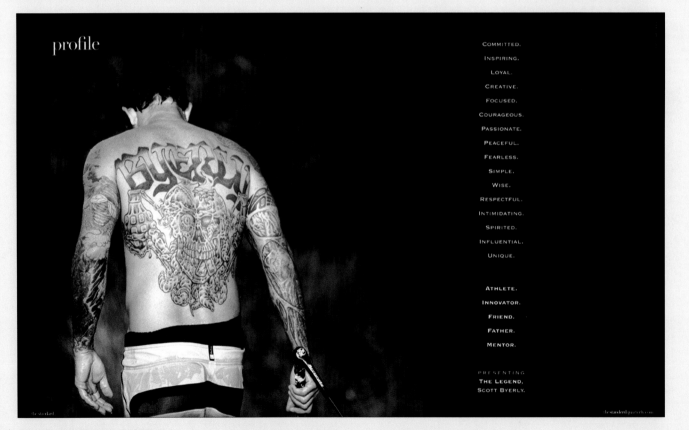

profile

COMMITTED.
INSPIRING.
LOYAL.
CREATIVE.
FOCUSED.
COURAGEOUS.
PASSIONATE.
PEACEFUL.
FEARLESS.
SIMPLE.
WISE.
RESPECTFUL.
INTIMIDATING.
SPIRITED.
INFLUENTIAL.
UNIQUE.

ATHLETE.
INNOVATOR.
FRIEND.
FATHER.
MENTOR.

PRESENTING
THE LEGEND,
SCOTT BYERLY.

Creative Firm: **THE STANDARD - ORLANDO, FL**
Creative Team: **JAMES KRAWCZYK, JOSH LETCHWORTH, JOEY MEDDOCK**
Client: **THE STANDARD**

The (P) *symbol designates a Platinum Award Winner, our Best in Category.*

Creative Firm: **INK PUBLISHING - LONDON, ENGLAND**
Creative Team: **CHLOE GREENBANK, MARTEN SEALBY**
Client: **BRUSSELS AIRLINES**

Creative Firm: **PLAYBOY ENTERPRISES INTERNATIONAL, INC. - CHICAGO, IL**
Creative Team: **ROB WILSON, JAMES IMBROGNO, JONATHAN LITTMAN**
Client: **PLAYBOY MAGAZINE**

Creative Firm: **JEFF HARRIS PHOTOGRAPHY - NEW YORK, NY**
Client: **MERILL LYNCH ADVISOR**

Creative Firm: **MORAD BOUCHAKOUR PHOTOGRAPHY - AMSTERDAM, THE NETHERLANDS**
Creative Team: **MORAD BOUCHAKOUR**
Client: **ESPN MAGAZINE**
WWW.MORADPHOTO.COM

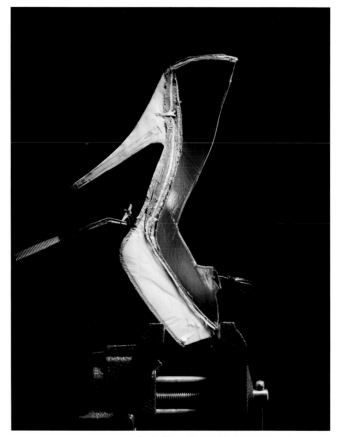

Creative Firm: **JEFF HARRIS PHOTOGRAPHY - NEW YORK, NY**
Creative Team: **JEFF HARRIS, BEN ADAMS**
Client: **MARIE CLAIRE**

Creative Firm: **JEFF HARRIS PHOTOGRAPHY - NEW YORK, NY**
Client: **SPREAD MAGAZINE**

Creative Firm: **MORAD BOUCHAKOUR PHOTOGRAPHY - AMSTERDAM, THE NETHERLANDS**
Creative Team: **MORAD BOUCHAKOUR**
Client: **VOLKSKRANT MAGAZINE**
WWW.MORADPHOTO.COM

Creative Firm: **MORAD BOUCHAKOUR PHOTOGRAPHY - AMSTERDAM**
Creative Team: **MORAD BOUCHAKOUR**
Client: **ESPN MAGAZINE**
WWW.MORADPHOTO.COM

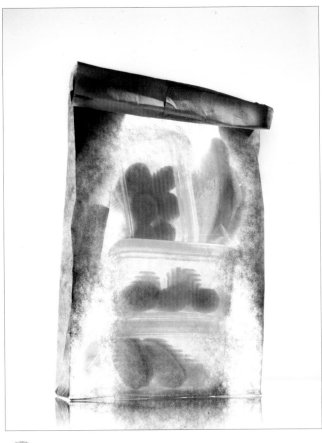

 Creative Firm: **JEFF HARRIS PHOTOGRAPHY - NEW YORK, NY**
Client: **CHILD**

Creative Firm: **INK PUBLISHING - LONDON, ENGLAND**
Creative Team: **DAN HAYES, MIKE WESCOMBE**
Client: **CNN**

Creative Firm: **INK PUBLISHING - LONDON, ENGLAND**
Creative Team: **CLARE BRUNDEL, SABINA FERNANDEZ, ARTHUR CHAN**
Client: **BANGKOK AIRWAYS**

Creative Firm: **MORAD BOUCHAKOUR PHOTOGRAPHY - AMSTERDAM, THE NETHERLANDS**
Creative Team: **MORAD BOUCHAKOUR**
Client: **LIFE MAGAZINE**
WWW.MORADPHOTO.COM

Creative Firm: **JEFF HARRIS PHOTOGRAPHY - NEW YORK, NY**
Client: **NEW YORK MOVES**

Creative Firm: **MORAD BOUCHAKOUR PHOTOGRAPHY -**
AMSTERDAM, THE NETHERLANDS
Creative Team: **MORAD BOUCHAKOUR**
Client: **DUTCH ELLE**
WWW.MORADPHOTO.COM

Creative Firm: **MORAD BOUCHAKOUR PHOTOGRAPHY - AMSTERDAM,**
THE NETHERLANDS
Creative Team: **MORAD BOUCHAKOUR**
Client: **DUTCH ELLE**
WWW.MORADPHOTO.COM

Creative Firm: **PLAYBOY ENTERPRISES INTERNATIONAL, INC. - CHICAGO, IL**
Creative Team: **ROB WILSON, TOM STAEBLER, JAMES IMBROGNO, PARI ESFANDIARI, RICHARD BUSKIN**
Client: **PLAYBOY MAGAZINE**

Creative Firm: **MORAD BOUCHAKOUR PHOTOGRAPHY - AMSTERDAM, THE NETHERLANDS**
Creative Team: **MORAD BOUCHAKOUR**
WWW.MORADPHOTOS.COM

Creative Firm: **INK PUBLISHING - LONDON, ENGLAND**
Creative Team: **CLARE BRUNDEL, SABINA FERNANDEZ, ARTHUR CHAN, LESTER LEDESMA**
Client: **BANGKOK AIRWAYS**

Creative Firm: **INK PUBLISHING - LONDON, ENGLAND**
Creative Team: **MADELEINE ENSOR, RITA CHEE, LESTER LEDESMA**
Client: **CEBU PACIFIC**

Creative Firm: **PRESPA STUDIOS - HUDSON, OH**
Creative Team: **PETE PASPALOVSKI**
Client: **PETE PASPALOVSKI**
WWW.PRESPASTUDIOS.COM

All good illustrations create a mood. Historical images must do so while also being factually accurate for their time period.

Before the artist started this design, he devoted a lot of time to researching the clothing, lifestyle and environment of pirates in an effort to capture their true essence.

"What I like most about this painting is his fierce expression and the sense of foreboding the background conveys," said artist Pete Paspalovski.

The ℗ *symbol designates a Platinum Award Winner, our Best in Category.*

 Creative Firm: **STUDIO NORTH - NOVATO, CA**
Creative Team: **CATHY LOCKE, MICHELE IOACBUCCI**
Client: **FLYING COLORS**

Creative Firm: **STUDIO NORTH - NOVATO, CA**
Creative Team: **CATHY LOCKE, ZHAOMING WU**
Client: **CREATIVE**

Bunnies jump
And bunnies run
Bunnies also sit in the sun
This is the song of the bunnies.

Creative Firm: **WENDELL MINOR DESIGN - WASHINGTON, CT**
Creative Team: **WENDELL MINOR, CARLA WEISE,**
MARTHA RAGO, PHOEBE YEH
Client: **HARPERCOLLINS**
WWW.MINORART.COM

Author Margaret Wise Brown, best known for her book "Good Night Moon," wrote many classic children's books that have won the hearts of children everywhere for more than sixty years. One of her works, "Nibble Nibble," a collection of five poems intended for preschool-aged children, was first published in 1959 in only two colors. When a 2007 condensed version of the book was set to be published in 2007, HarperCollins publishers turned to natural illustrator Wendell Minor to produce full-color art for the work.

The subject matter of the poems focuses primarily on rabbits. Typically, children's books dealing with similar subjects are illustrated in a cartoon style. For this book, Minor wanted to convey a sense of reality maintaining whimsical imagery that would make a child want to reach out and touch the creatures. His solution was to paint very simple, bright, bold images that would be appealing and attractive to today's children.

The **P** *symbol designates a Platinum Award Winner, our Best in Category.*

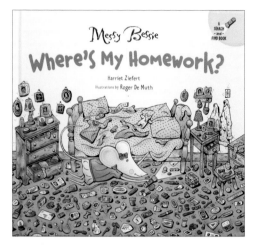

Creative Firm: **DEMUTH DESIGN - CAZENOVIA, NY**
Client: **BLUE APPLE BOOKS**

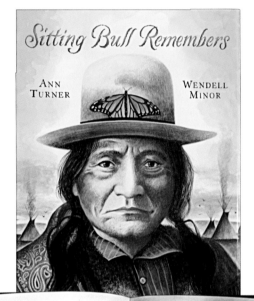

Creative Firm: **WENDELL MINOR DESIGN - WASHINGTON, CT**
Creative Team: **WENDELL MINOR, MATT ADAMEC, MARTHA RAGO, WHITNEY MANGER**
Client: **HARPERCOLLINS**
WWW.MINORART.COM

Creative Firm: **SABINGRAFIK, INC. - CARLSBAD, CA**
Creative Team: **TRACY SABIN**
Client: **SPIDERSKIN PRESS**

Creative Firm: **SUE TODD ILLUSTRATION - TORONTO, ON**
Creative Team: **SUE TODD, NOEL UPFIELD**
Client: **SCHOLASTIC CANADA**

Creative Firm: **WENDELL MINOR DESIGN - WASHINGTON, CT**
Creative Team: **WENDELL MINOR, LIZZY BROMLEY, DAN POTASH, PAULA WISEMAN**
Client: **SIMON & SCHUSTER**
WWW.MINORART.COM

Ever heard the saying,
"Don't get mad, get even?"

After Pearl Harbor, housewife Henrietta Bradbury invented a way to discharge torpedoes.

Discover Over 300 Black Inventors
CSC Celebrates Black History Month

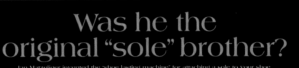

Wild Thing?
Who made our hearts sing?

Otis Boykin invented the artificial heart stimulator in 1961.

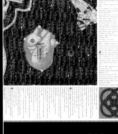

Was he the
original "sole" brother?

Jan Matzeliger invented the "shoe lasting machine" for attaching a sole to your shoe.

Discover Over 300 Black Inventors
CSC Celebrates Black History Month

Creative Firm: **CSC'S P2 COMMUNICATIONS SERVICES - FALLS CHURCH, VA**
Creative Team: **TERRY WILSON, HAP ATTILLIS, PETER GARFIELD, MAURICE COTTINGHAM, NANCY NAUGHTON**
Client: **CSC CORPORATE**

CSC stands for "Consulting, Systems Integration and Outsourcing." Essentially, the company guides clients through technical changes and upgrades.

CSC wanted a centerpiece for the corporation's observance of Black History Month and ultimately created inspirational posters to display in 10 of their facilities. The posters reflect the corporation's commitment to embracing and nurturing diversity.

Creative Director Terry Wilson created an original collage, later named "The Black Inventor," by merging 12 drawings of Black Americans. The border of each poster lists over 300 African American inventors and their inventions. The design intent was to capture the viewers' attention and elevate awareness of the accomplishments of a group of Americans.

Viewed by thousands of employees and visitors, plus thousands of views on the corporate Web site, the poster generated awareness of Black History Month and communicated the company's commitment to diversity in a thought-provoking way.

The (P) *symbol designates a Platinum Award Winner, our Best in Category.*

Creative Firm: **UNITED STATES POSTAL SERVICE - ARLINGTON, VA**
Creative Team: **HOWARD PAINE, KAZUHIKO SANO, ERIC KRIEMELMEYER, JEFF SYPECK**
Client: **UNITED STATES POSTAL SERVICE**

Creative Firm: **UNITED STATES POSTAL SERVICE - ARLINGTON, VA**
Creative Team: **ETHEL KESSLER, PAUL DAVIS, GREG VARNER**
Client: **UNITED STATES POSTAL SERVICE**

Creative Firm: **ECHO CHERNIK - CAPE CORAL, FL**
Creative Team: **ECHO CHERNIK**
Client: **HYPE MANUFACTURING**
HTTP://WWW.ECHO-X.COM

Creative Firm: **UNITED STATES POSTAL SERVICE - ARLINGTON, VA**
Creative Team: **DERRY NOYES, MICHAEL DEAS, KIM KOSTYAL**
Client: **UNITED STATES POSTAL SERVICE**

Creative Firm: **WONDRISKA RUSSO - CAPE CORAL, FL**
Creative Team: **ECHO CHERNIK, CHRISTOPHER EDDY**
Client: **CONNECTICUT OPERA**
HTTP://WWW.ECHO-X.COM

Creative Firm: **UNITED STATES POSTAL SERVICE - ARLINGTON, VA**
Creative Team: **ETHEL KESSLER, MICHAEL OSBORNE, REGINA SWYGER-SMITH**
Client: **UNITED STATES POSTAL SERVICE**

 Creative Firm: **UNITED STATES POSTAL SERVICE - ARLINGTON, VA**
Creative Team: **ETHEL KESSLER, TIM O'BRIEN, GREG BERGER, GREG VARNER**
Client: **UNITED STATES POSTAL SERVICE**

Creative Firm: **UNITED STATES POSTAL SERVICE - ARLINGTON, VA**
Creative Team: **PHIL JORDAN, WILLIAM PHILLIPS, REGINA SWYGERT-SMITH**
Client: **UNITED STATES POSTAL SERVICE**

Creative Firm: **UNITED STATES POSTAL SERVICE - ARLINGTON, VA**
Creative Team: **HOWARD PAINE, HOWARD KOSLOW, JOHN MCDONALD, MARY STEPHANOS**
Client: **UNITED STATES POSTAL SERVICE**

Creative Firm: **UNITED STATES POSTAL SERVICE - ARLINGTON, VA**
Creative Team: **RICHARD SHEAFF, STEVE BUCHANAN, VICTORIA COOPER**
Client: **UNITED STATES POSTAL SERVICE**

Creative Firm: **UNITED STATES POSTAL SERVICE - ARLINGTON, VA**
Creative Team: **TERRENCE MCCAFFREY, WILLIAM GICKER, DREW STRUZAN, REGINA SWYGERT-SMITH**
Client: **UNITED STATES POSTAL SERVICE**

Creative Firm: **UNITED STATES POSTAL SERVICE - ARLINGTON, VA**
Creative Team: **ETHEL KESSLER, JOHN DAWSON, LINDA NOLAN**
Client: **UNITED STATES POSTAL SERVICE**

Creative Firm: **UNITED STATES POSTAL SERVICE - ARLINGTON, VA**
Creative Team: **RICHARD SHEAFF, STEVE BUCHANAN, JEFF SYPECK**
Client: **UNITED STATES POSTAL SERVICE**

Creative Firm: **HILE DESIGN - ANN ARBOR, MI**
Creative Team: **DAVE HILE**
Client: **SELF PROMOTION FOR AD IN CREATE MAGAZINE**

Creative Firm: **DESIGN BY CHLOE - OAKLAND, CA**
Creative Team: **CHLOE HEDDEN**

Creative Firm: **TIM SPOSATO ILLUSTRATION - GORHAM, ME**
Creative Team: **TIM SPOSATO**
Client: **TIM SPOSATO ILLUSTRATION**

Creative Firm: **ZIMMERMAN ADVERTISING - CAPE CORAL, FL**
Creative Team: **ERICH STEFANOVICH, ECHO CHERNIK**
Client: **EL CONQUISTADOR RESORT / LXR**
HTTP://WWW.ECHO-X.COM

Creative Firm: **UNITED STATES POSTAL SERVICE - ARLINGTON, VA**
Creative Team: **CARL HERRMAN, CRAIG FRAZIER, HEIDI RIDGLEY**
Client: **UNITED STATES POSTAL SERVICE**

Creative Firm: **TIM SPOSATO ILLUSTRATION - GORHAM, ME**
Creative Team: **TIM SPOSATO**
Client: **TIM SPOSATO**

Creative Firm: **KINDRED DESIGN STUDIO, INC. - HINESBURG, VT**
Creative Team: **STEVE REDMOND**
Client: **MAGIC HAT BREWING COMPANY**

Creative Firm: **PLAYBOY ENTERPRISES INTERNATIONAL, INC. - CHICAGO, IL**
Creative Team: **ROB WILSON, TOM STAEBLER, DAVE MCKEAN, DENIS JOHNSON**
Client: **PLAYBOY MAGAZINE**

No specific design brief was supplied to the designer for this project; however, the story brought with it an overall mood—one that was dark and troubling.

The accompanying story goes like this: An inmate in a rehabilitation facility writes a series of letters explaining the chain of events that have led him to the facility. The letters are deeply personal, harshly honest and eye-opening to the inmate. As a result, the letters bring with them the possibility of healing and hope.

The designer wanted the illustration to communicate numerous things: an inward look at the soul, reflections of the inmate's past, and the fact that his prison is mostly self-imposed. The main intent, however, was to capture the moment when the inmate has two choices: give up completely or free himself with the words on the paper.

Because the inmate's letters were direct, the design needed to be direct as well. The colors are cool to match the dark and troubling mood of the story. The inmate's expression is equally as intense as his letters. To communicate that the man's prison is mainly self-imposed, the designer created the bars out of 'paper'.

Finally, the designer intended to communicate hope and freedom by placing light between the bars and warmer colors on his face, continuing the warm colors down to his hand, through his pen and onto the paper.

The P *symbol designates a Platinum Award Winner. This piece placed in a three-way tie for Best in Category in "Illustration, News & Editorial."*

CREATIVITY 37 *Annual Awards* | **243**

Creative Firm: **CHRIS HIERS ILLUSTRATOR - WOODSTOCK, GA**
Client: **THE DIRECTORSHIP**

(P) **This image** was created for the debut of the periodical "The Directorship." The illustrator added only a little color—to George Washington's face—to enhance the black eye and add more life to the image.

The **(P)** symbol designates a Platinum Award Winner. This piece placed in a three-way tie for Best in Category in "Illustration, News & Editorial."

244 | CREATIVITY 37 *Annual Awards*

Creative Firm: **PLAYBOY ENTERPRISES INTERNATIONAL, INC. - CHICAGO, IL**
Creative Team: **ROB WILSON, RYAN HESHKA, WOODY ALLEN**
Client: **PLAYBOY MAGAZINE**

This illustration for *PLAYBOY* magazine accompanied a short piece of fiction written by Woody Allen, entitled "This Nib For Hire."

The plot involved a novelist selling out his artistic integrity to write a Three Stooges screenplay for a Hollywood mogul. The accompanying image was designed to be a horrific exaggeration of the writer, tortured by the job of writing a trashy screenplay.

A hellish setting was a natural choice, with the Three Stooges hovering oppressively over the writer in the form of a demonic Hydra. Being a less concept driven and more character driven illustration, the key was to balance all the characters in the story without complicating the art, while also conveying the agony of the writer.

The (P) *symbol designates a Platinum Award Winner. This piece placed in a three-way tie for Best in Category in "Illustration, News & Editorial."*

Creative Firm: **PLAYBOY ENTERPRISES INTERNATIONAL, INC. - CHICAGO, IL**
Creative Team: **ROB WILSON, SCOTT ANDERSON, MIRKO ILIC, CHIP ROWE**
Client: **PLAYBOY MAGAZINE**

Creative Firm: **PLAYBOY ENTERPRISES INTERNATIONAL, INC. - CHICAGO, IL**
Creative Team: **ROB WILSON, TOM STAEBLER, MIRKO ILIC, PAT JORDAN**
Client: **PLAYBOY MAGAZINE**

Creative Firm: **PLAYBOY ENTERPRISES INTERNATIONAL, INC. - CHICAGO, IL**
Creative Team: **ROB WILSON, TOM STAEBLER, TOMER HANUKA, WALTER MOSLEY**
Client: **PLAYBOY MAGAZINE**

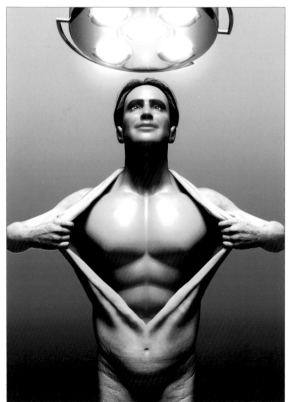

Creative Firm: **PLAYBOY ENTERPRISES INTERNATIONAL, INC. - CHICAGO, IL**
Creative Team: **TOM STAEBLER, ROB WILSON, KENT WILLIAMS, EDWARD FALCO**
Client: **PLAYBOY MAGAZINE**

Creative Firm: **PLAYBOY ENTERPRISES INTERNATIONAL, INC. - CHICAGO, IL**
Creative Team: **ROB WILSON, MIRKO ILIC, CHIP ROWE**
Client: **PLAYBOY MAGAZINE**

Creative Firm: **PLAYBOY ENTERPRISES INTERNATIONAL, INC. - CHICAGO, IL**
Creative Team: **ROB WILSON, GERARD DUBOIS, TOM STAEBLER**
Client: **PLAYBOY MAGAZINE**

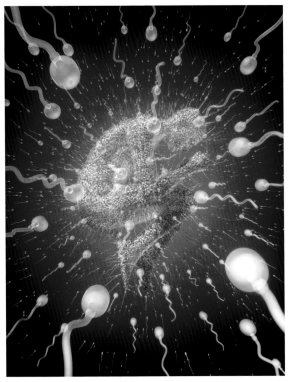

Creative Firm: INK PUBLISHING - LONDON, ENGLAND
Creative Team: GEMMA HARRIS, JONNY CLARK
Client: JET2.COM

Creative Firm: **PLAYBOY ENTERPRISES INTERNATIONAL, INC. - CHICAGO, IL**
Creative Team: **ROB WILSON, MATT GROLLER, JESS WALTER**
Client: **PLAYBOY MAGAZINE**

Creative Firm: INK PUBLISHING - LONDON, ENGLAND
Creative Team: ANDREW HUMPHREYS, BRENDAN ALTHORPE
Client: GULF AIR

Creative Firm: **ENERGY TIMES MAGAZINE - MELVILLE, NY**
Creative Team: **DONNA CASOLA**
Client: **ENERGY TIMES MAGAZINE**

This typography for an article in the health and wellness magazine Energy Times was created in-house. The article was about the benefits of lutein in preventing age-related vision loss. The design intent was typical and expected: to capture the essence of the story in a clever, noticeable manner.

Because art director Donna Casola is a fan of short, effective headlines, she wanted something bold and simple, explaining, "In designing this feature, the biggest challenge was coming up with a creative solution that would not only engage the reader with striking graphics, but also accommodate the half-page of copy on the opening spread".

There are many specific meanings for the various colors, numbers and shapes throughout the design. The fonts and colors on the left page emulate a typical eye chart with the numbered rows matching up with the headline, byline and deck. On the right page, the close-up shot of the eye is surrounded by brackets, alluding to a camera lens. The crosshairs within the eye's pupil further strengthen that intent.

It is the typography, however, that makes this opening spread especially creative and effective. Displaying the title of the article in the form of an eye chart is ideal, because it visually communicates the subject of the article and also manages to take the readers on a visual journey of their own.

VH1, a music television channel, has a sibling brand named VH1 Classics, which features the best rock, soul and pop artists from the 1960's through the 1990's. Because parts of VH1 Classic's logo contained elements that had been put to rest in 2002, a logo redesign proved necessary.

The objective was to convey a sense of nostalgia, specifically for the music from the 60's - 90's eras. The biggest challenge was to make a distinct connection to the VH1 brand and its logo while creating something distinct and unique.

The in-house design team used signature VH1 typography, but in a new shape that symbolized a vinyl record. The round shape acts as a customizable space, similar to elements of the VH1 logo. Customization allows the company to play with various colors and styles from past eras, and is a big part of the VH1 logo as well.

Creative Firm: **VH1 - NEW YORK, NY**
Client: **VH1**

The ⓟ symbol designates a Platinum Award Winner, our Best in Category.

Creative Firm: **BRIAN J. GANTON & ASSOCIATES - CEDAR GROVE, NJ**
Creative Team: **BRIAN J. GANTON, JR., CHRISTOPHER GANTON, MARK GANTON, PAT PALMIERI, MARC MILTON**
Client: **OLDCASTLE RETAIL**

Creative Firm: **KINDRED DESIGN STUDIO, INC. - HINESBURG, VT**
Creative Team: **STEVE REDMOND**
Client: **THE UNIVERSITY OF VERMONT**

Creative Firm: **THE STANDERD - ORLANDO, FL**
Creative Team: **JAMES KRAWCZYK, JOSH LETCHWORTH, JOEY MEDDOCK**
Client: **THE STANDERD**

Creative Firm: **SAMALOU.COM | THE ARTWORK OF LOUIS SIMEONE - BLOOMINGDALE, NJ**
Creative Team: **LOUIS SIMEONE**
Client: **SAMALOU.COM | THE ARTWORK OF LOUIS SIMEONE**

Creative Firm: **GRAPHICAT LTD. - WANCHAI, HONG KONG**
Creative Team: **COLIN TILLYER**
Client: **AUDENTIA CAPITAL INC**

Creative Firm: **ENERGY TIMES MAGAZINE - MELVILLE, NY**
Creative Team: **DONNA CASOLA**
Client: **ENERGY TIMES MAGAZINE**

5K Run & Pub Crawl

Creative Firm: **KINDRED DESIGN STUDIO, INC. - HINESBURG, VT**
Creative Team: **STEVE REDMOND**
Client: **TDK MEDICAL**

Creative Firm: **HITCHCOCK FLEMING & ASSOCIATES INC. - AKRON, OH**
Creative Team: **NICK BETRO, LENNY SPENGLER**
Client: **AKRUN & CRAWL**

THE ERLBAUM GROUP

Creative Firm: **VERY MEMORABLE DESIGN - NEW YORK, NY**
Creative Team: **MICHAEL PINTO**
Client: **THE ERLBAUM GROUP**

Creative Firm: **GRAPHICAT LTD. - WANCHAI, HONG KONG**
Creative Team: **COLIN TILLYER**
Client: **NOBLE GROUP LIMITED**

Creative Firm: **GRAPHICAT LTD. - WANCHAI, HONG KONG**
Creative Team: **COLIN TILLYER**
Client: **ANDREW MILLER**

Creative Firm: IDEO - SAN FRANCISCO, CA; TOLLESON DESIGN - SAN FRANCISCO, CA
Creative Team: MICHAEL GOUGH (ADOBE), RYAN HICKS (ADOBE), DAVID LEMON (ADOBE),
ROBERT SLIMBACH (ADOBE), SANDRA STOECKER (ADOBE), JIM CHRISTIE (ADOBE),
MICHELLE RICHARDS (ADOBE), RHETT WOODS (ADOBE)
Client: ADOBE SYSTEMS INCORPORATED

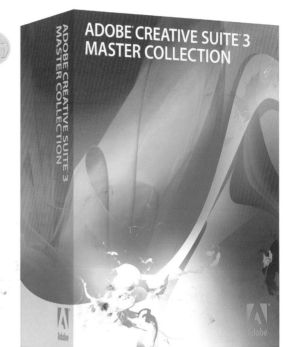

Creative Firm: PHILIPPE BECKER DESIGN - SAN FRANCISCO, CA
Creative Team: PHILIPPE BECKER, BARKHA WADIA, MELANIE HALIM
Client: HP

Creative Firm: G2 BRANDING AND DESIGN - NEW YORK, NY
Creative Team: PHIL KOUTSIS, MARIA SAMODRA, LOU ANTONUCCI,
JJ LARSON, BRIAN STAFFLINGER
Client: PANTONE

Creative Firm: **WALLACE CHURCH, INC. - NEW YORK, NY**
Creative Team: **STAN CHURCH, MARCO ESCALANTE**
Client: **WYATTZIER**

This darkly mysterious design is inspired by Shango, the powerful African god of lightning and love.

Shango's legend was brought to the Caribbean 500 years ago and is still celebrated today in Trinidad, Tobago, and Cuba.

Shango Rum's exotic matte black bottle, with red and silver graphics, was designed to appeal to the urban club crowd.

The Ⓟ *symbol designates a Platinum Award Winner, our Best in Category.*

Creative Firm: **MCGUFFIE DESIGN - NORTH VANCOUVER, BC**
Creative Team: **STEVE MCGUFFIE**
Client: **BLACK WIDOW WINERY**

Creative Firm: **THE SNAP ORGANISATION - MIAMI BEACH, FL**
Creative Team: **JAMES WAUGH, IAN THOMAS**
Client: **DIAGEO NORTH AMERICA**

Creative Firm: **P & W DESIGN CONSULTANTS - LONDON, ENGLAND**
Creative Team: **WESLEY ANSON, SIMON PEMBERTON**
Client: **TESCO STORES**

Creative Firm: **ANTHEM WORLDWIDE - SAN FRANCISCO, CA**
Creative Team: **RON VANDENBERG, BRIAN LOVELL, MICHAEL D. JOHNSON**
Client: **SAFEWAY INC.**

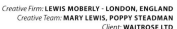

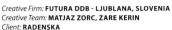

Creative Firm: **FUTURA DDB - LJUBLANA, SLOVENIA**
Creative Team: **MATJAZ ZORC, ZARE KERIN**
Client: **RADENSKA**

Creative Firm: **LEWIS MOBERLY - LONDON, ENGLAND**
Creative Team: **MARY LEWIS, POPPY STEADMAN**
Client: **WAITROSE LTD**

Creative Firm: **BRUKETA & ZINIC OM - ZAGREB, CROATIA**
Creative Team: **RUTH HOFFMAN, DAVOR BRUKETA, NIKOLA ZINIC,
MOE MINKARA, TANJA SKORIC, MIRNA GRZELJ**
Client: **CHIAVALON**

Creative Firm: **PURE DESIGN CO. LLC - LEVERETT, MA**
Creative Team: **DAN MISHKIND, MARY KATE MARCHAND**
Client: **GOOD FOOD ORGANICS**

Creative Firm: **DIDONATO DESIGN - CHICAGO, IL**
Creative Team: **PETER DIDONATO, DOUG MILLER**
Client: **AGAVE LOCO LLC**

Creative Firm: **SABINGRAFIK, INC. - CARLSBAD, CA**
Creative Team: **TRACY SABIN**
Client: **SEAFARER BAKING COMPANY**

Creative Firm: **MNA CREATIVE - DANBURY, CT**
Creative Team: **ASH OAT**
Client: **MNA CREATIVE**

Creative Firm: **MARK OLIVER, INC. - SOLVANG, CA**
Creative Team: **MARK OLIVER, PATTY DRISKEL, PAUL SLATER, MELANIE KRONNEMAN**
Client: **OCEAN BEAUTY SEAFOODS**

Creative Firm: **VOICEBOX CREATIVE - SAN FRANCISCO, CA**
Creative Team: **DAVID MURO, JACQUES ROSSOUW, OLAF BECKMAN, TUCKER AND HOSSLER**
Client: **RODNEY STRONG**

Creative Firm: **WEBB SCARLETT DEVLAM - CHICAGO, IL**
Client: **V & S PLYMOUTH**

Creative Firm: **THE SNAP ORGANISATION - MIAMI BEACH, FL**
Creative Team: **JAMES WAUGH, IAN THOMAS**
Client: **DIAGEO NORTH AMERICA**

Creative Firm: **THE BAILEY GROUP - PLYMOUTH MEETING, PA**
Creative Team: **DAVE FIEDLER, GARY LACROIX, ERIC YEAGER**
Client: **WELCH'S**

Creative Firm: **FLOWDESIGN INC. - NORTHVILLE, MI**
Creative Team: **DAN MATAUCH, DENNIS NALEZYTY**
Client: **HANSEN'S BEVERAGES**

Creative Firm: **HORNALL ANDERSON DESIGN WORKS - SEATTLE, WA**
Creative Team: **JACK ANDERSON, BRUCE STIGLER, DON STAYNER,**
VU NGUYEN, BETH GRIMM, ANDREW WELL
Client: **REDHOOD BREWERY**

Creative Firm: **P & W DESIGN CONSULTANTS - LONDON, ENGLAND**
Creative Team: **LEE NEWHAM, SIMON PEMBERTON**
Client: **HILL STATION PLC**

Creative Firm: **YELLOBEE STUDIO - ATLANTA, GA**
Creative Team: **ALISON SCHEEL, RHONDA DENNIS, MILLER MCMILLAN**
Client: **VIA ELISA**

Creative Firm: **FUTUREBRAND - NEW YORK, NY**
Creative Team: **KURT KRETTEN, JASON WONG**
Client: **DIAGEO**

Creative Firm: **HORNALL ANDERSON DESIGN WORKS - SEATTLE, WA**
Creative Team: **LISA CERVENY, JANA NISHI, BELINDA BOWLING, LEO RAYMUNDO**
Client: **TAHITIAN NONI INT'L.**

Creative Firm: **DESIGN OBJECTIVES PTE LTD - SINGAPORE**
Creative Team: **RONNIE S C TAN**
Client: **SHERATON TAIPEI HOTEL**
FTP.DESIGNOBJECTIVES.COM.SG

Creative Firm: **P & W DESIGN CONSULTANTS - LONDON, ENGLAND**
Creative Team: **WESLEY ANSON, SIMON PEMBERTON**
Client: **FRESH PASTA COMPANY**

Creative Firm: **CORNERSTONE STRATEGIC BRANDING, INC. - NEW YORK, NY**
Client: **SILVER BRANDS, INC.**

Creative Firm: **P & W DESIGN CONSULTANTS - LONDON, ENGLAND**
Creative Team: **WESLEY ANSON, ADRIAN WHITEFOORD**
Client: **STARBUCKS**

Creative Firm: **KLIM DESIGN, INC. - AVON, CT**
Client: **JOSE CUERVO INTERNATIONAL**

Creative Firm: **PHILIPPE BECKER DESIGN - SAN FRANCISCO, CA**
Creative Team: **PHILIPPE BECKER, HEATHER ALLEN, MELANIE HALIM**
Client: **ARTISAN WINE GROUP**

Creative Firm: **CORNERSTONE STRATEGIC BRANDING, INC. - NEW YORK, NY**
Client: **REDHOOK ALE BREWERY**

Creative Firm: **KLIM DESIGN, INC. - AVON, CT**
Client: **JOSE CUERVO INTERNATIONAL**

Creative Firm: **HORNALL ANDERSON DESIGN WORKS - SEATTLE, WA**
Creative Team: **JACK ANDERSON, DAVID BATES, BETH GRIMM, KATHLEEN GIBSON, JACOB CARTER**
Client: **WRIGLEY**

Creative Firm: **PHILIPPE BECKER DESIGN - SAN FRANCISCO, CA**
Creative Team: **PHILIPPE BECKER, MELANIE HALIM, MARIKO MUTO**
Client: **WILLIAMS-SONOMA**

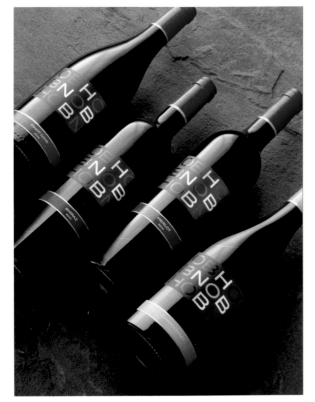

Creative Firm: **VOICEBOX CREATIVE - SAN FRANCISCO, CA**
Creative Team: **JEAN-FRANCOIS DE BUREN, JACQUES ROSSOUW, DAVID BISHOP**
Client: **GEORGES DUBOEUF**

Creative Firm: **VOICEBOX CREATIVE - SAN FRANCISCO, CA**
Creative Team: **JACQUES ROSSOUW, KRISTIE WISE, DAVID BISHOP**
Client: **LUNA VINEYARDS**

Creative Firm: **SAGON-PHIOR BRAND COMMUNICATIONS - LOS ANGELES, CA**
Client: **MCCORMICK DISTILLING CO.**

Creative Firm: **PHILIPPE BECKER DESIGN - SAN FRANCISCO, CA**
Creative Team: **PHILIPPE BECKER, MELANIE HALIM, COCO QIU**
Client: **WILLIAMS-SONOMA**

Creative Firm: **WEBB SCARLETT DEVLAM - CHICAGO, IL**
Client: **PROCTER AND GAMBLE**

Creative Firm: **ALEXANDER ISLEY INC. - REDDING, CT**
Creative Team: **ALEXANDER ISLEY, ALINE HILFORD, TARA BENYEI, CHERITH VICTORINO**
Client: **ELIZABETH ARDEN RED DOOR SPAS**

Creative Firm: **WALLACE CHURCH, INC. - NEW YORK, NY**
Creative Team: **STAN CHURCH, JOHN BRUNO, AKIRA YASUDA**
Client: **THE DIAL CORPORATION**

Creative Firm: **KYLE DESIGN - ROCKVILLE, MD**
Creative Team: **CATHY KYLE, DWIGHT SCHULTHEIS**
Client: **AMENITY**

Creative Firm: **WEBB SCARLETT DEVLAM - CHICAGO, IL**
Client: **PROCTER AND GAMBLE**

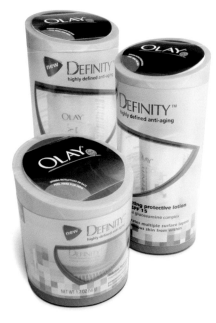

Classics

MAKER'S OLD FASHIONED
Maker's Mark Bourbon muddled with fresh orange, cherry and sugar.

LONG BEACH ICED TEA
ABSOLUT Vodka, Bacardi Superior Rum, Tanqueray Gin and Cointreau Orange Liqueur topped with cranberry juice.

BLOODY MARIA
Cuervo Tradicional Tequila and Bloody Mary Mix served with fresh lime, celery and olives.

RASPBERRY SEA BREEZE
Stoli Razberi Vodka, grapefruit and cranberry juices.

VANILLA COSMO
Ketel One Citroen, Navan Vanilla Liqueur with lime and cranberry juices.

Frozen

SPICED RUM RUNNER
Captain Morgan Original Spiced Rum, Bols Banana Liqueur, blackberry brandy and grenadine.

STRAWBERRY COLADA
Bacardi Superior Rum and strawberry purée swirled in the glass with piña colada mix.

TROPICAL DREAM
Malibu Coconut Rum, Kahlúa Coffee Liqueur, Bols Dark Crème de Cacao, ice cream and coconut.

MANGO MARGARITA
1800 Reposado Tequila, Cointreau Orange Liqueur and mango purée.

STRAWBERRY VANILLA DAIQUIRI
Mount Gay Rum, Navan Vanilla Liqueur and strawberry purée.

Tropicals

COCONUT MOJITO
Malibu Coconut Rum and club soda muddled with fresh mint and lime.

ATLANTIC COOLER
Bacardi Limón Rum and Bols Blue Curacao topped with lemon-lime soda.

SOUTHERN HURRICANE
Southern Comfort, grenadine, orange and pineapple juices.

CHAMBORD ECLIPSE
ABSOLUT CITRON Vodka, Chambord Raspberry Liqueur and Disaronno Amaretto topped with lemon-lime soda.

MELON MIST
SKYY Vodka, Midori Melon Liqueur orange and pineapple juices.

Martinis

CARIBBEAN MARTINI
Malibu Coconut Rum, Midori Melon Liqueur, Cointreau Orange Liqueur and pineapple juice.

ITALIAN LEMON DROP
Ketel One Vodka and Tuaca Italian Liqueur with a sugar rim.

MARGARITA MARTINI
Cuervo Tradicional Tequila and Cointreau Orange Liqueur with a float of Grand Marnier Liqueur.

MUDSLIDE TINI
Smirnoff Vanilla Vodka, Baileys Irish Cream, Kahlúa Coffee Liqueur and cream.

HENDRICK'S GIMLET
A combination of Hendrick's Gin and fresh lime juice.

BLUSH MARTINI
Belvedere Vodka, Chambord Raspberry Liqueur, lime and pineapple juices.

Creative Firm: **PATRICK HENRY CREATIVE PROMOTIONS, INC. - STAFFORD, TX**
Creative Team: **CHRISSY PERETTI, CHRISTY SEVIER, TIM TURNER**
Client: **INTERSTATE HOTELS & RESORTS**

Creative Firm: **PATRICK HENRY CREATIVE PROMOTIONS, INC. - STAFFORD, TX**
Creative Team: **SCOTT NAVA, SMITH PHOTOGRAPHY, MICHAEL HASKINS**
Client: **LOEWS HOTELS**

LOEWS SANTA MONICA BEACH HOTEL

№14

Raspberry Mojito
10 Cane Rum, mint leaves, brown sugar, lime juice, topped with Sprite and a float of Chambord Liqueur Royale.

LOS ANGELES, CA

Signature Cocktails

•LOEWS HOTELS

№10

Park Avenue Jewel
Bombay Sapphire Gin, DeKuyper Blue Curacao and sweet & sour mix, topped with tonic.

LOEWS MIAMI BEACH HOTEL

№08

Caribbean Sunshine
BACARDI Coco Rum, Pama Pomegranate Liqueur, mixed with orange and cranberry juices.

MIAMI, FL

LOEWS REGENCY HOTEL

NEW YORK, NY

Creative Firm: **WALLACE CHURCH, INC. - NEW YORK, NY**
Creative Team: **STAN CHURCH**
Client: **WALLACE CHURCH, INC**

Each year, creative firm Wallace Church designs a Thanksgiving wine bottle as a gift for clients and friends. Here, a simple twist on a classic saying—"Bottoms up"—suggests a nice way to end any Thanksgiving meal.

The ⓟ symbol designates a Platinum Award Winner, our Best in Category.

S *Creative Firm:* **INTEGRATED MARKETING SERVICES - NORWALK, CT**
Creative Team: **JULIA CONTACESSI, MATT NADLER, MELISSA FORD,**
KEVIN GIRONDA, DON COFFEY
Client: **UNILEVER**

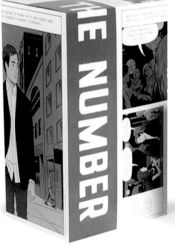

Gi *Creative Firm:* **MFP - NEW YORK, NY**
Creative Team: **NEIL POWELL, JOSH ROGERS, MARK SLOAN**
Client: **PERRY ELLIS**

Creative Firm: **THE SNAP ORGANISATION - MIAMI BEACH, FL**
Creative Team: **JAMES WAUGH, IAN THOMAS**
Client: **DIAGEO NORTH AMERICA** Gi

Creative Firm: **REVOLUCION - NEW YORK, NY**
Creative Team: **ALBERTO RODRIGUEZ, HENRY ALVAREZ, SARAH RAMSEY**
Client: **PALM BAY INTERNATIONAL**

 Creative Firm: **INTEGRATED MARKETING SERVICES - NORWALK, CT**
Creative Team: **JULIA CONTACESSI, SARAH DAVIS, MELISSA FORD,**
EMILY GRACE, CHRIS LOVELLO
Client: **UNILEVER**

Creative Firm: **OPEN STUDIO - NEW YORK, NY**
Creative Team: **SHELLY FUKUSHIMA**
Client: **OPEN STUDIO**

Creative Firm: **G2 BRANDING AND DESIGN - NEW YORK, NY**
Creative Team: **BEN GOLD, RAY MARRERO, DANIELA MASIELLO**
Client: **AVERY**

Creative Firm: **COMEDY CENTRAL OFF-AIR CREATIVE - NEW YORK, NY**
Creative Team: **ROLYN BARTHELMAN, ANGELINA BATTISTA**
Client: **COMEDY CENTRAL**

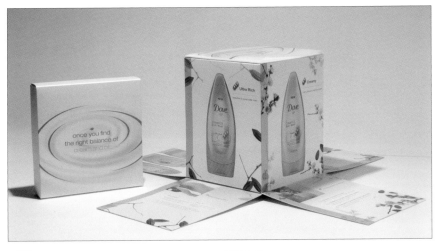

S
Creative Firm: **INTEGRATED MARKETING SERVICES - NORWALK, CT**
Creative Team: **JULIA CONTACESSI, SARAH DAVIS, MELISSA FORD, CHRIS LOVELLO**
Client: **UNILEVER**

Creative Firm: **THE SNAP ORGANISATION - MIAMI BEACH, FL**
Creative Team: **JAMES WAUGH, IAN THOMAS**
Client: **DIAGEO NORTH AMERICA**

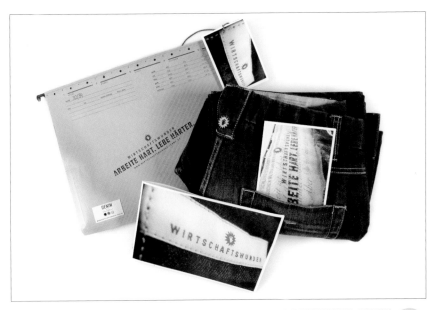

Creative Firm: **RTS RIEGER TEAM WERBEAGENTUR GMBH - LEINFELDEN-ECHTERDINGEN, GERMANY**
Creative Team: **JOERG DAMBACHER, THORSTEN HAUF, BORIS POLLIG, MARKUS KOCH, CHRISTINE GRAF,**
CLAUDIA GLÖCKLER
Client: **RTS RIEGER TEAM BUSINESS-TO-BUSINESS COMMUNICATION**
WWW.WIRTSCHAFTSWUNDER-JEANS.DE

S
Creative Firm: **G2 BRANDING AND DESIGN - NEW YORK, NY**
Creative Team: **ED TAUSSIG, SARA PRESS**
Client: **DUNHILL**

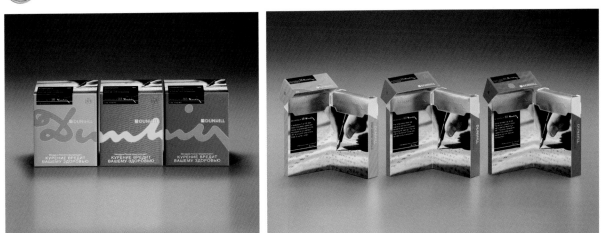

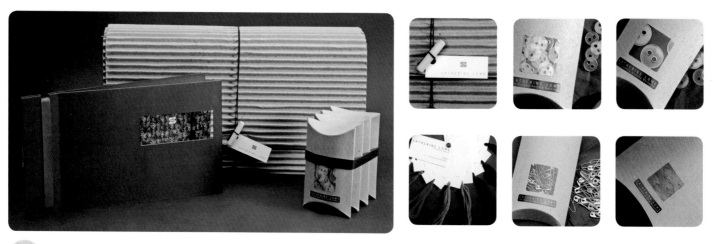

Creative Firm: **STUDIO TWO - LENOX, MA**
Creative Team: **HEATHER ROSE, KEVIN SPRAGUE**
Client: **CATHERINE LOWE**

Creative Firm: **DEFTELING DESIGN - PORTLAND, OR**
Creative Team: **ALEX WIJNEN**
Client: **CECILY INK**

Creative Firm: **AMPERSAND GCW - CD SATELITE, MEXICO**
Creative Team: **RAFAEL CORDOVA**
Client: **BIMBO**

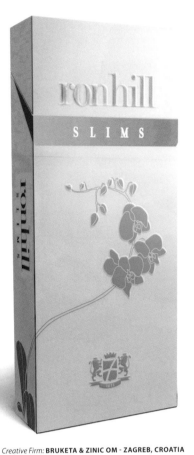

Creative Firm: **BBK STUDIO - GRAND RAPIDS, MI**
Creative Team: **SHARON OLENICZAK, JASON MURRAY, TIM CALKINS**
Client: **GRAND RAPIDS ART MUSEUM (GRAM)**

Creative Firm: **BRUKETA & ZINIC OM - ZAGREB, CROATIA**
Client: **TDR**

Creative Firm: **LEMLEY DESIGN COMPANY - SEATTLE, WA**
Creative Team: **DAVID LEMLEY, AMBER HAHTO, PAT SNAVELY, COVENTRY JANKOWSKI, JEREMY WHEAT**
Client: **SUGOI**

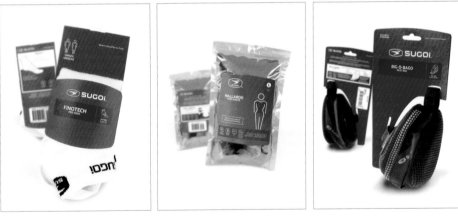

Creative Firm: **30SIXTY ADVERTISING+DESIGN, INC. - STUDIO CITY, CA**
Creative Team: **HENRY VIZCARRA, PÄR LARSSON, BRUCE VENTANILLA, YUJIN ONO, ERIC PEREZ, TUYET VONG**
Client: **20TH CENTURY FOX HOME ENTERTAINMENT**

Creative Firm: **30SIXTY ADVERTISING+DESIGN, INC. - STUDIO CITY, CA**
Creative Team: **HENRY VIZCARRA, PÄR LARSSON, BRUCE VENTANILLA, TUYET VONG**
Client: **20TH CENTURY FOX HOME ENTERTAINMENT**

Creative Firm: **30SIXTY ADVERTISING+DESIGN, INC. - STUDIO CITY, CA**
Creative Team: **HENRY VIZCARRA, DAVID FUSCELLARO, CHARLIE LE**
Client: **PARAMOUNT HOME ENTERTAINMENT GLOBAL**

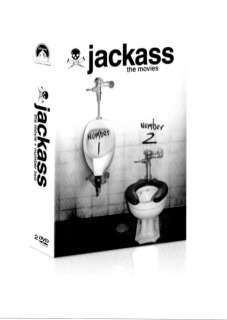

Creative Firm: **RIORDON DESIGN - OAKVILLE, ON**
Creative Team: **SHIRLEY RIORDON**
Client: **INTEGRITY MUSIC**

Creative Firm: **PLANET ADS AND DESIGN P/L - SINGAPORE**
Creative Team: **HAL SUZUKI, MAKOTO OISHI**
Client: **PLANET ADS & DESIGN P/L**

Creative Firm: **CHEN DESIGN ASSOCIATES - SAN FRANCISCO, CA**
Creative Team: **JOSHUA CHEN, MAX SPECTOR**
Client: **RICHARD GRIMES**

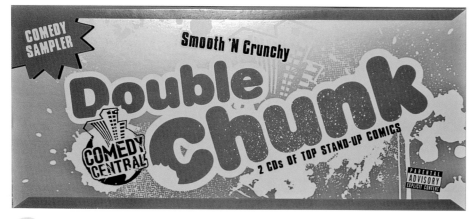

 Creative Firm: **COMEDY CENTRAL OFF-AIR CREATIVE - NEW YORK, NY**
Creative Team: **ROLYN BARTHELMAN, CHARLES HAMILTON**
Client: **COMEDY CENTRAL**

Creative Firm: **PATRICK HENRY CREATIVE PROMOTIONS, INC. - STAFFORD, TX**
Creative Team: **DAVID ROCABADO, MICHAEL HASKINS**
Client: **BENNIGAN'S GRILL & TAVERN**

Creative Firm: **COMPANY STANDARD - BROOKLYN, NY**
Creative Team: **MELISSA GORMAN**
Client: **CRYSTALTOP MUSIC**

The Point of Passion.

Creative Firm: **ICONTENT INC - 126 FIFTH AVE. NEW YORK, NY**
Creative Team: **DOUGLAS SLOAN - DIRECTOR, TANIA SETHI -
EXECUTIVE PRODUCER, JEFFREY M. BROOKS - COPY WRITER,
GAIL KERSHNER - PRODUCER/DESIGNER, TONY JANNELLI -
DIRECTOR OF PHOTOGRAPHY**
Client: **CONDE NAST MEDIA GROUP**

Being asked to create the first ever brand positioning and tagline for Conde Nast is no small order. Icontent, Inc. was asked to do not only that, but also to create a short film to articulate the positioning and bring the brand to life.

The biggest challenge for Icontent was creating a language and visual imagery that transcended the individual magazine titles of Conde Nast, which are incredibly diverse and range from Vogue to Wired, Architectural Digest to Glamour, and Vanity Fair to The New Yorker.

Conde Nast specifically wanted the film to define passion through the voices of the celebrity editors of Conde Nast magazines. The intent was to demonstrate that the editors all shared an intense passion for their magazines. In turn, the readers shared a strong passion for the subject matter of various magazines.

This is the theme that runs throughout the film: A connection is made at the point of passion.

The symbol designates a Platinum Award Winner, our Best in Category.

Creative Firm: **G2 BRANDING AND DESIGN - NEW YORK, NY**
Creative Team: **VICTOER MAZZEO, PHIL KOUTSIS, JASON BORZOUYEH, JOHN RESNIK, KC TAGLIARENI, TRACY DENNIS, MATT EGAN, REBECCA GINSBERG**
Client: **UL**

Creative Firm: **G2 BRANDING AND DESIGN - NEW YORK, NY**
Creative Team: **CHRIS YOUNG, JASON BORZOUYEH, DREW COBURN, MATT EGAN, SABINA MATHEWSON, FLYINGFISH PRODUCTION COMPANY, KC TAGLIARENI**
Client: **COCA-COLA**

 Creative Firm: **FELIX DESIGN - PHILADELPHIA, PA**
Creative Team: **PENNY ASHMAN, DANIELA KUEHN,**
MARA KONALIAN
Client: **GSK/PEARRE, INC**

Creative Firm: **G2 BRANDING AND DESIGN - NEW YORK, NY**
Creative Team: **PHIL KOUTSIS, MARIA SAMODRA,**
ARON BUTCHER, FLYINGFISH PRODUCTION COMPANY,
KC TAGLIARENI, KICK (UK), RICK MULHALL, TERRY NEALE
Client: **LEVEL VODKA**

 Creative Firm: **MERESTONE - SCOTTSDALE, AZ**
Creative Team: **DAVID DEROSIER, ROB HILL, JANET ERICKSON**
Client: **GOLD CANYON CANDLES**

Not only do we offer cutting edge treatment,
but we look at generic medications as well.

When my daughter recovered, I was very pleased
because Coartem healed her in a manner

NOVARTIS

Creative Firm: BETH SINGER DESIGN - ARLINGTON, VA
Creative Team: BETH SINGER, SUHEUN YU, SUCHA SNIDVONGS
Client: AMERICAN ISRAEL PUBLIC AFFAIRS COMMITTEE (AIPAC)

Creative Firm: RUDER FINN - NEW YORK, NY
Creative Team: LISA GABBAY, MARYANN CAMMARATA,
GUY MELLITZ, ASHLEY ISER
Client: NOVARTIS

 Creative Firm: MTV NETWORKS CREATIVE SERVICES - NEW YORK, NY
Creative Team: L. LEVENTMAN, S. WADLER, C. FAMILY, M. HERRON, M. BUCCAFUSCO, T. ARNOLD, J. ZELENAK,
E. BOSCOE, H. CARDENAS, A. PECHARSKY, N. JOHNNIDES, G. PAYNE, K. SAJI, P. O'SULLIVAN
Client: MTV NETWORKS

Creative Firm: **SYRUP - NEW YORK, NY**
Creative Team: **JAKOB DASCHEK, KATE CUNNINGHAM, SESSE LIND, DANIEL DE VICIOLA**
Client: **GENERAL ELECTRIC**
HTTP://GE.ECOMAGINATION.COM/SITE/QT.HTML

Creative Firm: **DOUBLEJAY CREATIVE - KNOXVILLE, TN**
Client: **SCHOOL OF ART INSTITUTE, CHICAGO**

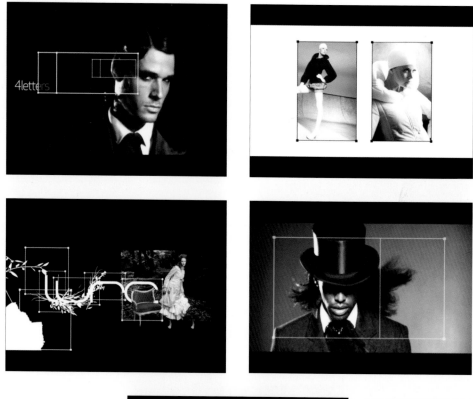

Creative Firm: **LOOPMEDIA INC. - TORONTO, ON**
Creative Team: **CRAIG KIRKHAM, DAN LIM, BILL BELL, PAUL SYCH**
Client: **DAN LIM**

The name of the film is "Forte," and it is collaboration between four artists with four different stories. It is a journey through the world of fashion.

This self-promotion film was created for Dan Lim Photography, who wanted to give its clients an opportunity to experience an artistic vision beyond the realm of print.

To bring the stories to life, Loopmedia's Creative Director Craig Kirkham worked with Dan Lim's team to design and build the motion graphics. "We wanted to create an exciting and visually stunning piece to reflect the individual beauty of the images. The challenge was to uphold all four artists' visions while maintaining flow and movement in the piece." The resulting film is a splendid blend of differing styles.

The (P) *symbol designates a Platinum Award Winner, our Best in Category.*

Creative Firm: **MTV NETWORKS - NEW YORK, NY**
Creative Team: **THERESA FITZGERALD, TAMAR SAMIR, COMPANY: ADOLESCENT**
Client: **NICKELODEON ON-AIR**

Creative Firm: **RUDER FINN DESIGN - NEW YORK, NY**
Creative Team: **LISA GABBAY, KAVEN LAM**
Client: **RUDER FINN DEIGN**

Creative Firm: **DENVER HIGHDEF - DENVER, CO**
Client: **STARZ ENTERTAINMENT**

Creative Firm: **OVERLAND AGENCY - PORTLAND, OR**
Creative Team: **NECIA DALLAS, JACK JOHNSON, RICHARD JACKSON, GREG TOZIAN, CHRIS KENNY, COLETTE SONAFRANK, JENNIFER SEAVEY**
Client: **NEW EDGE NETWORKS**
HTTP://WWW.NEWEDGENETWORKS.COM/_APPS/IPSTORY.HTML

The client, New Edge Networks, is a subsidiary of Earthlink, Inc, a leading provider of private IP network solutions. They were looking for an innovative way to showcase the depth and benefits of their network solutions while also enhancing their brand against larger network competitors.

Overland Agency scripted, designed and built a unique, Flash-based product demonstration for the NEN sales force to use at trade shows or when traveling and meeting with clients. The demo also appears on the company's Web site.

The film features a fictitious furniture manufacturer named "Sit" and shows how NEN created network solutions that benefited the entire company, from IT to operations to sales.

One result is that highly complex solutions like "multiprotocol label switching" are communicated in layman's terms. Additionally, the demo is also a brand-building tool that helps NEN's sales force compete on cost-of-ownership, efficiency and project management.

The **P** *symbol designates a Platinum Award Winner, our Best in Category.*

In The Global Sourcing Race,
Are You The Tortoise or The Hare?

CONTENDER #1
★ TORTOISE ★
★ TALE OF THE TAPE ★

Top Speed:	0.1 MPH
Weight:	20 lbs
Height:	12 inches
Reach:	5 inches
Strengths:	Determined, Steady
	Cautious, Experienced
Weaknesses:	Slow to Market
	Mired in Spreadsheets
	Lacks Visibility

CONTENDER #2
★ H A R E ★
★ TALE OF THE TAPE ★

Top Speed:	35 MPH
Weight:	10 lbs
Height:	15 inches
Reach:	7 inches
Strengths:	Fast To Market
Weaknesses:	Poor Quality Control
	Takes Unecessary Risk
	Poor Communication
	No Consistency

The Secret Sourcing Advantage.*

*Caution. Do not attempt.
Professional Stunt Tortoise.

Creative Firm: **HAPPY TRAILS ANIMATION - PORTLAND, OR**
Creative Team: **ANDY COLLEN, EDGAR ALLEN POE, JOE MCMURRIN, ANDREW REFF, TRAVIS HANOUR, AMY COLLEN**
Client: **SELF PROMOTION (HAPPY TRAILS ANIMATION)**
HTTP://WWW.HAPPYTRAILSANIMATION.COM/

Creative Firm: **BSY ASSOCIATES INC. - HOLMDEL, NJ**
Creative Team: **GORDON FORSYTH, SCOTT SALTZ, BARBARA YENINAS, JANE BIDDLE, OLWYN SPIERS, KIMBERLY KASTNER**
Client: **EQOS**

Creative Firm: **HAWTHORNE DIRECT - FAIRFIELD, IA**
Creative Team: **PAUL ALLEN, STEVE SCHOTT**
Client: **MEDIFAST**

The biggest challenge surrounding this infomercial for Medifast weight loss program was time. Hawthorne Direct had only two weeks to coordinate the shoot, tape the commercial and shoot all new food footage. They were then given an additional two weeks to edit, add graphics and music, and post five separate spots.

The client specifically wanted the following features to be conveyed: ease of use, low cost, high results, and free shipping. The ads are targeted to women, aged 25 - 45. The colors and overall look of the spots are contemporary, with an intentional "E! Channel" look and feel.

The ⓟ symbol designates a Platinum Award Winner. This piece tied for Best in Category in "Infomercial."

on the spot car recovery

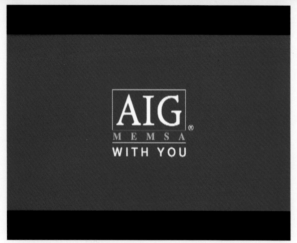

AIG
M E M S A
WITH YOU

Creative Firm: **JWT - DUBAI**
Creative Team: **NIZAR SWAILEM,**
ELIAS HADDAD, CHAFIC HADDAD,
ASH CHAGLA
Client: **AIG**

The ⓟ symbol designates a Platinum Award Winner. This piece tied for Best in Category in "Infomercial."

CREATIVITY 37 *Annual Awards* | **285**

INFOMERCIAL

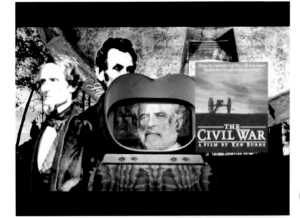

 Creative Firm: **MERESTONE - SCOTTSDALE, AZ**
Creative Team: **CAMILLE HILL, DAVID DEROSIER**
Client: **RYLAND**

SALES FILM/VIDEO

 Creative Firm: **DENVER HIGHDEF - DENVER, CO**
Client: **BARNHART ADVERTISING**

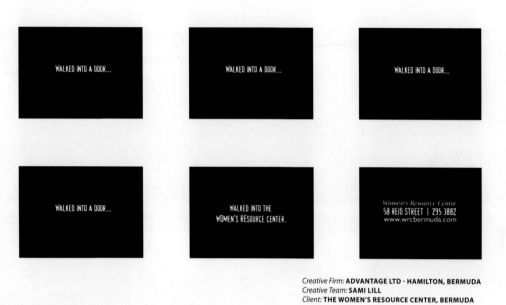

Creative Firm: **ADVANTAGE LTD - HAMILTON, BERMUDA**
Creative Team: **SAMI LILL**
Client: **THE WOMEN'S RESOURCE CENTER, BERMUDA**

 AdVantage, Ltd. was asked to create a thirty-second public service film, focusing on domestic abuse in Bermuda. The film needed to generate awareness of this issue in a country where domestic abuse is often overlooked, and educate the public about the programs available to abused persons through the Women's Resource Centre in Bermuda.

AdVantage, Ltd. decided to focus on the excuses that victims often give to cover up their physical injuries. The challenge was conveying the message without the help of images. While the words in the frames point out the abuse, the final message is one of hope.

The ⓟ symbol designates a Platinum Award Winner, our Best in Category.

Creative Firm: **MCCANN ERICKSON - NEW YORK, NY**
Creative Team: **JOYCE KING THOMAS, STEVE OHLER, MIKE JOINER,**
YANA GOODSTEIN, SALLY HOTCHKISS
Client: **VERIZON WIRELESS**

"Director's Chair" is a two minute in-theater commercial created to support the partnership between Verizon Wireless and "On The Lot," a reality show created by Steven Spielberg and Mark Burnett. "On The Lot" gave aspiring directors a chance to win a million dollar development deal at DreamWorks Studios.

According to McCann Erickson, the biggest challenge when creating this in-theater commercial was coming up with an idea that would build excitement for the show while also promoting the fact that you could watch exclusive content and meet all the contestants on your V CAST phone exclusively from Verizon Wireless. Another challenge was having Steven Spielberg as a client.

McCann Erickson overcame both hurdles. Working closely with Director Frank Todaro, they were able to bring to life every pressure, challenge, and hot-seat situation that a first-time director might face if he were to suddenly find himself in the Director's Chair of an action movie.

The (P) symbol designates a Platinum Award Winner, our Best in Category.

Creative Firm: **MTV NETWORKS - NEW YORK, NY**
Creative Team: **JAMES HITCHCOCK,**
MICHAEL ENGLEMAN, AMIE NGUYEN,
EMILIE SCHNICK DISHNO, PURE NY
Client: **CMT**

In 2007, CMT launched its film division, producing feature-length theatrical and television releases. As a title sequence, the piece needed to be an immediate representation of what happens when a country-centric brand like CMT takes on the movie business.

Using a combination of live-action cows and 3-D modeling, MTV Networks created a piece that lauds the cinematic scope of filmmaking through big, pastoral landscapes, while simultaneously using a comic twist to lighten the mood. This combination of reverence and irreverence is central to the CMT brand in all of its forms.

The (P) *symbol designates a Platinum Award Winner, our Best in Category.*

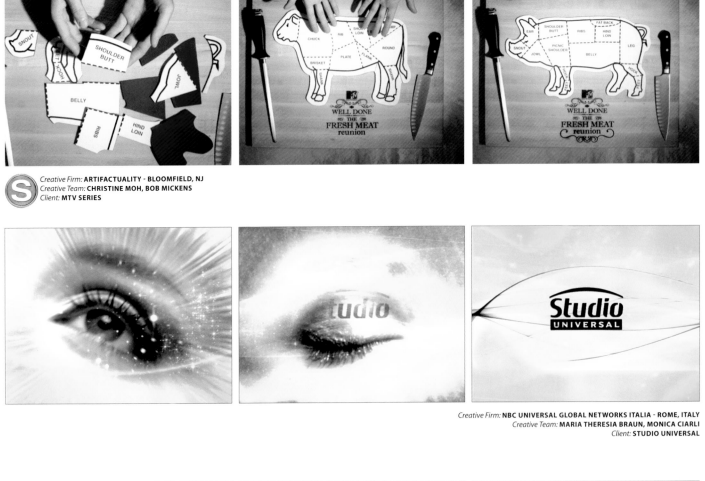

Creative Firm: **ARTIFACTUALITY - BLOOMFIELD, NJ**
Creative Team: **CHRISTINE MOH, BOB MICKENS**
Client: **MTV SERIES**

Creative Firm: **NBC UNIVERSAL GLOBAL NETWORKS ITALIA - ROME, ITALY**
Creative Team: **MARIA THERESIA BRAUN, MONICA CIARLI**
Client: **STUDIO UNIVERSAL**

Creative Firm: **LOOPMEDIA INC - TORONTO, ON**
Creative Team: **CRAIG KIRKHAM**
Client: **INSIGHT PRODUCTIONS**

Creative Firm: **MTV NETWORKS - NEW YORK, NY**
Creative Team: **JAMES HITCHCOCK, MICHAEL ENGLEMAN, AMIE NGUYEN, EMILIE SCHNICK DISHNO, ADAM GAULT**
Client: **CMT**

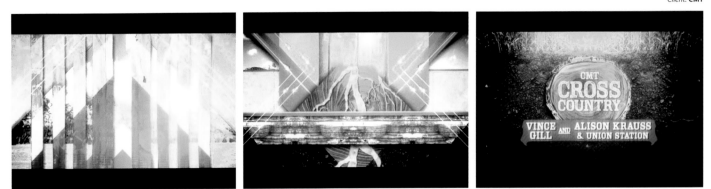

Creative Firm: **MTV NETWORKS - NEW YORK, NY**
Creative Team: **JAMES HITCHCOCK, MICHAEL ENGLEMAN, AMIE NGUYEN, EMILIE SCHNICK DISHNO, LEFTCHANNEL**
Client: **CMT**

Creative Firm: **KRISTER FLODIN ILLUSTRATION - INGARÖ, SWEDEN**
Creative Team: **KRISTER FLODIN**
Client: **MTV PORTUGAL**

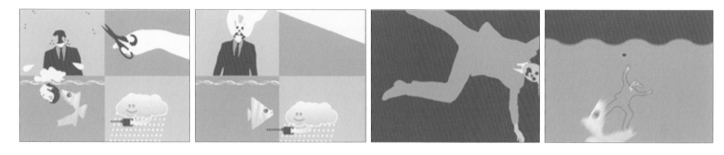

Creative Firm: **MTV ON AIR DESIGN - NEW YORK, NY**
Creative Team: **RODGER BELKNAP, SUSANNAH NILOSEK, ROMY MANN, JEFFREY KEYTON, PRODUCTION CO.**
Client: **MTV**

Creative Firm: **NBC UNIVERSAL GLOBAL NETWORKS ITALIA - ROME, ITALY**
Creative Team: **MARIA THERESIA BRAUN, MONICA CIARLI, ALESSANDRA VINCENTI**
Client: **STUDIO UNIVERSAL**

Creative Firm: **MTV ON AIR DESIGN - NEW YORK, NY**
Creative Team: **DAVID MCELWAINE, SUZANNE BARR, ROMY MANN, JEFFREY KEYTON**
Client: **MTV**

Creative Firm: **BLACKSTONE EDGE STUDIOS - PORTLAND, OR**
Creative Team: **PHILIP CLAYTON-THOMPSON, TOM GRISSOM, RALPH WELLS,**
MARSHAL SERNA, COREY HISKEY, WILLIAM STROMBERG
Client: **WILLAMETTE CONCERT OPERA**
WWW.BLACKSTONEEDGE.COM

Creative Firm: **MTV NETWORKS - NEW YORK, NY**
Creative Team: **JAMES HITCHCOCK, MICHAEL ENGLEMAN, AMIE NGUYEN,**
SCOTT GERLOCK, JOSH LIBITSKY (INNERCIRCLE), INNERCIRCLE
Client: **CMT**

Creative Firm: **MTV NETWORKS - NEW YORK, NY**
Creative Team: **JAMES HITCHCOCK, MICHAEL ENGLEMAN, AMIE NGUYEN,**
EMILIE SCHNICK DISHNO, JUSTIN MCCLURE
Client: **CMT**

Creative Firm: **MTV NETWORKS - NEW YORK, NY**
Client: **VH1**

Creative Firm: **MTV NETWORKS - NEW YORK, NY**
Creative Team: **JAMES HITCHCOCK, MICHAEL ENGLEMAN, AMIE NGUYEN, EMILIE SCHNICK DISHNO, CAPACITY**
Client: **CMT**

Creative Firm: **MTV NETWORKS - NEW YORK, NY**
Creative Team: **JAMES HITCHCOCK, MICHAEL ENGLEMAN, AMIE NGUYEN, EMILIE SCHNICK DISHNO, ADOLESCENT**
Client: **CMT**

Creative Firm: **NBC UNIVERSAL GLOBAL NETWORKS ITALIA - ROME, ITALY**
Creative Team: **MARIA THERESIA BRAUN, MONICA CIARLI**
Client: **STUDIO UNIVERSAL**

Creative Firm: **MTV NETWORKS - NEW YORK, NY**
Creative Team: **THERESA FITZGERALD, TAMAR SAMIR, ANDREW HARRISON, COMPANY: ROGER**
Client: **NICKELODEON ON-AIR**

 Creative Firm: **MTV NETWORKS - NEW YORK, NY**
Creative Team: **CATHERINE CHESTERS, SUSANNAH NILOSEK, CROBIN, CHRIS GALLAGHER, ROMY MANN, JEFFREY KEYTON**
Client: **MTV**

Creative Firm: **PCI COMMUNICATIONS - ALEXANDRIA, VA**
Client: **AMERICAN ASSOCIATION OF MUSEUMS**

Creative Firm: **MTV ON AIR DESIGN - NEW YORK, NY**
Creative Team: **RODGER BELKNAP, KYLE MCDONALD, ROMY MANN, JEFFREY KEYTON**
Client: **MTVU**

Creative Firm: **PCI COMMUNICATIONS - ALEXANDRIA, VA**
Client: **FANNIE MAE**

 Creative Firm: **MTV NETWORKS - NEW YORK, NY**
Creative Team: **JAMES HITCHCOCK, MICHAEL ENGLEMAN, JEFF NICHOLS, AMIE NGUYEN, COURTNEY YOUNGS, EYEBALL NYC**
Client: **CMT**

Creative Firm: **HITCHCOCK FLEMING & ASSOCIATES INC. - AKRON, OH**
Creative Team: **NICK BETRO, MILISSA SHRAKE, TONY FANIZZI**
Client: **GOODYEAR TIRE & RUBBER CO.**

Creative Firm: **BAYCREATIVE - SAN FRANCISCO, CA**
Creative Team: **ARNE HURTY, BARBARA ASSADI, MICHAEL JOHNSON**
Client: **PROSPER**
HTTP://WWW.BAYCREATIVE.COM/BC2/MULTIMEDIA_PSP_SHOW.HTML

Creative Firm: **MCCANN ERICKSON KOREA - SEOUL, SOUTH KOREA**
Creative Team: **JUNG HYUN SHON, YONG BEOM SHIN, GUNWOO KIM, WON KUK KIM**
Client: **COCA-COLA KOREA**

This summer promotion from Coca-Cola™ involved a chance to win one of 100 scooters. Coca-Cola's intent was to enable consumers to get the most out of their on-the-go lifestyle.

McCann Erickson Korea needed to associate both Coke™ and Coke Zero™ with "summer", "fun" and "refreshing". This commercial was a quick glimpse at how all those factors came together with the bonus of a chance to "Grab and Go!" a scooter.

The ⓟ symbol designates a Platinum Award Winner, our Best in Category.

Creative Firm: **TAXI CANADA INC. - MONTRÉAL, QC**
Creative Team: **STÉPHANE CHARIER, ROBERTO BAIBICH, ANDREA USHER JONES, BRIAN GILL, ÉMILIE TRUDEAU, JULIE SIMON**
Client: **REITMANS**

It's a Sierra Mist Free. It's just like Sierra Mist but it doesn't have sugar or calories.   Look hold on to the sides, and like this.   It's that refreshing.

Creative Firm: **DIESTE HARMEL & PARTNERS - DALLAS, TX**
Creative Team: **ALDO QUEVEDO, JAIME ANDRADE, MIGUEL MORENO, ROBERTO SAUCEDO, SALVADOR NORIEGA, JOSE SUASTE**
Client: **PEPSI-SIERRA MIST**

Creative Firm: **DIESTE HARMEL & PARTNERS - DALLAS, TX**
Creative Team: **ALDO QUEVEDO, ALEX DUPLAN, CHRISTIAN HOYLE, ALEX ARELLANO, FLORENCIA LEIBASCHOFF, FRANCISCO CARDENAS**
Client: **SALSA XOCHITL**

Creative Firm: **DIESTE HARMEL & PARTNERS - DALLAS, TX**
Creative Team: **ALDO QUEVEDO, JAVIER GUEMES, GABRIEL PUERTO, FRANCISCO CARDENAS, ALEX ARELLANO, ANGEL LA RIVA**
Client: **FRITO LAY**

My grandson, Alfonso Posada,   lost his Latino blood in a blood transfusion.   Lay's. 100% pure joy.

CREATIVITY 37 *Annual Awards* | **297**

 Creative Firm: **THE VIA GROUP - PORTLAND, ME**
Creative Team: **RON CLAYTON, JASON MCCURRY, JON ROBERTS, AMOS GOSS, GREG SMITH, WAYNE HOLLOWAY**
Client: **HP HOOD**

Creative Firm: **DIESTE HARMEL & PARTNERS - DALLAS, TX**
Creative Team: **ALDO QUEVEDO, CARLOS TOURNE, RAYMUNDO VALDEZ, PATRICIA MARTINEZ, ALEX TOEDTLI, JOHN COSTELLO**
Client: **CLOROX**

 Creative Firm: **GREY WORLDWIDE INC. - SHIBUYA-KU, JAPAN**
Creative Team: **YOICHIRO SERIZAWA, MASANORI TAGAYA, KOUJIRO KAWADA, TERUHITO SHIRAISHI, YASUO INOUE, TOSHITAKA SAITO**
Client: **P&G**

Creative Firm: **SCHEER ADVERTISING GROUP - SOUTH ORANGE, NJ**
Creative Team: **H ROBERT GREENBAUM, DON JACOBS, LISA KALB SCHAFFER**
Client: **BURLINGTON COAT FACTORY**

 Creative Firm: **MCCANN ERICKSON KOREA - SEOUL, SOUTH KOREA**
Creative Team: **JUNG HYUN SHON, JUNG HYUN CHO, SANG JIN KIM, MOON SUN CHOI, MIN JUNG SONG**
Client: **MICROSOFT KOREA**

Creative Firm: **MCCANN ERICKSON KOREA - SEOUL, SOUTH KOREA**
Creative Team: **JUNG HYUN SHON, BYUNG HO AHN, GUNWOO KIM, CHUN UN KIM, WON KUK KIM**
Client: **DAEDONG CONSTRUCTION**

 Creative Firm: **THE MCCARTHY COMPANIES - DALLAS, TX**
Client: **CHASE CHEVROLET**

Creative Firm: **NORTHLICH - CINCINNATI, OH**
Creative Team: **DON PERKINS, JEFF CHAMBERS, JEFFREY WARMAN, CAREY MCGUIRE, DIANE FREDERICK**
Client: **KENTUCKY LOTTERY CORPORATION**

 Creative Firm: **ADVANTAGE LTD - HAMILTON, BERMUDA**
Creative Team: **SAMI LILL, RANDY SCOTT**
Client: **PARLIAMENTARY REGISTRY, BERMUDA**

Creative Firm: **MCCANN ERICKSON KOREA - SEOUL, SOUTH KOREA**
Creative Team: **JUNG HYUN SHON, JUNG HYUN CHO, YOUNG CHUL PARK, SANG JIN KIM, MOON SUN CHOI, MIN JUNG SONG**
Client: **NIKON**

299

Creative Firm: **DIESTE HARMEL & PARTNERS - DALLAS, TX**
Creative Team: **ALDO QUEVEDO, CARLOS TOURNE, RAYMUNDO VALDEZ, PATRICIA MARTINEZ, ALEX TOEDTLI, JOHN COSTELLO**
Client: **CLOROX**

Creative Firm: **DIESTE HARMEL & PARTNERS - DALLAS, TX**
Creative Team: **ALDO QUEVEDO, CARLOS TOURNE, RAYMUNDO VALDEZ, PATRICIA MARTINEZ, ALEX TOEDTLI, ANGEL LA RIVA**
Client: **GLAD**

Creative Firm: **DIESTE HARMEL & PARTNERS - DALLAS, TX**
Creative Team: **ALDO QUEVEDO, JAIME ANDRADE, MIGUEL MORENO, ROBERTO SAUCEDO, SALVADOR NORIEGA, JOSE SUASTE**
Client: **PEPSI - SIERRA MIST**

Creative Firm: **NORTHLICH - CINCINNATI, OH**
Creative Team: **DON PERKINS, JEFF CHAMBERS, JEFFREY WARMAN, CAREY MCGUIRE, DIANE FREDERICK**
Client: **KENTUCKY LOTTERY CORPORATION**

Creative Firm: **MTV NETWORKS - NEW YORK, NY**
Creative Team: **THERESA FITZGERALD, TAMAR SAMIR, TIM WILDER, SHANNON MACNEILAGE**
Client: **NICKELODEON ON-AIR**

Creative Firm: **NORTHLICH - CINCINNATI, OH**
Creative Team: **DON PERKINS, JEFF CHAMBERS, JEFFREY WARMAN, CAREY MCGUIRE, DIANE FREDERICK**
Client: **KENTUCKY LOTTERY CORPORATION**

Creative Firm: **LITTLE FLUFFY CLOUDS ANIMATION STUDIO - MILL VALLEY, CA**
Creative Team: **JERRY VAN DE BEEK, BETSY DE FRIES, BILLY COLLINS**
Client: **SUNDANCE CHANNEL**

Creative Firm: **MTV ON-AIR PROMOS - NEW YORK, NY**
Creative Team: **GEORGIA GREVILLE, GRAYSON ROSS, JOE ARCIDIACONO, PETER BROWER, ROB CAMPBELL, MARK SZUMSKI, BRITT MYERS**
Client: **MTV / L'OREAL**

Creative Firm: **MTV NETWORKS - NEW YORK, NY**
Creative Team: **JAMES HITCHCOCK, MICHAEL ENGLEMAN, JEFF NICHOLS, AMIE NGUYEN, SCOTT GERLOCK, DENNIS GO**
Client: **CMT**

Creative Firm: **DIESTE HARMEL & PARTNERS - DALLAS, TX**
Creative Team: **ALDO QUEVEDO, JAIME ANDRADE, MIGUEL MORENO, ROBERTO SAUCEDO, SALVADOR NORIEGA, JOSE SUASTE**
Client: **PEPSI - SIERRA MIST**

Creative Firm: **HEYE & PARTNER GMBH - UNTERHACHING, GERMANY**
Creative Team: **JAN OKUSLUK, OLIVER DIEHR, MARCO KALFF, MAGNUS AUGUSTIN, MARCO LUDWIG**
Client: **VKB VERSICHERUNGSKAMMER BAYERN (INSURANCE)**

Creative Firm: **GARGOYLE - PRINCETON, NJ**
Creative Team: **DAN VELTRI, WILL PANG, PAUL FEDERICO, SAUL KATZ, DAVE WETZEL, CHRIS SULLIVAN**
Client: **WESTERN PEST SERVICES**

Creative Firm: **BRUKETA & ZINIC OM - ZAGREB, CROATIA**
Creative Team: **MOE MINKARA, DANIEL VUKOVIC,
KRUNOSLAV FRANETIC, IVAN CADEZ, MIHA MLAKER**
Client: **TELE 2**

 ## This humorous commercial

for Tele 2, a telecom operator, was created
to poke fun at the company's giant
competitors: T-mobile and Vip.

The goal was to position TELE 2 as the price
leader and to generate word-of-mouth buzz.

To increase their customer base, TELE 2 needed to position
itself as having the best prices, something that would be
especially attractive to younger subscribers. The hip, edgy
commercial was created to grab their attention, make them
laugh, and help them see that TELE 2 could save them
money.

The (P) *symbol designates a Platinum Award Winner. This piece tied for Best in Category in "Consumer TV, Self-Promotion, Campaign."*

come on up.

Creative Firm: **MCCANN ERICKSON - NEW YORK, NY**
Creative Team: **JOYCE KING THOMAS, CRAIG MARKUS, SHALOM AUSLANDER, TRACEY SMITH, TONI LIPARI**
Client: **LABATT**

 The creative firm McCann Erickson provided the following background story about this platinum winning entry:

"The client introduced creative firm McCann Erickson to a 'guy' named Steve. According to reams of research, Steve lives somewhere in the vast northeastern United States, close to the Canadian border. He's a good guy, Steve. Late 20's. Probably married, with a good job and not as much time with his friends as he used to have. But still loves to hang out with them. Whether it's for a beer or a weekend fishing trip. Steve loves to connect with Canada but not Canada with a capital 'C'—the hockey-playing, tuke-wearing Canada. For Steve, Canada represents weekends fishing, camping or hiking (cottaging, I think they call it), or a pickup game of hockey on a frozen pond. But because of his life, he has less time for these activities. And in the areas below the Canadian border, the northeastern part of the United States, there are A LOT of 'Steves'.

This is where Labatt Blue and Blue light come in. The client wanted McCann Erickson to reconnect with the thousands of 'Steves' out there and remind them that when they open a Labatt Blue or Blue Light, they are reconnecting with that part of themselves. And who better to remind them, than a talking fish and a few buddies who are waiting for Steve to show?

The most challenging part of all this? Finding a talking fish. But not nearly as hard as a talking sheet of ice, a group of talking boulders, or a pissed off deer.

or

We've been trying to get a talking fish into a commercial for a few years. We finally found a client brave enough to live the dream."

The (P) symbol designates a Platinum Award Winner. This piece tied for Best in Category in "Consumer TV, Self-Promotion, Campaign."

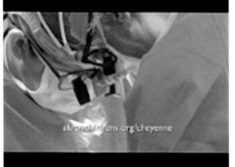

Creative Firm: **MARCUS THOMAS LLC - CLEVELAND, OH**
Creative Team: **LAURA SEIDEL, JOANNE KIM, KEVIN KERWIN, NIKKI DIFRANCO**
Client: **AKRON CHILDREN'S HOSPITAL**

Creative Firm: **FRY HAMMOND BARR - ORLANDO, FL**
Creative Team: **TIM FISHER, JOHN LOGAN, SHANNON HALLARE**
Client: **BRIGHT HOUSE NETWORKS**

Creative Firm: **MTV NETWORKS - NEW YORK, NY**
Creative Team: **JAMES HITCHCOCK, MICHAEL ENGLEMAN, JEFF NICHOLS, VALERIE CARRILLO, NATIONAL TV, CASEY MOULTON**
Client: **CMT**

305

Creative Firm: **PHP COMMUNICATIONS, INC. - BIRMINGHAM, AL**
Creative Team: **BRYAN CHACE**
Client: **BRADFORD HEALTH SERVICES**

Creative Firm: **MCCANN ERICKSON - NEW YORK, NY**
Creative Team: **JOYCE KING THOMAS, STEVE OHLER, GEORGE DEWEY,**
CHRIS QUILLEN, DAN DONOVAN, MARCO CIGNINI
Client: **VERIZON WIRELESS ESPN**

Creative Firm: **BRUKETA & ZINIC OM - ZAGREB, CROATIA**
Creative Team: **MOE MINKARA, DANIEL VUKOVIC, TANJA SKORIC, ANA BELIC, DAVOR RUKOVANJSKI, VANJA OSREDECKI**
Client: **PODRAVKA**

Creative Firm: **ENGINE, LLC - SAN FRANCISCO, CA**
Creative Team: **GEOFF SKIGEN, ROBERT SOLIS**
Client: **MEDJOOL**
WWW.ENGINELLC.COM

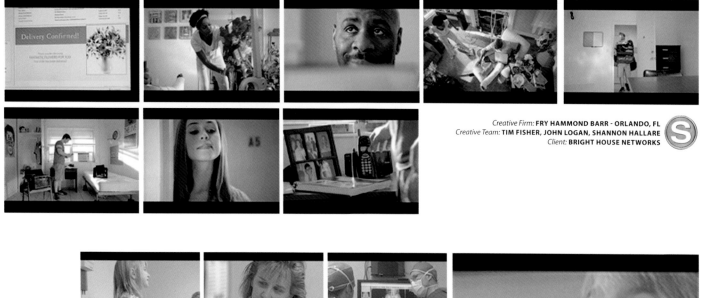

Creative Firm: **FRY HAMMOND BARR - ORLANDO, FL**
Creative Team: **TIM FISHER, JOHN LOGAN, SHANNON HALLARE**
Client: **BRIGHT HOUSE NETWORKS**

Creative Firm: **MARCUS THOMAS LLC - CLEVELAND, OH**
Creative Team: **LAURA SEEIDEL, JOANNE KIM, KEVIN KERWIN, NIKKI DIFRANCO**
Client: **AKRON CHILDREN'S HOSPITAL**

Creative Firm: **BRUKETA & ZINIC OM - ZAGREB, CROATIA**
Creative Team: **DAVOR BRUKETA, NIKOLA ZINIC, TOMISLAV JURICA KACUNIC,**
KRAS GANCEV, HRVOJE STEFOTIC, MIRNA GRZELJ
Client: **ZAGREB ACKA PIOVOVARA**

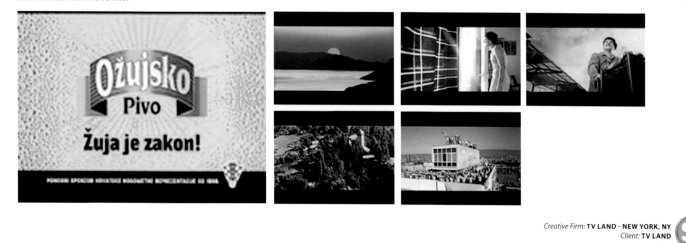

Creative Firm: **TV LAND - NEW YORK, NY**
Client: **TV LAND**

Creative Firm: **NORTHLICH - CINCINNATI, OH**
Creative Team: **DON PERKINS, JEFF CHAMBERS, JEFFREY WARMAN, CAREY MCGUIRE, DIANE FREDERICK**
Client: **KENTUCKY LOTTERY CORPORATION**

Creative Firm: **MTV NETWORKS - NEW YORK, NY**
Client: **VH1**

Creative Firm: **MCCANN ERICKSON KOREA - SEOUL, SOUTH KOREA**
Creative Team: **JUNG HYUN SHON, YOUNG CHUL PARK, GUNWOO KIM, MIN JUNG SONG**
Client: **AIG**

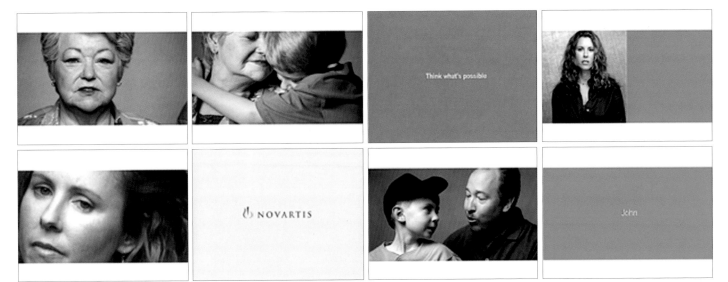

Creative Firm: **RUDER FINN - NEW YORK, NY**
Creative Team: **MICHAEL SCHUBERT, LISA GABBAY, JOHN GRUEN, MARYANN CAMMARATA**
Client: **NOVARTIS**

 Creative Firm: **MTV ON-AIR PROMOS - NEW YORK, NY**
Creative Team: **EVAN SILVER, GINA FORTUNATO, SHEREE SHU, JOE ARCIDIACONO, NATHAN BYRNE, MICHAEL WOLF, SUSAN BLOCK**
Client: **MTV**

Creative Firm: **GREY WORLDWIDE INC. - SHIBUYA-KU, JAPAN**
Creative Team: **YOICHIRO SERIZAWA, CHIKAKO MATSUSHIMA, TOMOYA YOSHIMOTO, TERUHITO SHIRAISHI, AKIRA MURAKAMI, NAOTO OKAYASU**
Client: **BRISTOL-MYERS LION LTD.**

Creative Firm: **NBC UNIVERSAL GLOBAL NETWORKS ITALIA - ROME, ITALY**
Creative Team: **MARIA THERESIA BRAUN, MONICA CIARLI, ADRIANO FILIPPUCCI**
Client: **STUDIO UNIVERSAL**

Creative Firm: **MTV ON-AIR PROMOS - NEW YORK, NY**
Creative Team: **SOPHIA CRANSHAW, STEPHANIE WANG-BREAL, JOE ARCIDIACONO, PAUL GOLDMAN, BEN WILLIAMS, ERICSON CORE, DAX MARTINEZ-VARGAS**
Client: **MTVU**

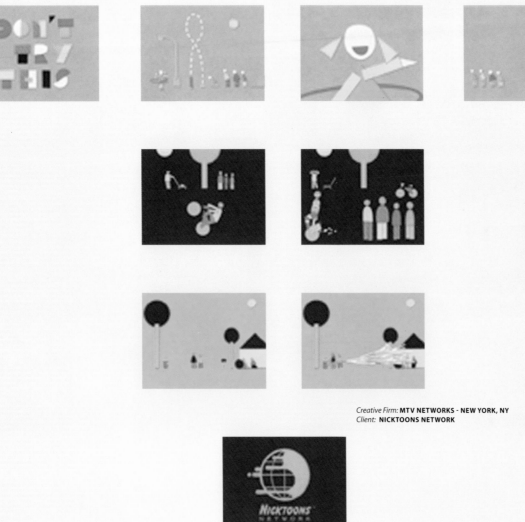

Creative Firm: **MTV NETWORKS - NEW YORK, NY**
Client: **NICKTOONS NETWORK**

Nicktoons Network originally contracted with HunterGatherer Studio to create a few logo IDs. As time went on, the idea grew into a longer self-promotion piece, resulting in a mini-network image campaign.

"Don't Try This" employs a unique visual style and sensibility that capture the essence of the Nicktoon's brand—that of an eleven-year-old boy. The spots exploit the notion that if you tell an eleven-year-old boy not to do something, he will make every effort to do just that.

Ever mindful of Standards and Practices, HunterGatherer purposely utilized an animated approach that feels more "fun and funny" than "dangerous". The spots fit perfectly with the Nicktoons color palette and had a low-key sound design that put most of the focus on the visuals.

The (P) *symbol designates a Platinum Award Winner, our Best in Category.*

Creative Firm: **MTV ON-AIR PROMOS - NEW YORK, NY**
Creative Team: **ALAN HARRIS, WILL KOEHL, SHEREE SHU, KIP BOGDAHN, MARK SNELGROVE, BEN WILLIAMS**
Client: **MTVU**

Creative Firm: **MTV ON-AIR PROMOS - NEW YORK, NY**
Creative Team: **TED PAULY, SHEREE SHU, BRYAN NEWMAN, BRAD TURNER, NATHAN BYRNE, PETER BUCCELLATO, AMY SILVER, JEN RODDIE, LINDSAY NOWAK**
Client: **MTV**

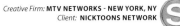

Creative Firm: **MTV NETWORKS - NEW YORK, NY**
Client: **NICKTOONS NETWORK**

Creative Firm: **MTV ON-AIR PROMOS - NEW YORK, NY**
Creative Team: **EVAN SILVER, GINA FORTUNATO, FERNANDO VALLEJO, MATTHEW GIULVEZAN, HARLAN BOSMAJIAN, NICOLAS STAMPE, PETER BROWER, ERIC THOMPSON**
Client: **MTV TR3S**

Creative Firm: **MTV ON-AIR PROMOS - NEW YORK, NY**
Creative Team: **EVAN SILVER, DAVID GRAD, JERRY RISIUS, IRENE ADSUAR, PAUL GOLDMAN, CHRIS HOFFMAN, EBEN BULL, BRAD TURNER, NATHAN BYRNE**
Client: **MTV TR3S**

Creative Firm: **MTV NETWORKS - NEW YORK, NY**
Client: **NICKTOONS NETWORK**

Creative Firm: **MTV ON-AIR PROMOS - NEW YORK, NY**
Creative Team: GINA FORTUNATO, EVAN SILVER, KRIS WALTER, DAVE GORN, BRIAN CAIAZZA, ALEX JUDSON, MORGAN Z, LEE WHITTIER, MILES MICHAEL
Client: **MTV**

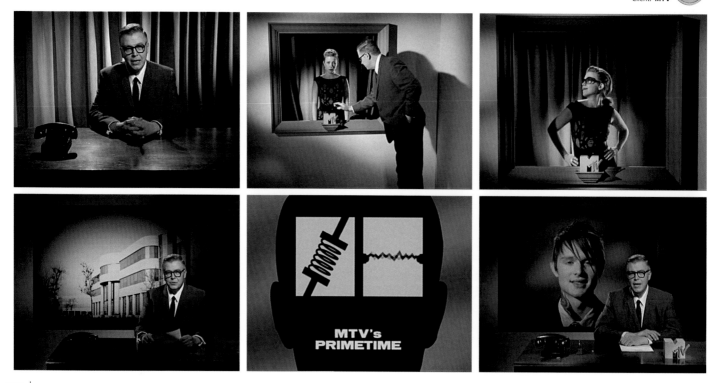

Creative Firm: **NORTHLICH - CINCINNATI, OH**
Creative Team: **DON PERKINS, JEFFREY WARMAN, CAREY MCGUIRE, DIANE FREDERICK**
Client: **OHIO TOBACCO PREVENTION FOUNDATION**

To convince Ohio residents that smoke-free sections within restaurants are not as safe as they seem, creative firm Northlich established a visual metaphor that was impossible to ignore.

Shot in a real diner, this TV shoot involved forty live snakes, two snake wranglers and a group of actors who had 'promised' they were comfortable working with snakes.

The message that non-smoking sections are not safe was powerfully conveyed by using snakes to symbolize cigarette smoke. It showed that smoke, like snakes, will not stay contained to one area.

The result was that a few months later, Ohio residents voted to make Ohio a smoke-free state.

The ⓟ *symbol designates a Platinum Award Winner, our Best in Category.*

Creative Firm: **NORTHLICH - CINCINNATI, OH**
Creative Team: **DON PERKINS, JEFFREY WARMAN, CAREY MCGUIRE, DIANE FREDERICK, JEFF CHAMBERS**
Client: **OHIO TOBACCO PREVENTION FOUNDATION**

Creative Firm: **NORTHLICH - CINCINNATI, OH**
Creative Team: **DON PERKINS, JEFFREY WARMAN, CAREY MCGUIRE, DIANE FREDERICK, JEFF CHAMBERS**
Client: **OHIO TOBACCO PREVENTION FOUNDATION**

Creative Firm: **NORTHLICH - CINCINNATI, OH**
Creative Team: **DON PERKINS, JEFFREY WARMAN, CAREY MCGUIRE, DIANE FREDERICK**
Client: **OHIO TOBACCO PREVENTION FOUNDATION**

Creative Firm: **NORTHLICH - CINCINNATI, OH**
Creative Team: **DON PERKINS, JEFFREY WARMAN, CAREY MCGUIRE, DIANE FREDERICK, JEFF CHAMBERS**
Client: **OHIO TOBACCO PREVENTION FOUNDATION**

Creative Firm: **SCANAD - AARHUS C, DENMARK**
Creative Team: **HENRY RASMUSSEN, ERIK REFNER, MARTIN JORGENSEN**
Client: **COPENHAGEN THEATERS**

Creative Firm: **NORTHLICH - CINCINNATI, OH**
Creative Team: **DON PERKINS, JEFF CHAMBERS, MIKE PETERSON, TODD LIPSCOMB, DIANE FREDERICK**
Client: **CITY OF CINCINNATI**

Creative Firm: **NORTHLICH - CINCINNATI, OH**
Creative Team: **DON PERKINS, JEFFREY WARMAN, CAREY MCGUIRE, DIANE FREDERICK, JEFF CHAMBERS**
Client: **OHIO TOBACCO PREVENTION FOUNDATION**

Creative Firm: **MTV ON-AIR PROMOS - NEW YORK, NY**
Creative Team: **MICHAEL BELLINO**
Client: **MTV**

Creative Firm: **MTV ON-AIR PROMOS - NEW YORK, NY**
Creative Team: **ALAN HARRIS, LINDSAY NOWAK, PAT DONNELLY, BEN WILLIAMS, DAN O'SULLIVAN, JODI ASNES**
Client: **MTV**

Creative Firm: **NORTHLICH - CINCINNATI, OH**
Creative Team: **DON PERKINS, JEFF CHAMBERS, MIKE PETERSON, TODD LIPSCOMB, DIANE FREDERICK**
Client: **OHIO CABLE TELEVISION ASSOCIATION**

Creative Firm: **NORTHLICH - CINCINNATI, OH**
Creative Team: **DON PERKINS, JEFFREY WARMAN, CAREY MCGUIRE, DIANE FREDERICK**
Client: **OHIO TOBACCO PREVENTION FOUNDATION**

Ohio creative firm Northlich shot two television spots for this campaign. One was about the myth that non-smoking sections are safe; the other focused on the false belief that 'Everybody smokes, so I should too'.

Their goal was simple: Debunk both myths.

Both commercials were strong and to-the-point. Northlich says the real reward is with the results: Voters passes a law to make Ohio a smoke-free state, teen smoking in the state has decreased, and 'quit-attempts' have increased.

The Ⓟ *symbol designates a Platinum Award Winner, our Best in Category.*

Creative Firm: **REVOLUCION - NEW YORK, NY**
Creative Team: **ALBERTO RODRIGUEZ, ROBERTO ALCAZAR, MERCY LEONARD**
Client: **AD COUNCIL FOR ADOPT US KIDS**

Creative Firm: **MTV NETWORKS - NEW YORK, NY**
Creative Team: **JAMES HITCHCOCK, MICHAEL ENGLEMAN, LESLIE LEGARE, SCOTT MCDONALD, JOSEFINA NADURATA, LENA BEUG**
Client: **CMT**

Creative Firm: **MCCANN ERICKSON - NEW YORK, NY**
Creative Team: **JOYCE KING THOMAS, BILL OBERLANDER, GIB MARQUARDT, SASHA SHOR, GAIL BARLOW, CORI RANZER BOUDIN**
Client: **AD COUNCIL MEDIA MANAGEMENT**

Creative Firm: **NORTHLICH - CINCINNATI, OH**
Creative Team: **DON PERKINS, JEFFREY WARMAN, CAREY MCGUIRE, DIANE FREDERICK, JEFF CHAMBERS**
Client: **OHIO TOBACCO PREVENTION FOUNDATION**

Creative Firm: **IMAGINATION PUBLISHING - CHICAGO, IL**
Creative Team: **BUD CADDELL**
Client: **INFORMATIONAL**
HTTP://WWW.PASSION2PUBLISH.COM/

RADIO, *SINGLE*

Creative Firm: **RLR ADVERTISING - PASADENA, CA**
Creative Team: **HANS CASTRO-GALLO, DAVID MUCHNIK, DAN NEIRA**
Client: **LA CARE**

RADIO, *CAMPAIGN*

Creative Firm: **ADVANTAGE LTD - HAMILTON, BERMUDA**
Creative Team: **SAMI LILL, YVONNE DECOUTE, RANDY SCOTT**
Client: **PARLIAMENTARY REGISTRY**

Creative Firm: **ADVANTAGE LTD - HAMILTON, BERMUDA**
Creative Team: **SAMI LILL, STEVE EASTON, PENNY DILL**
Client: **THE WOMEN'S RESOURCE CENTER, BERMUDA**

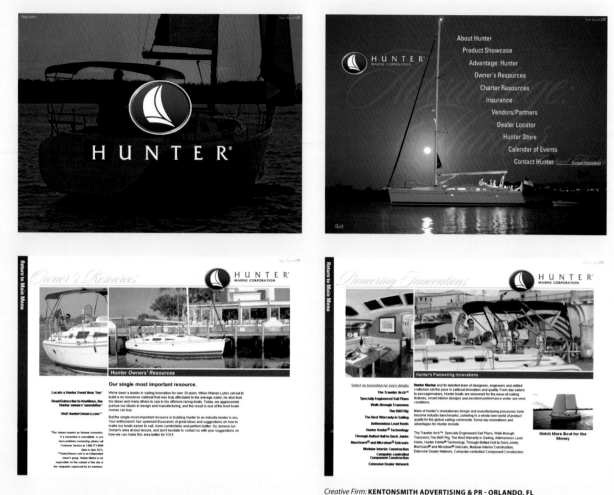

Creative Firm: **KENTONSMITH ADVERTISING & PR - ORLANDO, FL**
Creative Team: **WANDA KENTON SMITH, MARK KELLUM, SCOTT SAYLOR, MARK GREENWALD**
Client: **HUNTER MARINE**

When long-term client Hunter Marine, one of the world's leading manufacturers of sailboats, came to Kenton Smith Advertising & PR with a problem, they knew we had to think outside of the box.

The problem: Hunter was overspending in its print collateral category to the tune of more than $5 per brochure, with another $1- $2 per unit in shipping. Their collateral featured high-end, oversized 9 x 12 glossy brochures—one each for small and large boat audiences. To compound the problem, this was the primary sales tool used for distribution at boat shows—a costly proposition for prospects who might be simply browsing, or not yet ready to buy at the time.

After extensive internal brainstorming, the agency developed a winning solution. Kenton Smith Advertising resegmented the larger brochures into three categories including trailerable, mid-size boats and yachts. They reduced the size and scope of each brochure, but packaged it in an overall carrier package that could

be used as a stand-alone for boat show distribution, or could hold one or more of the brochures for the more qualified prospects. They also integrated an interactive CD as a unifying piece to the campaign. It provided the "cool factor" and offered much more than the previous glossy brochures, including video, diagrams, local dealer links, etc.

As a result, Hunter printed and shipped the smaller brochures at a fraction of the original cost. They could also use the brochure carrier at boat shows, or pass out the CD, which only costs $.40 apiece. The client feedback was very positive. Over 50,000 CDs later, Hunter has seen savings of well over $100,000 in marketing costs!

Best of all, the agency provided a hip new package perceived as cutting edge among prospective sailboat buyers who loved the targeted approach to information, as well as the ability to watch sailing videos and link directly to the company Web site and/or authorized dealers.

CD/DVD ROM DESIGN

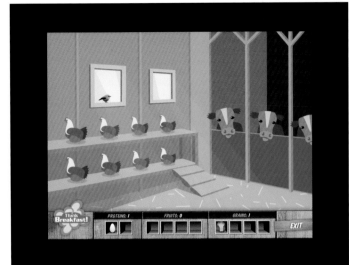

Creative Firm: **FUTUREMEDIA INTERACTIVE - SARATOGA SPRINGS, NY**
Creative Team: **JASON NEMEC, THOMAS ADAMS, LINDA DEMERS, ERICA SCHWAB**
Client: **IMAGINE THAT MKTG & COMM. AND NYS EDUCATION DEPT.**

GRAPHIC USER INTERFACE

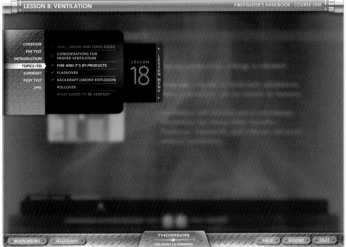

Creative Firm: **FUTUREMEDIA INTERACTIVE - SARATOGA SPRINGS, NY**
Creative Team: **JASON NEMEC, THOMAS ADAMS**
Client: **THOMSON DELMAR LEARNING**

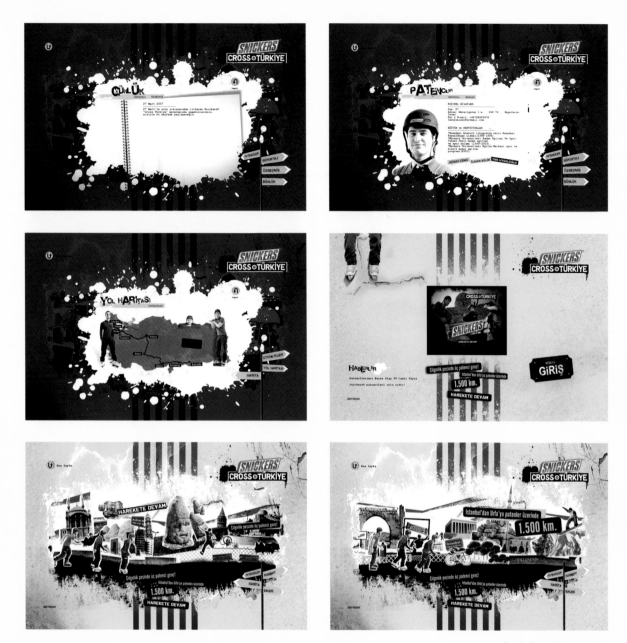

Creative Firm: **2FRESH - ISTANBU**
Client: **MASTER FOODS SNICKERS**
WWW.SNICKERS.COM.TR/CROSSTURKIYE/

This web site was created as part of an online communications for a "Snickers® Cross Türkiye" event. The event followed three roller skaters as they traveled through Türkiye over the span of two months. To be consistent with the event, the web site design solution reflects the street culture and the spirit of rollerblading, while appealing to the core target group of Snickers®—mainly youth.

The art direction is based on street life, textures and road signs. The core of the design features an illustration of the route on a sliding strip, which moves along with the three skaters as they make their way across the country. The 2-D character animations of the skaters are intentionally sloppy and are combined with 3-D street sign navigation. A selective yellow-brown color palette and flat, textured graphics were used to communicate the visual style of the event in a 'Snickers®-branded' way.

To develop continuous online communication and numerous site revisits, the design firm employed skater diaries, an event calendar, an interactive map and photo/video galleries, which were updated daily. New video clips were posted three times a week on both the web site and YouTube.

The (P) *symbol designates a Platinum Award Winner, our Best in Category.*

Golf is a game in which you yell "fore," shoot six, and write down five. – PAUL HARVEY

To view and download more golf signatures for your e-mail, visit www.thedyepreserve.com

Golf is not a game of great shots. It's a game of the most accurate misses. – GENE LITTLER

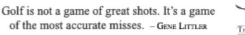

Golf is not a fair game, so why build a course fair? – PETE DYE

To view and download more golf signatures for your e-mail, visit www.thedyepreserve.com

If you think it's hard to meet new people, try picking up the wrong golf ball. – JACK LEMMON

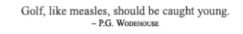

The ardent golfer would play Mount Everest if somebody would put a flagstick on top. – PETE DYE

To view and download more golf signatures for your e-mail, visit www.thedyepreserve.com

Golf, like measles, should be caught young. – P.G. WODEHOUSE

To view and download more golf signatures for your e-mail, visit www.thedyepreserve.com

It's good sportsmanship to not pick up lost golf balls while they are still rolling. – MARK TWAIN

To view and download more golf signatures for your e-mail, visit www.thedyepreserve.com

The reason the pro tells you to keep your head down is so you can't see him laughing. – PHYLLIS DILLER

To view and download more golf signatures for your e-mail, visit www.thedyepreserve.com

My favorite alibi is The Dye Preserve.

To view and download more golf signatures for your e-mail, visit www.thedyepreserve.com

Creative Firm: **CAREY O'DONNELL PR GROUP - WEST PALM BEACH, FL**
Creative Team: **CAREY O'DONNELL**
Client: **THE DYE PRESERVE, A PRIVATE GOLF CLUB**

Creative Firm: **CSC'S P2 COMMUNICATIONS SERVICES - FALLS CHURCH, VA**
Creative Team: **TERRY WILSON, LAURIE ANNE ERNST, JENNIFER VOLTAGGIO**
Client: **CSC CORPORATE**

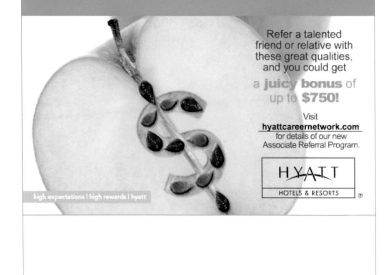

© 2005 NAS
(Media: delete copyright notice)
This material is developed by, and is the property of, NAS Recruitment Communications and is to be used only in connection with services rendered by NAS Recruitment Communications. It is not to be copied, reproduced, published, exhibited or otherwise used without the express written consent of NAS Recruitment Communications. Color depicted is for presentation purposes only and may not be an exact representation of the final product. Every effort has been made to simulate the colors of the finished product.

Creative Firm: **NAS RECRUITMENT COMMUNICATIONS - CLEVELAND, OH**
Creative Team: **JAMES HERRINGSHAW, MAGGIE LYALL, FRED KIML, JENNIFER DOOP**
Client: **HYATT**

Creative Firm: **TORRE LAZUR MCCANN - PARSIPPANY, NJ**
Creative Team: **ADAM SCHIRMER, BRETT NICHOLS, MAX DIVAK**
Client: **BRISTOL-MYERS SQUIBB / SANOFI AVENTIS**
HTTP://WWW.TORRELAZUR.COM/_PLAVIX_EMAILS/IT_TAKES_TWO.HTML

Creative Firm: **NAS RECRUITMENT COMMUNICATIONS - CLEVELAND, OH**
Creative Team: **JAMES HERRINGSHAW, TERRENCE WALSH, LINDA MANTHEY**
Client: **GENESCO**

Creative Firm: **POP - SEATTLE, WA**
Creative Team: **AARON ELLIOTT, JOEL EBY, DAVE CURRY, JASON FORBES, JOE LARRABEE**
Client: **NINTENDO**
HTTP://MARIO.NINTENDO.COM/

To coincide with the release of the new Super Mario Bros. game, Nintendo was seeking to capture the "quintessential Mario feeling" with their graphics. Design firm POP was asked to focus on those elements that established Mario as a cultural icon. The goal was to set this game apart from the numerous other titles that linked Mario with tennis, racing, etc.

While the nostalgic appeal of Mario was a major factor, the most important message to convey was that these elements were new. POP utilized modern 3-D graphics, of course, but they also incorporated many of the special moves that are uniquely Mario. Copy was kept light to let the video tell as much of the story as possible

The ℗ *symbol designates a Platinum Award Winner, our Best in Category.*

 Creative Firm: **ANGELVISION TECHNOLOGIES, INC. - PORTLAND, OR**
Client: **RIVERMARK COMMUNITY CREDIT UNION**
WWW.IMPACTMOVIE.COM/RIVERMARK/

Creative Firm: **ANGELVISION TECHNOLOGIES, INC. - PORTLAND, OR**
Client: **CHALLENGER SPORTS - BRITISH SOCCER**
WWW.IMPACTMOVIE.COM/BRITISHSOCCER/

 Creative Firm: **ANGELVISION TECHNOLOGIES, INC. - PORTLAND, OR**
Client: **BRIDGESTREET WORLDWIDE**
WWW.IMPACTMOVIE.COM/BRIDGESTREET/

 *Creative Firm:* **ANGELVISION TECHNOLOGIES, INC. - PORTLAND, OR**
WWW.IMPACTMOVIES.COM

What can you do in a few minutes? Kick some butt Hear the latest gossip

Creative Firm: **ADVANTAGE LTD - HAMILTON, BERMUDA**
Creative Team: **SAMI LILL, RANDY SCOTT, YVONNE DECOUTE**
Client: **PARLIAMENTARY REGISTRY**

Creative Firm: **MATRIXX PRODUCTIONS - SANTA MONICA, CA**
Creative Team: **VAN VANDEGRIFT, MIKE GOEDECKE, STEPHEN CHOW, ROBERT GEE**
Client: **COBY ELECTRONICS**
WWW.MATRIXXPICTURES.COM/CA/CA.HTML

Creative Firm: **MARTIN RANDAL COMMUNICATIONS - CAMBRIDGE, MA**
Creative Team: **ERIC ROTRAMEL**
Client: **ZE-GEN**

Waste not. Want not.

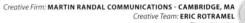

Creative Firm: **PUBLICIS NET - PARIS, FRANCE**
Creative Team: **MATHIEU GALLOUX, JULIEN BENMOUSSA, U-MAN U-MAN, CHRISTIAN MERRET-PALMAIR**
Client: **THOMSON**
HTTP://WWW.DAILYMOTION.COM/VIDEO/XNGJM_LA-COURSE-A-LELYSEE

Creative Firm: **AGENCYNET -
FORT LAUDERDALE, FL**
Client: **IN DEMAND**
HTTP://WWW.MOJOHD.COM/

The ℗ *symbol designates a Platinum Award Winner, our Best in Category.*

Creative Firm: **FAHRENHEIT STUDIO - LOS ANGELES, CA**
Creative Team: **DYLAN TRAN, ROBERT WEITZ**
Client: **VIRGIN RECORDS AMERICA**
HTTP://WWW.VIRGINRECORDS.COM

Creative Firm: **GRINLOCK LIMITED - KIDDERMISNTER, ENGLAND**
Creative Team: **PHILIPPE INGELS, TERSIA INGELS, ANDREW HADLINGTON**
Client: **PINEAPPLE SQUARED ENTERTAINMENT**
HTTP://WWW.ORSUMISLAND.COM

Creative Firm: **DOMANI STUDIOS - BROOKLYN, NY**
Client: **NEW LINE CINEMA**
HTTP://WWW.RUSHHOURMOVIE.COM/GAME/

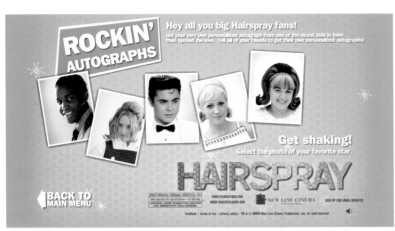

Creative Firm: **VERY MEMORABLE DESIGN - NEW YORK, NY**
Creative Team: **MICHAEL PINTO, GWENEVERE SINGLEY, MARJ KLEINMAN**
Client: **SCHOLASTIC**
HTTP://WWW.ISPYFUNHOUSE.COM/

Creative Firm: **DOMANI STUDIOS - BROOKLYN, NY**
Client: **NEW LINE CINEMA**
HTTP://WWW.HAIRSPRAYMOVIE.COM/AUTOGRAPH.HTML

Creative Firm: **FAHRENHEIT STUDIO - LOS ANGELES, CA**
Creative Team: **DYLAN TRAN, ROBERT WEITZ**
Client: **VIRGIN RECORDS AMERICA**
HTTP://WWW.JOSSSTONE.COM

Creative Firm: **VERY MEMORABLE DESIGN - NEW YORK, NY**
Creative Team: **MICHAEL PINTO, GWENEVERE SINGLEY, JON NIELSEN**
Client: **KIDZ BOP**

Gestalt is the name of an interactive web campaign, developed to meet the following objectives for Getty Images:

Creative Firm: **REMERINC - SEATTLE, WA**
Creative Team: **DAVE REMER, ANDREA JONES, CHRIS HARWOOD, NAOMI MENAHEM, ANDREW FARLEY, BENJAMIN ATHAY**
Client: **GETTY IMAGES**
HTTP://WWW.WONDERFULUNION.COM/GESTALT/?COUNTRY=USA

• Increase repeat traffic to the Getty Images web site by existing accounts
• Increase awareness of the quality of Getty's royalty-free images
• Increase the number of new accounts

The campaign was targeted toward individuals responsible for selecting or recommending imagery at advertising agencies, design firms or publishing houses, namely art and creative directors, photo editors, designers and production managers. Creating a game that encourages multiple visits to the Getty Images web site, and for longer periods of time, was the natural choice to reinforce and strengthen the company's standing as the #1 choice for image searches.

The premise of the game was this: Every weekday for a month, players were invited to visit the Gestalt web site. Once there, they were challenged to look at Rorschach-style inkblots and try to determine which of the ten Getty royalty-free images was hidden within the inkblot.

Participants could play three different inkblot games per day and be entered to win daily prizes each time. Prizes included a winner of $1,000 per day and six grand prize trips to exotic locations.

The game not only allowed creatives to actively use their imaginations, but by studying the inkblots closely, participants were interacting with the newest royalty-free imagery in an intense and concentrated way.

The (P) *symbol designates a Platinum Award Winner, our Best in Category.*

Creative Firm: **PROJECTIONS, INC. - NORCROSS, GA**
Creative Team: **BEN LANGBERG, CHRIS CRADDOCK, JACQUI GREGORY, MATT HULGAN**
Client: **ATLANTA BREAD COMPANY**
HTTP://WWW.PROJECTIONSINC.COM/ABC/MAIN.HTML

Creative Firm: **BRIAN J. GANTON & ASSOCIATES - CEDAR GROVE, NJ**
Client: **OLDCASTLE GLASS**

Creative Firm: **OVERLAND AGENCY - PORTLAND, OR**
Creative Team: **GREG TOZIAN, HEATHER MARCROFT, JACK JOHNSON,
NATE BEDORTHA, JIRO FEINGOLD, JENNIFER MCKENZIE, MAIA ENGEL**
Client: **DOLPHIN SOFTWARE**
WWW.DOLPHINSAFESOURCE.COM

Creative Firm: **DON SCHAAF & FRIENDS, INC. - WASHINGTON, DC**
Creative Team: **MIKE RASO, JOHN PUNSALAN, DON SCHAAF, RICK MORRIS**
Client: **WESTINGHOUSE**
WWW.WESTINGHOUSENUCLEAR.COM

Creative Firm: **FRANKE+FIORELLA - MINNEAPOLIS, MN**
Creative Team: **LAURA GULZINSKI, CRAIG FRANKE**
Client: **CRAMER STUDIO**
WWW.CRAMERSTUDIO.COM

Creative Firm: **NO|INC - BALTIMORE, MD**
Creative Team: **MARK MALONEY, MATTHEW CUMMINGS, ANDY SPANGLER, ALEX MARKSON, SAM GOLDMAN, NICK HAMILL**
Client: **ADVERTISING.COM**
HTTP://WWW.ADVERTISING.COM

Creative Firm: **ALL WEB CAFE - BERWYN, PA**
Client: **JSP INTERNATIONAL**
WWW.ARPRO.COM

Creative Firm: **ALL WEB CAFE - BERWYN, PA**
Client: **JSP INTERNATIONAL**
WWW.JSP.COM

Creative Firm: **ZERO GRAVITY DESIGN GROUP - SMITHTOWN, NY**
Creative Team: **ZERO GRAVITY DESIGN GROUP**
Client: **SRS SOFTWARE**
HTTP://SRSSOFT.COM/

Creative Firm: **RAINCASTLE COMMUNICATIONS - NEWTON, MA**
Creative Team: **TONY CATLIN, CARRI MULLANEY, DAVID BETZ, JOHN CANESTRARO, PAUL REGENSBURG**
Client: **MARK RICHEY WOODWORKING**
WWW.MARKRICHEY.COM

Creative Firm: **SPROKKIT - LOS ANGELES, CA**
Client: **BOOSTER JUICE**
HTTP://BJFRANCHISE.COM

Creative Firm: **SYRUP - NEW YORK, NY**
Creative Team: **JAKOB DASCHEK, ERIK JARLSSON, ALEX LINS, VINEET CHOUDHARY, ILING CHEN**
Client: **GENERAL ELECTRIC**
HTTP://WWW.GE.COM/ECOMAGINATION

Creative Firm: **MTV NETWORKS CREATIVE SERVICES - NEW YORK, NY**
Creative Team: **SCOTT WADLER, CHERYL FAMILY, ANDREW LOPEZ, KEN SAJI, DAVID LANFAIR**
Client: **MTV NETWORKS**
HTTP://WWW.MTVN.COM

Creative Firm: **PEAK SEVEN ADVERTISING - DEERFIELD BEACH, FL**
Creative Team: **CHRIS WILSON, JONATHAN BERG**
Client: **THE PUGLIESE COMPANY**
WWW.PUGLIESECO.COM

Creative Firm: **RED MEAT DESIGN - VENICE, CA**
Client: **MARKETPLACE CAPITAL GROUP**
HTTP://WWW.MARKETPLACECAPITALGROUP.COM/

Creative Firm: **STEADFAST DATA SYSTEMS - EVANSTON, IL**
Creative Team: **LAWRENCE NEISLER, LAURENCE MINSKY, MARK INGRAHAM, KRISTEN ALTHOFF**
Client: **TRANS UNITED INC.**
WWW.TRUCKISMO.COM

Creative Firm: **BEHAVIOR - NEW YORK, NY**
Creative Team: **RALPH LUCCI, NICK KEPPOL, BRAD CARTER**
Client: **LEE HECHT HARRISON**
HTTP://WWW.LHH.COM

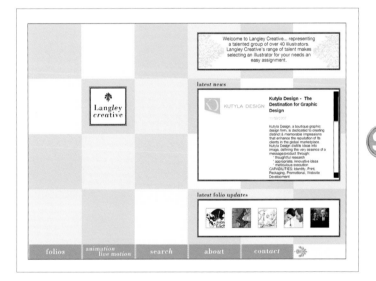

Creative Firm: **KRISTER FLODIN ILLUSTRATION - INGARÖ, SWEDEN**
Creative Team: **KRISTER FLODIN, JOHAN ÖBRINK, JÖRGEN WIDMARK**
Client: **LANGLEY CREATIVE**
WWW.LANGLEYCREATIVE.COM

Creative Firm: **BEHAVIOR - NEW YORK, NY**
Creative Team: **RALPH LUCCI, THOMAS MAHER**
Client: **ADECCO**
HTTP://WWW.ADECCOUSA.COM

Creative Firm: **HELENA SEO DESIGN - SUNNYVALE, CA**
Creative Team: **HELENA SEO, NANCY TOMKINS, BILL FLEMING**
Client: **VIVENDI DEVELOPMENT**
WWW.VIVENDIDEVELOPMENT.COM

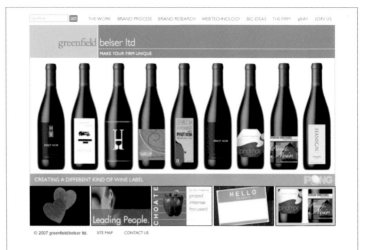

Creative Firm: **GREENFIELD/BELSER LTD. - WASHINGTON, DC**
Creative Team: **BURKEY BELSER, JOE WALSH, STEVE GALLAGHER, FABRICE SARCIAUX, PAUL CHANG, DAVID RANKIN**
Client: **GREENFIELD/BELSER, LTD.**
WWW.GREENFIELDBELSER.COM

Creative Firm: **BREEDWORKS - ONEONTA, NY**
Creative Team: **SUSAN MUTHER, JASON BURNS, HAZEN REED, HEATH STEIN**
Client: **GLIMMERGLASS ALPACAS**
HTTP://WWW.GLIMMERGLASSALPACAS.COM

Creative Firm: **CONRY DESIGN - TOPANGA, CA; SEVEN SHADOW INTERACTIVE - NEW YORK, NY/TOPANGA, CA**
Creative Team: **RHONDA CONRY, CHARLIE STROUT, GLEN ADAMIK**
Client: **PSAV PRESENTATION SERVICES**
WWW.PSAV.COM

Creative Firm: **SINGULARITY DESIGN, INC. - PHILADELPHIA, PA**
Creative Team: **OWEN LINTON, JOSHUA COHEN**
Client: **GROUNDWATER & ENVIRONMENTAL SERVICES**
HTTP://WWW.GESONLINE.COM

Creative Firm: **NAS RECRUITMENT COMMUNICATIONS - CLEVELAND, OH**
Creative Team: **JAMES HERRINGSHAW, CHARLES KAPEC, KATHERINE SANDLIN, TOM MACKO**
Client: **VERIZON BUSINESS**
HTTP://WWW.VERIZONBUSINESS.JOBS/

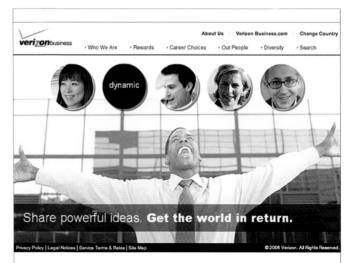

339

Creative Firm: **BRAND NEW WORLD - NEW YORK, NY**
Creative Team: **MARK RISIS, ALAN SCHULMAN, BRIAN BROWN, MICHAEL MEIKSON, WAYNE WU**
Client: **INTERACTIVE ADVERTISING BUREAU**
HTTP://WWW.IAB.NET/MEDIAMOREENGAGING/

Creative Firm: **OVERLAND AGENCY - PORTLAND, OR**
Creative Team: **ARVE OVERLAND, DANA RIERSON, CHRIS KENNY, DANE HESSELDAHL, JENNIFER SEAVEY**
Client: **OREGON MEMORIALS**
WWW.OREGONMEMORIALS.COM

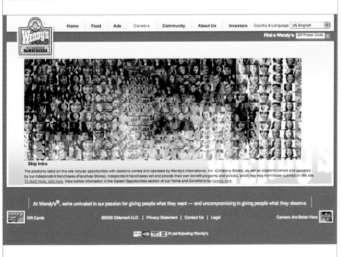

Creative Firm: **NAS RECRUITMENT COMMUNICATIONS - CLEVELAND, OH**
Creative Team: **JAMES HERRINGSHAW, CHARLES KAPEC, PATTIRA SRISUK**
Client: **WENDY'S**
HTTP://WWW.WENDYS.COM/CAREERS/

Creative Firm: **PLEXIPIXEL - SEATTLE, WA**
Creative Team: **JESSE HIBERT, DEVI PELLERIN, ROB CHAPPLE, KRISTI TORGRIMSON**
Client: **MICROSOFT**
HTTP://WWW.PLEXIPIXEL.COM/PORTFOLIO/MSRESEARCH/

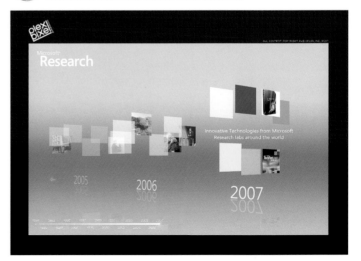

Creative Firm: **ALL WEB CAFE, INC - BERWYN, PA**
Creative Team: **STEPHEN WILLIAMS, MAGNUS SEPP, ERICA PARADISI,**
TRAVIS LAMBERT, RYAN HOY
Client: **JSP**
HTTP://WWW.ARPROAUTOMOTIVE.COM

Creative Firm: **GREENFIELD/BELSER LTD. - WASHINGTON, DC**
Creative Team: **AARON THORNBURGH, JOE WALSH, STEVE GALLAGHER,**
PAUL CHANG, DAVID RANKIN, FABRICE SARCIAUX
Client: **BOWNE**
HTTP://BOWNE.COM/

Creative Firm: **FRANK. - MIAMI, FL**
Creative Team: **TODD HOUSER, RAYMOND ADRIAN, STEFAN KOSEL**
Client: **CAPE HORN GROUP**
WWW.FRANKWORLDWIDE.COM/55WW/

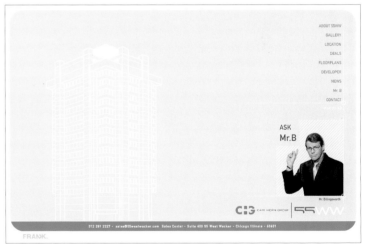

Creative Firm: **DAVIS DESIGN PARTNERS - HOLLAND, OH**
Creative Team: **MATT DAVIS, KAREN DAVIS, NICK WILCOX, PATRICK POER**
Client: **THE MATTINGLY CORPORATION**
HTTP://CLIENTS2.SERVERSIDE.NET/MATTINGLYCORP/

341

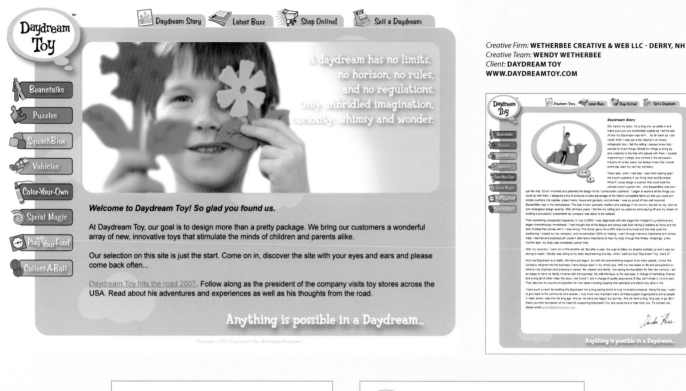

Creative Firm: **WETHERBEE CREATIVE & WEB LLC - DERRY, NH**
Creative Team: **WENDY WETHERBEE**
Client: **DAYDREAM TOY**
WWW.DAYDREAMTOY.COM

DaydreamToy.com, a start-up company, wanted to showcase their fun and innovative product line of children's toys in a distinctive way. To fulfill their vision, the company turned to Wetherbee Creative and Web, LLC, which proved to be a perfect match.

Wetherbee Creative believes that working with start-up companies can be tremendously rewarding, even when budgets are limited. Partner Wendy Weatherbee explained, "The fact that we were working with a client who was driven to ensure that their web site evoked everything they felt their brand was trying to communicate helped us bring the vision to reality. Also, how can you not have fun designing for a toy company?"

Innovation was a large part of the inspiration for the web site. The toys themselves are innovative, and the site needed to be as well. Wetherbee Creative and Web, LLC worked with DaydreamToy.com to step out of the box. Rather than focus on the traditional method

of "sales" and "e-commerce," the site was instead created to be an online product catalog, easily browse-able, fun to look through and filled with photos and detailed descriptions.

To reinforce DaydreamToy.com's branding, the design firm created dreamy blue-sky and cloud packaging, a brightly colored thought-bubble logo and a technologically advanced, easy-to-navigate, intuitive and engaging online environment. To enhance the site experience and make the toys and company come to life, videos of key product lines and a message from the founder were incorporated into the design. Wetherbee incorporated the idea of innovation again when they created wonderfully polished flash videos, set within thought bubbles, to echo the logo and reinforce the branding.

The result was a match of fun and function, establishing a professional on-line image while maintaining the fun and innovation of the brand.

The **P** *symbol designates a Platinum Award Winner, our Best in Category.*

Creative Firm: **MTV NETWORKS - NEW YORK, NY**
Creative Team: **LUCIA FOLK, DONNA PRIESMEYER, LORI REEVES, ROBIN RICHARDSON, BEN FRANK, JASON HILL**
Client: **CMT**
HTTP://WWW.CMT.COM/ONE_COUNTRY/

BANNER ADVERTISING

Creative Firm: **CRITICAL MASS - CHICAGO, IL**
Client: **ALBERTSONS**

Creative Firm: **FOODMIX - WESTMONT, IL**
Creative Team: **FOODMIX CREATIVE**
Client: **NAKANO**

Creative Firm: **CRITICAL MASS - CHICAGO, IL**
Client: **DELL USA**

343

Creative Firm: **MCCANN ERICKSON - NEW YORK, NY**
Creative Team: **JOYCE KING THOMAS, BILL OBERLANDER, TOM SULLIVAN, LARRY PLATT, WENDY LEAHY**
Client: **NIKON**
WWW.STUNNINGNIKON.COM

To promote the Nikon D80 camera, traditional thinking would prompt design firms to place the camera in the hands of a professional photographer and show the results. McCann Erickson decided to do something a bit more risky, but a lot smarter.

The camera, which is designed for photography enthusiasts who are not (yet) professionals, was given to 16 promising photo bloggers, along with simple instructions to photograph whatever tickled their fancy. The results were spectacular in many regards.

First, the images themselves were tremendous, which helped draw attention to the project, resulting in over 368,000 unique visitors to the web site stunningnikon.com.

Second, by placing the camera in the hands of its target market—folks who were already active on social networking sites like Flickr.com—the project was tremendously successful. The Nikon D80 became the #1 selling DSLR in the hotly contested photo enthusiast segment.

The (P) *symbol designates a Platinum Award Winner, our Best in Category.*

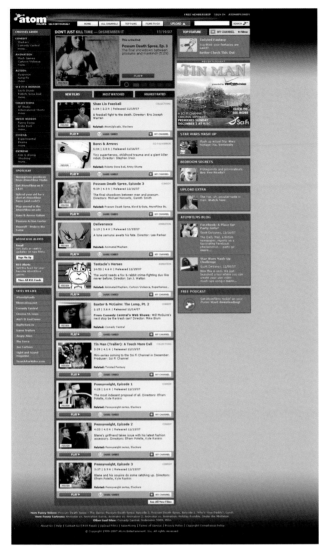

Creative Firm: **MTV NETWORKS - NEW YORK, NY**
Creative Team: **SCOTT ROESCH, CHRIS ALBRECHT, JOEL SANDERS,**
JOHN BARRERA, MEGAN O'NEILL, PETER IGNACIO
Client: **ATOMFILMS**
HTTP://WWW.ATOMFILMS.COM/

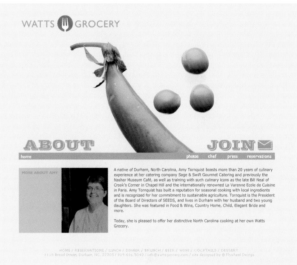

Creative Firm: **FLYWHEEL DESIGN - DURHAM, NC**
Creative Team: **WOODY HOLLIMAN, AMY COCHRAN**
Client: **SAGE & SWIFT GOURMET CATERERS**
WWW.WATTSGROCERY.COM

Creative Firm: **TOLL BROTHERS - HORSHAM, PA**
Creative Team: **KIERAN EVANS**
Client: **TOLL BROTHERS**
HTTP://WWW.HAMPTONHALLSC.COM/

Creative Firm: **ANCHOR POINT DESIGN - LA MESA, CA**
Creative Team: **DON MAES, DAVID ORDAZ**
Client: **SUCCESSFUL SOLUTIONS**
WWW.SUCCESSFULSOLUTIONS.COM

Creative Firm: **SINGULARITY DESIGN, INC. - PHILADELPHIA, PA**
Creative Team: **CHRIS COUNTER, JOSHUA COHEN**
Client: **ALLEGIANCE TECHNOLOGY PARTNERS**
HTTP://WWW.ALLTP.COM

Creative Firm: **TOLL BROTHERS - HORSHAM, PA**
Creative Team: **KATIE WAHN**
Client: **TOLL BROTHERS**
HTTP://WWW.OCEANSEDGEATSINGERISLAND.COM/

Creative Firm: **FINE DESIGN GROUP - SAN FRANCISCO, CA**
Creative Team: **KENN FINE, JOSH KELLY, JESSICA CHRISTEN, DEREK RUDD, JOHN BOUTELLE**
Client: **HITACHI AMERICA, LTD. / SERVER SYSTEMS GROUP**
HTTP://WWW.SELLYOURCTO.COM/

Creative Firm: **CRITICAL MASS - CHICAGO, IL**
Client: **ALBERTSONS**
HTTP://WWW.ALBERTSONS.COM/TRADITIONS/INDEX.ASP

Creative Firm: **POP - SEATTLE, WA**
Creative Team: **BRAD HOLST, ARUNA MALL, DAVE CURRY, AVRAM EISNER, ANNE SANGIOVANNI, LORI TATE**
Client: **TULLY'S COFFEE**
HTTP://WWW.TULLYS.COM/

Creative Firm: **THOMSON-FINDLAW - EAGAN, MN**
Creative Team: **JOE LOVER**
Client: **LAW OFFICES OF TIMOTHY DAVID KOSNOFF**
WWW.KOSNOFF.COM

Creative Firm: **ARKANSASWEB.COM - LITTLE ROCK, AR**
Creative Team: **JOSHUA BAKER**
Client: **PRIMROSE CREEK**
WWW.PRIMROSECREEKAR.COM

Creative Firm: **CRITICAL MASS - CHICAGO, IL**
Client: **MERCEDES-BENZ USA**
HTTP://WWW.MBUSA.COM/THENEWC

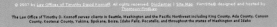

Creative Firm: **CRITICAL MASS - CHICAGO, IL**
Client: **SUPERVALU**
WWW.SELECTION07.COM

Creative Firm: **CRITICAL MASS - CHICAGO, IL**
Client: **ROLEX**
WWW.ROLEX.COM

Creative Firm: **ELLEN BRUSS DESIGN - DENVER, CO**
Creative Team: **ELLEN BRUSS, JORGE LAMORA, CHARLES CARPENTER**
Client: **TURNBERRY PROPERTIES**
WWW.ZIDENVER.COM

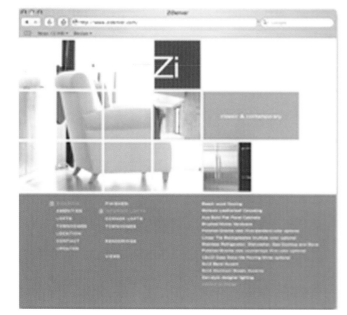

Creative Firm: **CODE AND THEORY - NEW YORK, NY**
Creative Team: **MARK FORSCHER, BRIAN HONOHAN, JON ROGOFF, DONNIE COLEMAN,**
ROBERTO GONZALEZ-REY
Client: **CHARLIE ROSE**
HTTP://WWW.CHARLIEROSE.COM

Creative Firm: **FLYWHEEL DESIGN - DURHAM, NC**
Creative Team: **WOODY HOLLIMAN, STEPHEN BECKER**
Client: **SAGE & SWIFT GOURMET CATERING**
WWW.SAGEANDSWIFT.COM

Creative Firm: **TOLL BROTHERS - HORSHAM, PA**
Creative Team: **MEGHAN FISHER**
Client: **TOLL BROTHERS**
HTTP://WWW.REGENCYDOMINIONVALLEY.COM.COM/

Creative Firm: **SINGULARITY DESIGN, INC. - PHILADELPHIA, PA**
Creative Team: **OWEN LINTON, JOSHUA COHEN**
Client: **NEW ENGLAND HOME MAGAZINE**
HTTP://WWW.NEHOMEMAG.COM

Creative Firm: **WHITTMANHART - LOS ANGELES, CA**
Client: **SIDNEY KIMMEL ENTERTAINMENT**
WWW.CHARLIEBARTLETT-THEMOVIE.COM

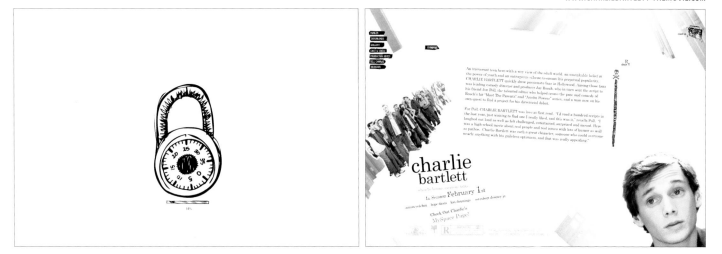

Creative Firm: **JPL PRODUCTIONS - HARRISBURG, PA**
Creative Team: **MATT BYERS, SERENA FEDOR, DAN LIESTER, STEPHEN CRUMP**
Client: **THE HERSHEY COMAPNY**
HTTP://WWW.HERSHEYS.COM/REESES/ELVIS/

Creative Firm: **WHITTMANHART - LOS ANGELES, CA**
Client: **TOYOTA**
WWW.SCION.COM/BROADBAND

Creative Firm: **POP - SEATTLE, WA**
Creative Team: **BRAD HOLST, TOM MORAN, TARA GRUMM, DAVE CURRY, CHRIS NELSON**
Client: **NOBLE HOUSE**
HTTP://WWW.LITTLEPALMISLAND.COM/

Creative Firm: **ELLEN BRUSS DESIGN - DENVER, CO**
Creative Team: **ELLEN BRUSS, JORGE LAMORA, GORDON CHISLETT**
Client: **OPUS DEVELOPMENT**
WWW.WYNKOOPRESIDENCES.COM

Creative Firm: **TOLL BROTHERS - HORSHAM, PA**
Creative Team: **MEGHAN FISHER**
Client: **TOLL BROTHERS**
HTTP://WWW.DRAYTONWOODSATPROVIDENCE.COM/

Creative Firm: **FLUILINK SRL - ROME, ITALY**
Creative Team: **GIULIO GIORGETTI, EMILIANO SPADA,**
ELEONORA DI PIETRO, SARA QUINTORIO
Client: **NBC UNIVERSAL GLOBAL NETWORKS ITALIA SRL**
WWW.STUDIOUNIVERSAL.IT

Creative Firm: **PEAK SEVEN ADVERTISING - DEERFIELD BEACH, FL**
Creative Team: **ROBERT MILLER, DARREN SEYS**
Client: **LIBRARY COMMONS**
WWW.LIBRARYCOMMONSBOCA.COM

Creative Firm: **CODE AND THEORY - NEW YORK, NY**
Creative Team: **BRANDON RALPH, JEREMY LANDIS, MATT CALOS, JEREMY DAVIS,**
VINCENT TUSCANO, MICHAEL KELLY
Client: **CADBURY SCHWEPPES AMERICAS BEVERAGE**
HTTP://CODEANDTHEORY.COM

Creative Firm: **TOLL BROTHERS - HORSHAM, PA**
Creative Team: **KATIE WAHN**
Client: **TOLL BROTHERS**
HTTP://WWW.CROSSINGSATMORTONGROVE.COM

Creative Firm: **POP - SEATTLE, WA**
Creative Team: **GREG NATIONS, TOM MORAN, ANNE SANGIOVANNI, JASON FORBES, DEBORAH SWAN**
Client: **BROWN FORMAN**
HTTP://WWW.B-F.COM/

Creative Firm: **PROCONCEPTS INTERNATIONAL - COLORADO SPRINGS, CO**
Creative Team: **GREG WILLIAMS, JEREMY WILLER, CHELSY OFFUTT, LAURIE HOFFMAN**
Client: **PACIFIC MARKETING ASSOCIATES**
WWW.FILLMOREHERITAGE.COM

Creative Firm: **PUBLICIS NET - PARIS, FRANCE**
Creative Team: **PHILIPPE SIMONET, NATHALIE HUNI, OLIVIER BIENAIME, NICOLAS LEPALLEC, DIANE ATTAR, GREGOIRE ASSEMAT-TESSANDIER**
Client: **COCA-COLA**
HTTP://WWW.COCA-COLABLAK.FR

Creative Firm: **DARLING DESIGN - NEW YORK, NY**
Creative Team: **COURTNEY DARLING, SARAH SKAPIK, JONATHAN SCHNAPP**
Client: **LUXO|RIO CONDOMINIUMS**
WWW.LUXORIO.COM

Creative Firm: **ISLAND OASIS MARKETING - WALPOLE, MA**
Creative Team: **PETE BUHLER, YONGCHI CHEN**
Client: **ISLAND OASIS**

Creative Firm: **ZERO GRAVITY DESIGN GROUP - SMITHTOWN, NY**
Creative Team: **ZERO GRAVITY DESIGN GROUP**
Client: **KEIRAN MURPHY**
HTTP://KIERANMURPHYMUSIC.COM/

Creative Firm: **THE VIA GROUP - PORTLAND, ME**
Creative Team: **GREG SMITH, RON CLAYTON, JON ROBERTS,**
AMOS GOSS, KRISTIN COLLINS, JASON MCCURRY
Client: **MONSTER**
WWW.MYJOBSIGN.COM

Creative Firm: **JPL PRODUCTIONS - HARRISBURG, PA**
Creative Team: **KATY JACOBS, CHELSIE MARKEL, BOB WOLFE,**
SHANE HOFFA, DAN LEISTER, STEVE CRUMP
Client: **THE HERSHEY COMPANY**
HTTP://WWW.HERSHEYS.COM/PAISLEY/

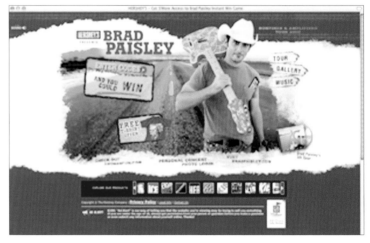

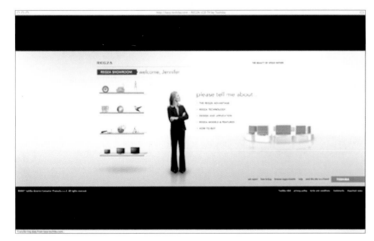

Creative Firm: **LISKA + ASSOCIATES - CHICAGO, IL**
Creative Team: **TANYA QUICK, EMILY VERBA, JASMINE PROBST,**
SEAN KENNEDY SANTOS, ADAM JOHNSON
Client: **LEVIEV FULTON CLUB**
WWW.DISTRICTNY.COM

Creative Firm: **FUTUREMEDIA INTERACTIVE - SARATOGA SPRINGS, NY**
Creative Team: **JASON NEMEC, TIM SCHAPKER, THOM ADAMS,**
JOHN LENSS, BRIAN KOHN
Client: **TOSHIBA AMERICA CONSUMER PRODUCTS**
HTTP://WWW.REGZALCDTV.COM

Creative Firm: **TOLL BROTHERS - HORSHAM, PA**
Creative Team: **JON GREYSON**
Client: **TOLL BROTHERS**
HTTP://WWW.LIVETHEMARK.COM/

Creative Firm: **ZERO GRAVITY DESIGN GROUP - SMITHTOWN, NY**
Creative Team: **ZERO GRAVITY DESIGN GROUP**
Client: **FAIRYTALE FASHION**
HTTP://FAIRYTALEFASHION.COM/

Creative Firm: **WHITTMANHART - LOS ANGELES, CA**
Client: **ANHEUSER-BUSCH, INC.**
WWW.BUDWEISER.COM

Creative Firm: **MCCANN ERICKSON - NEW YORK, NY**
Client: **MASTERCARD**
WWW.PRICELESS.COM

355

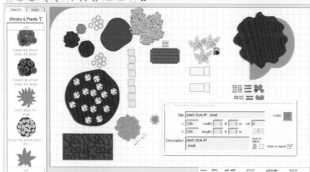

Creative Firm: **LBI (FORMERLY CREATIVE DIGITAL GROUP) - ATLANTA, GA**
Creative Team: **DAWN ELMORE, BRAD BARNETT, NICK WEBB, BRYAN SCOTT, JOEL BOORSTEIN, WHITLOCK DUNBAR**
Client: **THE HOME DEPOT**
HTTP://WWW.HDLANDSCAPESUPPLY.COM/

Creative Firm: **WE ARE GIGANTIC - NEW YORK, NY**
Creative Team: **NEIL POWELL, JOSH ROGERS, BRAD DIXON, KRISTOFER DELANEY, MARY WILLIAMS**
Client: **MIKE'S HARD LEMONADE**
HTTP://MIKESOLOGY.COM/

Creative Firm: **ASU HERBERGER COLLEGE OF THE ARTS - TEMPE, AZ**
Creative Team: **TANYA AMOS, SYLWIA WALERYS, LAURA TOUSSAINT-NEWKIRK, HEATHER LE FUR, TIM TRUMBLE**
Client: **ASU HERBERGER COLLEGE OF THE ARTS**
HTTP://HERBERGERTEST.HC.ASU.EDU/MAINSTAGE/

Creative Firm: **CRITICAL MASS - CHICAGO, IL**
Client: **PAMPERS**
WWW.PAMPERS.COM

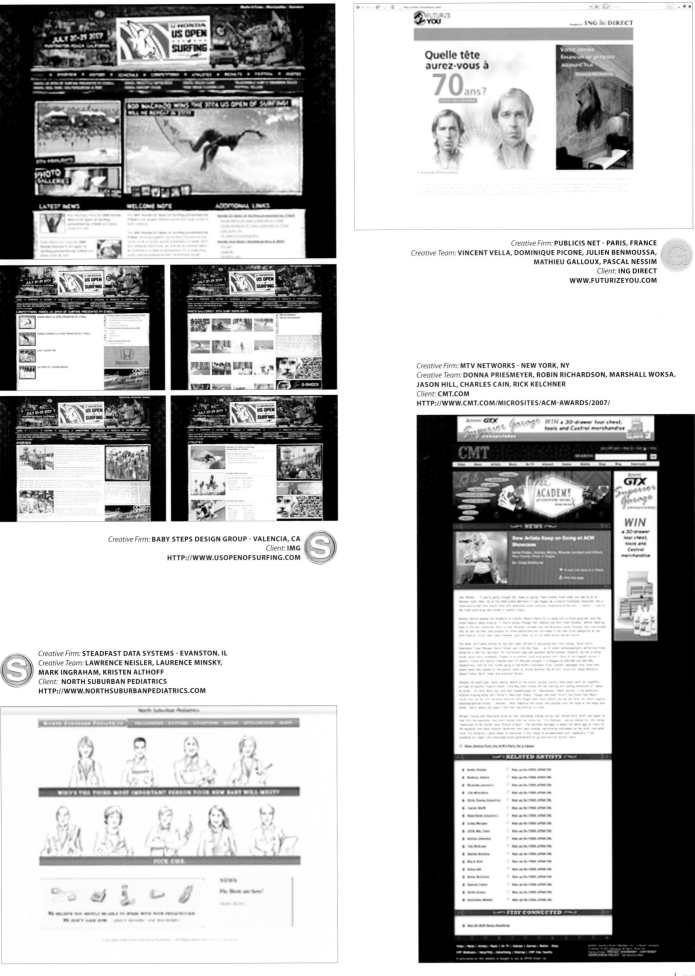

Creative Firm: **PUBLICIS NET - PARIS, FRANCE**
Creative Team: **VINCENT VELLA, DOMINIQUE PICONE, JULIEN BENMOUSSA,
MATHIEU GALLOUX, PASCAL NESSIM**
Client: **ING DIRECT**
WWW.FUTURIZEYOU.COM

Creative Firm: **MTV NETWORKS - NEW YORK, NY**
Creative Team: **DONNA PRIESMEYER, ROBIN RICHARDSON, MARSHALL WOKSA,
JASON HILL, CHARLES CAIN, RICK KELCHNER**
Client: **CMT.COM**
HTTP://WWW.CMT.COM/MICROSITES/ACM-AWARDS/2007/

Creative Firm: **BABY STEPS DESIGN GROUP - VALENCIA, CA**
Client: **IMG**
HTTP://WWW.USOPENOFSURFING.COM

Creative Firm: **STEADFAST DATA SYSTEMS - EVANSTON, IL**
Creative Team: **LAWRENCE NEISLER, LAURENCE MINSKY,
MARK INGRAHAM, KRISTEN ALTHOFF**
Client: **NORTH SUBURBAN PEDIATRICS**
HTTP://WWW.NORTHSUBURBANPEDIATRICS.COM

Creative Firm: **OVERLAND AGENCY - PORTLAND, OR**
Creative Team: **NECIA DALLAS, JACK JOHNSON, DANE HESSELDAHL, RICHARD JACKSON, CHRIS KENNY, HEIN HAUGLAND, JULIE BYUN, JENNIFER MCKENZIE**
Client: **VERDERO**
WWW.VERDERO.COM

Creative Firm: **ZERO GRAVITY DESIGN GROUP - SMITHTOWN, NY**
Creative Team: **ZERO GRAVITY DESIGN GROUP**
Client: **THE GRAPES OF ROTH**
HTTP://THEGRAPESOFROTH.COM/

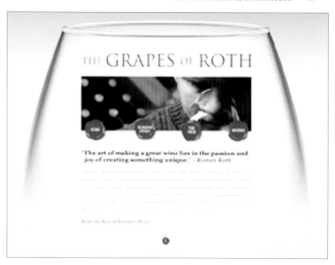

Creative Firm: **PUBLICIS NET - PARIS, FRANCE**
Creative Team: **MATHIEU GALLOUX, JULIEN BENMOUSSA, XAVIER MESSAGER, PASCAL NESSIM**
Client: **THOMSON**
WWW.THOMSONBLACKDIAMOND.COM

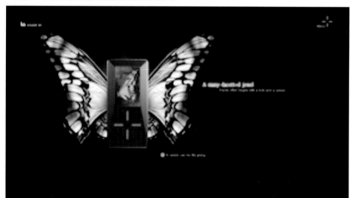

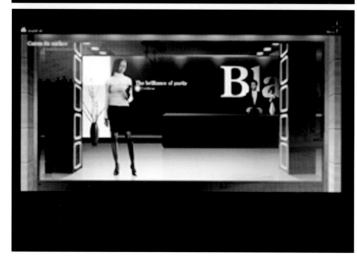

Creative Firm: **FAHRENHEIT STUDIO - LOS ANGELES, CA**
Creative Team: **DYLAN TRAN, ROBERT WEITZ**
Client: **AXISS AUDIO**
HTTP://WWW.AXISSAUDIO.COM

Creative Firm: **CODE AND THEORY - NEW YORK, NY**
Creative Team: **BRANDON RALPH, JEREMY LANDIS, VINCENT TUSCANO**
Client: **MASTERCARD/MRM**
HTTP://GOLF.PRICELESS.COM

Creative Firm: **CRITICAL MASS - CHICAGO, IL**
Client: **MERCEDES-BENZ USA**
WWW.MBUSA.COM/LIFESTYLE

Creative Firm: **THOMSON-FINDLAW - EAGAN, MN**
Creative Team: **PETER OTTO**
Client: **DENNER PELLEGRINO, LLP**
WWW.DENNERLAW.COM

Creative Firm: **LBI / MASTERMIND - ATLANTA, GA**
Creative Team: **DAWN ELMORE, BRAD HANNA, NICK WEBB,**
JAKE WARHAFTIG, PARTNER AGENCY - MASTERMIND
Client: **UPS**
HTTP://CHALLENGE.UPS.COM/

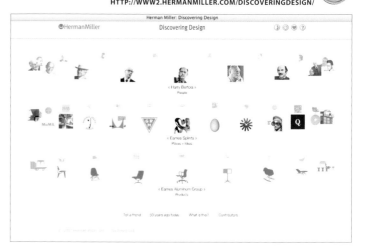

Creative Firm: **BBK STUDIO - GRAND RAPIDS, MI**
Creative Team: **GEOFFREY MARK, RYAN LEE, MARIE-CLAIRE CAMP, JOHN WINKELMAN**
Client: **HERMAN MILLER**
HTTP://WWW2.HERMANMILLER.COM/DISCOVERINGDESIGN/

Creative Firm: **CODE AND THEORY - NEW YORK, NY**
Creative Team: **BRANDON RALPH, BRIAN HONOHAN, BOBBY FITZPATRICK, JEREMY DAVIS, ANDREW WENDLING**
Client: **VICE MAGAZINE**
HTTP://VBS.TV

Creative Firm: **LBI (FORMERLY CREATIVE DIGITAL GROUP) - ATLANTA, GA**
Creative Team: **JEFF WYLIE, DAWN ELMORE, BRAD BARNETT, JAKE WARHAFTIG, WHITLOCK DUNBAR, BROOKE HAYNES, JOEL BOORSTEIN**
Client: **THE HOME DEPOT**
HTTP://WWW.HOMEDEPOTRENTS.COM/

Creative Firm: **ELLEN BRUSS DESIGN - DENVER, CO**
Creative Team: **ELLEN BRUSS, CHARLES CARPENTER, JORGE LAMORA**
Client: **WESTERN DEVELOPMENT**
WWW.NORTHCREEKDENVER.COM

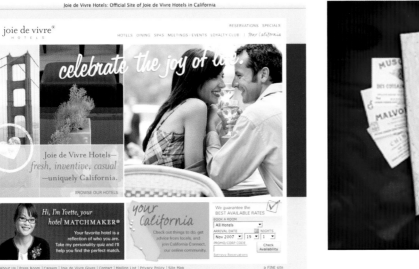

Joie de Vivre Hotels: Official Site of Joie de Vivre Hotels in California

Creative Firm: **NO - SAN FRANCISCO, CA**
Creative Team: **KENN FINE, TSILLI PINES, MELISSA CHAN, LORI DUNKIN, SCOTT BRISKO, JASON FINE**
Client: **JOIE DE VIVRE HOSPITALITY**
HTTP://WWW.JDVHOTELS.COM/

Creative Firm: **NINTH DEGREE INC. - DANA POINT, CA**
Client: **THE WINERY**
WWW.THEWINERYRESTAURANT.NET

Creative Firm: **LBI (FORMERLY CREATIVE DIGITAL GROUP) - ATLANTA, GA**
Creative Team: **PHIL KINZLER, CHRIS REBEL, NICK WEBB, BRAD HANNA, JAKE WARHAFTIG, BRAD BARNETT**
Client: **KODAK**
WWW.THINKLIKERYAN.COM

Creative Firm: **WHITTMANHART - LOS ANGELES, CA**
Client: **ANHEUSER-BUSCH, INC.**
WWW.BUDLIGHT.COM

Creative Firm: **THOMSON-FINDLAW - EAGAN, MN**
Creative Team: **LORI ZURN**
Client: **STRELLIS & FIELD INJURY LAWYERS**
WWW.STRELLISLAW.COM

Creative Firm: **PROCONCEPTS INTERNATIONAL - COLORADO SPRINGS, CO**
Creative Team: **GREG WILLIAMS, JEREMY WILLER, JEREMY WILLER, LAURIE HOFFMAN**
Client: **VALENCIA DEVELOPMENT**
WWW.VALENCIA-LIVING.COM

Creative Firm: **MTV NETWORKS - NEW YORK, NY**
Creative Team: **DONNA PRIESMEYER, ROBIN RICHARDSON, MARSHALL WOKSA,**
JASON HILL, CHARLES CAIN, RICK KELCHNER
Client: **CMT / CMT.COM**
HTTP://WWW.CMT.COM/MICROSITES/CMA/2006/

Creative Firm: **DESIGN 446 - MANASQUAN, NJ**
Creative Team: **BRIAN STERN**
Client: **JP BARRY HOSPITALITY**
HTTP://WWW.MOLLYPITCHER-OYSTERPOINT.COM/OYSTERPOINT/INDEX.HTML

Creative Firm: **DEVELISYS - HUMMELSTOWN, PA**
Creative Team: **AARON SHERRICK, IAN SCHAEFER, NATHAN BAKER**
Client: **HAIRDIRECT**
HTTP://WWW.HAIRDIRECT.COM

Creative Firm: *JPL PRODUCTIONS - HARRISBURG, PA*
Creative Team: **CHELSIE MARKEL, DAVE MINGOS, BARBRA SUGGS, KATY JACOBS**
Client: **HERSHA HOTELS**
HTTP://WWW.HERSHAHOTELS.COM/

Creative Firm: **PUBLICIS NET - PARIS, FRANCE**
Creative Team: **PASCAL NESSIM, CATHY KARSENTY, JULIEN BENMOUSSA, THIERRY GUERCHET, MYRIAM CHARVET, LEA BERTRAND**
Client: **PETIT BATEAU**
HTTP://AWARDS.PUBLICISNET.FR/PETITBATEAU/CAMPAIGN/

Creative Firm: **VIEWSOURCE, INC. - CINCINNATI, OH**
Creative Team: **KIERSTIN PAYNE, PHIL RUSSELL, ANDREW GEISER**
Client: **CLOPAY BPC**
HTTP://WWW.CLOPAYDOOR.COM

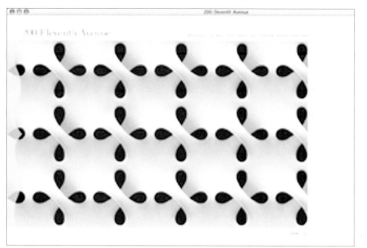

Creative Firm: LISKA + ASSOCIATES - CHICAGO, IL
Creative Team: TANYA QUICK, MEGHAN EPLETT, JASMINE PROBST, ADAM JOHNSON, HAYES DAVIDSON
Client: YOUNGWOO
WWW.200ELEVENTH.COM

Creative Firm: JPL PRODUCTIONS - HARRISBURG, PA
Creative Team: MATT BYERS, DAVE ROBERTSON, BOB WOLFE, KIM QUIGLEY, EUGENE CRISTOAICA
Client: THE HERSHEY COMPANY
HTTP://WWW.HERSHEYSTRACKANDFIELD.COM/

Creative Firm: TOLL BROTHERS - HORSHAM, PA
Creative Team: KATIE WAHN
Client: TOLL BROTHERS
HTTP://WWW.TOLLBROTHERSDESIGNSTUDIO.COM/

Creative Firm: OCTAVO DESIGNS - FREDERICK, MD
Creative Team: SUE HOUGH, MARK BURRIER, HARRIET WISE
Client: THE PERFECT TRUFFLE
HTTP://WWW.THEPERFECTTRUFFLE.COM

Creative Firm: **SIGNATURE ADVERTISING - DENVER, CO**
Creative Team: **DAVE PICCONE**
Client: **RIVERSTONE RESIDENTIAL**
WWW.ALEXANBELLAVISTA.COM

Creative Firm: **MTV NETWORKS - NEW YORK, NY**
Creative Team: **DONNA PRIESMEYER, ROBIN RICHARDSON, BEN FRANK, JASON HILL, CHARLES CAIN, TYSON TUNE**
Client: **CMT**
HTTP://WWW.CMT.COM/MICROSITES/CMT-MUSIC-AWARDS/2007/

Creative Firm: **BEHAVIOR - NEW YORK, NY**
Creative Team: **ANTHONY ARMENDARIZ, MATT ARMENDARIZ, BRAD CARTER**
Client: **IMAGINOVA CORP**
HTTP://WWW.LIVESCIENCE.COM

Creative Firm: **DESIGN 446 - MANASQUAN, NJ**
Creative Team: **BRIAN STERN**
Client: **EASTMAN COMPANIES**
HTTP://LIVINGSTONTOWNCENTER.COM/RETAIL/INDEX.HTML

365

Creative Firm: **OCTAVO DESIGNS - FREDERICK, MD**
Creative Team: **SUE HOUGH, MARK BURRIER, RICHY SHARSHAN**
Client: **FREDERICK WINE TRAIL**
HTTP://WWW.FREDERICKWINETRAIL.COM

Creative Firm: **JPL PRODUCTIONS - HARRISBURG, PA**
Creative Team: **KATY JACOBS, CHELSIE MARKEL, ALISON FETTERMAN, DAVE ROBERTSON**
Client: **THE PENNSYLVANIA EMPLOYEES BENEFIT TRUST FUND**
HTTP://WWW.PEBTF.ORG/

Creative Firm: **PEAK SEVEN ADVERTISING - DEERFIELD BEACH, FL**
Creative Team: **CHRIS WILSON, JONATHAN BERG**
Client: **OCALA PARTNERS**
WWW.EQUISOCALA.COM

Creative Firm: **RED MEAT DESIGN - VENICE, CA**
Client: **MY WATER BOTTLE**
HTTP://WWW.MYWATERBOTTLE.COM/

Creative Firm: **BLUE CROSS BLUE SHIELD OF MA - BOSTON, MA**
Creative Team: **KATHY VARNEY, PATRICK HNATH, DJ MIN, SARAH DEMAYO,**
EFFIE KAZAKOS, BOB PARIURY
Client: **BLUE CROSS BLUE SHIELD OF MASSACHUSETTS**
WWW.WHYGETIT.COM

Creative Firm: **MTV NETWORKS - NEW YORK, NY**
Creative Team: **DONNA PRIESMEYER, ROBIN RICHARDSON, MARSHALL WOKSA, JASON**
HILL, CHARLES CAIN, RICK KELCHNER
Client: **CMT / CMT.COM**
HTTP://WWW.CMT.COM/MICROSITES/LOADED-AWARDS/2007/

Creative Firm: **SIGNATURE ADVERTISING - DENVER, CO**
Creative Team: **MICHAEL GRAHAM**
Client: **RIVERSTONE RESIDENTIAL**
WWW.ALEXANCITYCENTER.COM

Creative Firm: **BABY STEPS DESIGN GROUP - VALENCIA, CA**
Client: **USA SEVENS**
HTTP://WWW.USASEVENS.COM

Creative Firm: **ANCHOR POINT DESIGN - LA MESA, CA**
Creative Team: **DAVID ORDAZ, DON MAES**
Client: **LA CHATIE DESIGNS**
WWW.LACHATIEDESIGNS.COM

Creative Firm: **VERY MEMORABLE DESIGN - NEW YORK, NY**
Creative Team: **MICHAEL PINTO, RITA STOKES, BILL STOKES**
Client: **MODERN CONCEPTS**

Creative Firm: **FITTING GROUP - PITTSBURGH, PA**
Creative Team: **TRAVIS NORRIS, VICTORIA TAYLOR, JEFF FITTING**
Client: **AMBIANCE BOUTIQUE**
WWW.AMBIANCEBOUTIQUE.ORG

Creative Firm: **MFP - NEW YORK, NY**
Creative Team: **NEIL POWELL, JOSH ROGERS, MARY WILLIAMS,
ADAM KENNEDY, BRANDON**
Client: **GRINCH**

Creative Firm: **BEHAVIOR - NEW YORK, NY**
Creative Team: **RALPH LUCCI, ANTHONY ARMENDARIZ, THOMAS MAHER,
BRAD CARTER, MATT ARMENDARIZ, NATALIE VI THAI**
Client: **SIRIUS SATELLITE RADIO**
HTTP://WWW.SIRIUS.COM/JEEP
HTTP://WWW.SIRIUS.COM/CHRYSLER
HTTP://WWW.SIRIUS.COM/DODGE

Creative Firm: **FAHRENHEIT STUDIO - LOS ANGELES, CA**
Creative Team: **DYLAN TRAN, ROBERT WEITZ**
Client: **NAVELLIER & ASSOCIATES**
HTTP://WWW.NAVELLIER.COM

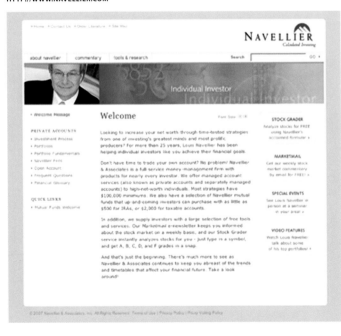

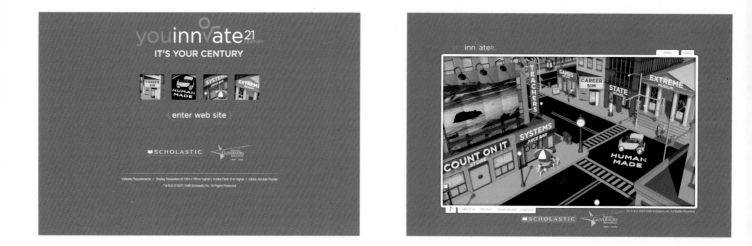

Creative Firm: **EMBER MEDIA - NEW YORK, NY**
Creative Team: **CLAYTON BANKS, ALEXANDER GRINSHPOON, ROBERT FEUGATE, JASON FREENY, HALDANE HENRY, COURTNEY LIDDELL**
Client: **SCHOLASTIC AND NATIONAL GOVERNORS ASSOCIATION**
WWW.YOUINNOVATE21.NET

The goal of youinnovate21.com was to generate excitement among middle school students about science, technology, engineering, and math (STEM).

Ember Media approached the project with the idea of creating original 3-D animations to give the viewer a truly immersive experience. Scholastic provided key learning assets that Ember Media was able to incorporate into the site without losing the integrity of the design.

The web site features standards-based content that encourages young people to convey their own ideas about innovation, and offers teachers information to augment their curriculum.

The (P) *symbol designates a Platinum Award Winner. This piece tied for Best in Category in "Website, Public Service."*

Creative Firm: **AGENCYNET - FORT LAUDERDALE, FL**
Client: **STATE OF COLORADO/ CACTUS**
HTTP://WWW.OWNYOURC.COM

The design of OwnYourC.com blends traditional and digital media. The site was created as a place where kids could "exercise their choices." The opening page reads:

"Everyday, life is full of choices. Some choices are simple (what to wear). Some choices are harder (should we break up). And some choices are huge (what am I passionate about and what do I want to do with my life.) One thing is certain. Every choice you make defines you. Own your choice."

The design intent was to allow kids to explore a virtual world and discover nuggets of information on their own. Rather than using a traditional method of preaching to kids about tobacco use, for example, the site aims to instill the idea that every choice defines you, and encourage kids to make positive choices on their own.

The site can be customized, with choices ranging from making it rain, adding romance or buying trinkets with accumulated c-coins.

The ⓟ symbol designates a Platinum Award Winner. This piece tied for Best in Category in "Website, Public Service."

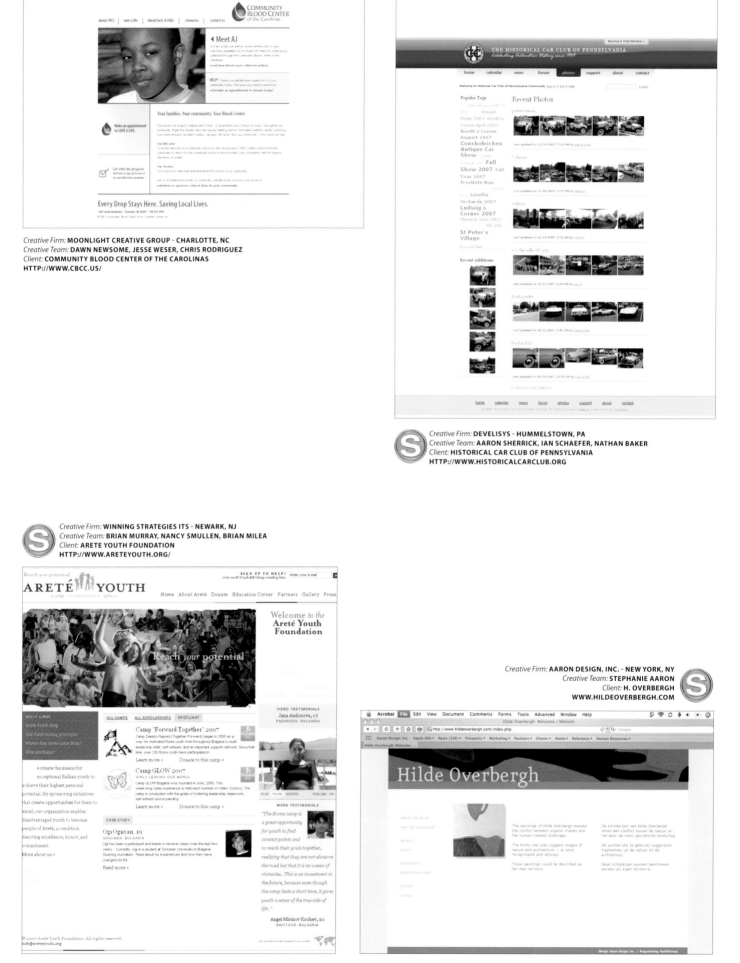

Creative Firm: **MOONLIGHT CREATIVE GROUP - CHARLOTTE, NC**
Creative Team: **DAWN NEWSOME, JESSE WESER, CHRIS RODRIGUEZ**
Client: **COMMUNITY BLOOD CENTER OF THE CAROLINAS**
HTTP://WWW.CBCC.US/

Creative Firm: **DEVELISYS - HUMMELSTOWN, PA**
Creative Team: **AARON SHERRICK, IAN SCHAEFER, NATHAN BAKER**
Client: **HISTORICAL CAR CLUB OF PENNSYLVANIA**
HTTP://WWW.HISTORICALCARCLUB.ORG

Creative Firm: **WINNING STRATEGIES ITS - NEWARK, NJ**
Creative Team: **BRIAN MURRAY, NANCY SMULLEN, BRIAN MILEA**
Client: **ARETE YOUTH FOUNDATION**
HTTP://WWW.ARETEYOUTH.ORG/

Creative Firm: **AARON DESIGN, INC. - NEW YORK, NY**
Creative Team: **STEPHANIE AARON**
Client: **H. OVERBERGH**
WWW.HILDEOVERBERGH.COM

Creative Firm: **INSITE INTERACTIVE - DALLAS, TX**
Creative Team: **JEREMY BERNSTEIN, BRUCE FRISCH**
Client: **MICHAEL J. FOX FOUNDATION**

Creative Firm: **ECLECTIV - ROWLAND HEIGHTS, CA**
Creative Team: **JAY LEE**
Client: **THE OPEN DOOR**
WWW.LAOPENDOOR.COM

Creative Firm: **DEVELISYS - HUMMELSTOWN, PA**
Creative Team: **AARON SHERRICK, IAN SCHAEFER, NATHAN BAKER**
Client: **AACA MUSEUM**
HTTP://WWW.AACAMUSEUM.ORG

Creative Firm: **DAVIS DESIGN PARTNERS - HOLLAND, OH**
Creative Team: **MATT DAVIS, KAREN DAVIS, NICK WILCOX, PATRICK POER**
Client: **ONSLOW COUNTY, N.C. GOVERNMENT**
HTTP://WWW.ONSLOWCOUNTYNC.GOV/

Creative Firm: **ZERO GRAVITY DESIGN GROUP - SMITHTOWN, NY**
Creative Team: **ZERO GRAVITY DESIGN GROUP**
Client: **RAUCH FOUNDATION**
HTTP://RAUCHFOUNDATION.ORG/

Creative Firm: **OVERLAND AGENCY - PORTLAND, OR**
Creative Team: **ARVE OVERLAND, NECIA DALLAS, DANA RIERSON, CHRIS
KENNY, DANE HESSELDAHL, SHANE WESTWOOD, COLETTE SONAFRANK**
Client: **MT. HOOD HABITAT FOR HUMANITY**
WWW.MTHOODHABITAT.ORG

Creative Firm: **FATHOM CREATIVE - WASHINGTON, DC**
Creative Team: **MARIBEL COSTA, SHERI GRANT, AARON HANSEN, JAMES SHARPER**
Client: **AID FOR AFRICA**
WWW.AIDFORAFRICA.ORG

Creative Firm: **VERY MEMORABLE DESIGN - NEW YORK, NY**
Creative Team: **MICHAEL PINTO, GWENEVERE SINGLEY, ROGER WIDICUS, SCOTT KELLUM**
Client: **SCHOLASTIC/PBS KIDS**
HTTP://PBSKIDS.ORG/CLIFFORD/

Creative Firm: **RED MEAT DESIGN - VENICE, CA**
Client: **LUPUS LA**
HTTP://WWW.LUPUSLA.ORG/

Creative Firm: **THE VIA GROUP - PORTLAND, ME**
Creative Team: **GREG SMITH, IAN DUNN, JOANNE DIXON, TIM BEIDEL**
Client: **MAINE READINESS COUNCIL**
WWW.KICKSTARTMAINE.COM

Creative Firm: **G2 MEDIA GROUP INC. - CANTON, OH**
Creative Team: **GEORGE MILNES II, MATT MCCOMB, JUSTIN MCCREA, MALLORY BAIR**
WWW.G2MEDIAGROUP.COM

The design intent of G2 Media Group's web site was to deliver a clear message of 'simple and clean,' so they decided to go back to the basics: pencil, paper and imagination.

Lighthearted design elements and simple navigation were perfect choices for the company. Since hardbound sketchbooks are often used by employees to develop projects, they decided to incorporate them as the backdrop for the web site.

One challenge they had to overcome was presenting their diverse skills while maintaining an overall sketchy, simplistic design theme. Another hurdle was optimizing web assets to provide a fluid user experience while maintaining quality. "Simplicity" and "creativity" are sometimes difficult partners, but the web site benefited from matching the two. This was accomplished through the use of fun and entertaining animation in the intro.

The (P) *symbol designates a Platinum Award Winner, our Best in Category.*

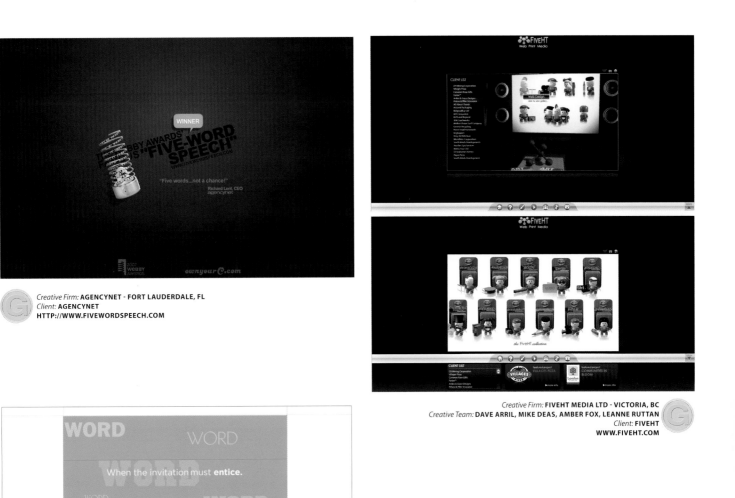

Creative Firm: **AGENCYNET - FORT LAUDERDALE, FL**
Client: **AGENCYNET**
HTTP://WWW.FIVEWORDSPEECH.COM

Creative Firm: **FIVEHT MEDIA LTD - VICTORIA, BC**
Creative Team: **DAVE ARRIL, MIKE DEAS, AMBER FOX, LEANNE RUTTAN**
Client: **FIVEHT**
WWW.FIVEHT.COM

Creative Firm: **BETH SINGER DESIGN - ARLINGTON, VA**
Creative Team: **BETH SINGER, SUHEUN YU, SUCHA SNIDVONGS**
Client: **MARGE LEE**
HTTP://WWW.MUSEUMWORD.COM/

Creative Firm: **RIORDON DESIGN - OAKVILLE, ON**
Creative Team: **RIC RIORDON, SHIRLEY RIORDON, ALAN KRPAN,**
MAT SANDFORD, ALEX BECKETT
Client: **RIORDON DESIGN**
HTTP://WWW.RIORDONDESIGN.COM

Creative Firm: **THE BRAND FACTORY - WOODBRIDGE, ON**
Creative Team: **ULYSSIS CRISOSTOMO, MOHAN SWAMINATHAN**
Client: **THE BRAND FACTORY**
WWW.THEBRANDFACTORY.COM

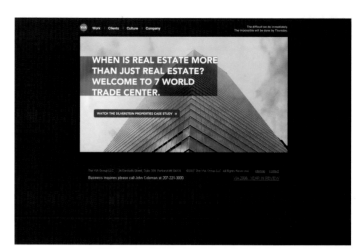

Creative Firm: **TAXI CANADA INC. - MONTRÉAL, QC**
Creative Team: **STÉPHANE CHARIER, DOMINIQUE TRUDEAU, DAVID LAMARCHE,**
ACHIM BRAUWEILER, MARIO LABERGE, JEAN-ALEXANDRE SARRAZIN
Client: **TAXI MONTRÉAL**
HTTP://WWW.VOYEZLESEFFETSTAXI.CA/BILINGUAL/

Creative Firm: **THE VIA GROUP - PORTLAND, ME**
Creative Team: **GREG SMITH, IAN DUNN, STEVE LACHANCE, RAKA**
Client: **THE VIA GROUP**
WWW.VIANOW.COM

Creative Firm: **DESIGN NUT - KENSINGTON, MD**
Creative Team: **BRENT ALMOND, GENE RO, JOHN WOJCIECH**
Client: **DESIGN NUT, LLC**
HTTP://WWW.DESIGNNUT.COM

Creative Firm: **THINK CREATIVE ADVERTISING INC. - AVON, MN**
Creative Team: **KEVIN EHLINGER, CHRIS HANSEN-EHLINGER, JON RUPRECHT,**
NICK PELTON, TRAVIS TOTZ
Client: **THINK CREATIVE ADVERTISING INC.**
HTTP://WWW.ITHINKCREATIVE.COM

Creative Firm: **FUTUREMEDIA INTERACTIVE - SARATOGA SPRINGS, NY**
Creative Team: **JASON NEMEC, THOMAS ADAMS, JOHN LENSS**
Client: **FUTUREMEDIA INTERACTIVE**
HTTP://WWW.FUTUREMEDIAINTERACTIVE.COM/HOLIDAY2006/

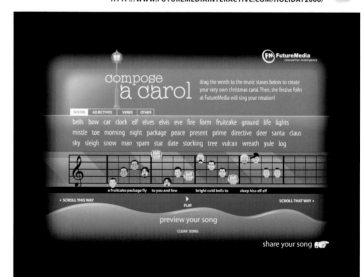

Creative Firm: **PUBLICIS NET - PARIS, FRANCE**
Creative Team: **PHILIPPE SIMONET, NATHALIE HUNI, HELLOHIKIMORI HELLOHIKIMORI, MAXIME MONTEGNIES, GUILLAUME CARTIGNY, GREGOIRE ASSEMAT-T**
Client: **SFR**
HTTP://AWARDS.PUBLICISNET.FR/CKOICEHOLDUP/WEBSITE/

Creative Firm: **MTV NETWORKS - NEW YORK, NY**
Client: **NICKTOONS NETWORK**
WWW.NICKTOONSNETWORK.COM

Creative Firm: **FLUILINK SRL - ROME, ITALY**
Creative Team: **GIULIO GIORGETTI, EMILIANO SPADA**
Client: **NBC UNIVERSAL GLOBAL NETWORKS ITALIA SRL**

Creative Firm: **HOLOHAN DESIGN - PHILADELPHIA, PA**
Creative Team: **KELLY HOLOHAN**
Client: **RICHARD CORNISH**
HTTP://WWW.RICHARDCORNISHHAIR.COM

Creative Firm: **BERENTER, GREENHOUSE & WEBSTER - NEW YORK, NY**
Creative Team: **SHARON OCCHIPINTI, DAN TRINIC, HEATHER EYRICH, DAVID WANDER, AMP**
Client: **BERENTER, GREENHOUSE & WEBSTER**
WWW.BGWAD.COM

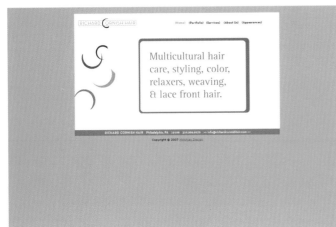

Creative Firm: **TORRE LAZUR MCCANN - PARSIPPANY, NJ**
Creative Team: **CHRISTOPHER BEAN, KATHARINE IMBRO, BRETT NICHOLS,**
MAX DIVAK, JENNIFER ALAMPI, MARCIA GODDARD
Client: **TORRE LAZUR MCCANN**
HTTP://WWW.TORRELAZUR.COM

Creative Firm: **INFORMATION EXPERTS - RESTON, VA**
Creative Team: **JERRY SMITH, MARK HENRY, DAVE WHITRAP, DENNIS SCHULTE,**
BEN STERLING, BAKER MAKTABI
Client: **INFORMATION EXPERTS**
HTTP://WWW.INFORMATIONEXPERTS.COM

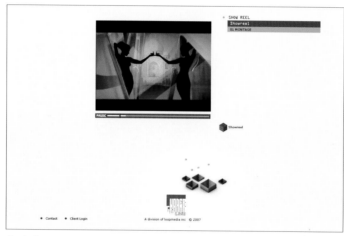

Creative Firm: **LOOPMEDIA INC - TORONTO, ON**
Creative Team: **AARON WHITE**
Client: **LOOPMEDIA INC**
WWW.UNDERGROUNDLANE.COM

Creative Firm: **NOVOCENT PARTNERS - SUCCASUNNA, NJ**
Creative Team: **AL CRISAFULLI, DAN ARABIA, JESSICA VAN**
EMBDEN, CARRIE LITTMAN
WWW.NOVOCENTPARTNERS.COM

Creative Firm: **LTD CREATIVE - FREDERICK, MD**
Creative Team: **TIMOTHY FINNEN, LOUANNE WELGOSS, EVAN WIEGAND, MARLENE ENGLAND**
Client: **LTD CREATIVE**
WWW.LTDCREATIVE.COM

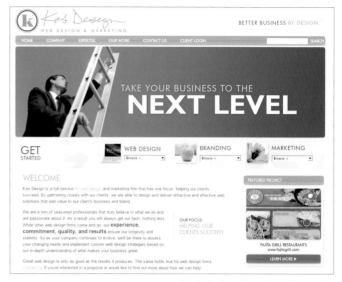

Creative Firm: **SURF U SOFT - JACKSONVILLE, FL**
Creative Team: **PATHIK SHAH, SHANE BAILEY, ANKUR CHOTAI**
Client: **SURF U SOFT**
HTTP://WWW.SURFUSOFT.COM

Creative Firm: **KAS DESIGN, LLC - FREEHOLD, NJ**
Creative Team: **JEFF KASTNING**
Client: **KAS DESIGN, LLC**
HTTP://WWW.KASDESIGNLLC.COM

Creative Firm: **ZYGO COMMUNICATIONS - WYNCOTE, PA**
Creative Team: **SCOTT LASEROW, JESSICA HISCHE, JOE SCORSONE, ALICE DRUEDING**
Client: **TEMPLE UNIVERSITY/TYLER SCHOOL OF ART**

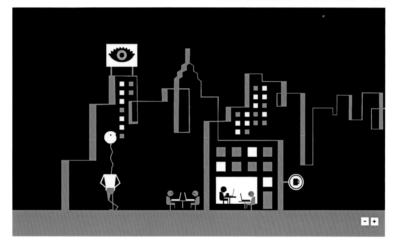

Creative Firm: **LTD CREATIVE - FREDERICK, MD**
Creative Team: **LOUANNE WELGOSS, TIMOTHY FINNEN, KIMBERLY DOW, RICHY SHARSHAN**
Client: **AMG EVENTS**
WWW.AMGEVENTSLLC.COM

Creative Firm: **GALVANEK & WAHL ADVERTISING AGENCY - MANVILLE, NJ**
Creative Team: **PAXTON GALVANEK, JESSICA GALVANEK, CHRIS CASO, JUSTIN LERN, KIM ALTHAUSEN**
Client: **GALVANEK & WAHL LLC**
HTTP://WWW.GWADAGENCY.COM

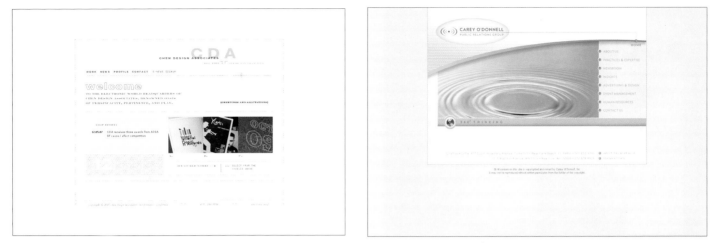

Creative Firm: **CHEN DESIGN ASSOCIATES - SAN FRANCISCO, CA**
Creative Team: **JOSHUA CHEN, LAURIE CARRIGAN, MAX SPECTOR,**
CAROL MILLER, KATHRYN HOFFMAN
Client: **CHEN DESIGN ASSOCIATES**
WWW.CHENDESIGN.COM

Creative Firm: **CAREY O'DONNELL PR GROUP - WEST PALM BEACH, FL**
Creative Team: **JENNIFER SULLIVAN, CAREY O'DONNELL**
HTTP://WWW.CODPR.COM

Creative Firm: **OCTAVO DESIGNS - FREDERICK, MD**
Creative Team: **SUE HOUGH, MARK BURRIER, ANDREA JACOBSON**
Client: **ANDREA JACOBSON PHOTOGRAPHY**
HTTP://WWW.ANDREA-JACOBSON.COM

Creative Firm: **BUCK CONSULTANTS, AN ACS COMPANY - ST. LOUIS, MO**
Creative Team: **JENNIFER WHITLOW, AIME LAURENT, STAN SAMS, ROBERT GRIMM**
Client: **BUCK CONSULTANTS, AN ACS COMPANY**
WWW.BUCKDESIGNSOLUTIONS.COM

Creative Firm: **FINE DESIGN GROUP - SAN FRANCISCO, CA**
Creative Team: **KENN FINE, JOSH KELLY, KIRK ROBERTS, MATTHIAS BASKE**
Client: **FINE DESIGN GROUP**
WWW.FINEDESIGNGROUP.COM

Creative Firm: **CUNNING COMMUNICATIONS - NEW YORK, NY**
Creative Team: **MARK VOYSEY, FLOYD HAYES, ANNETTE DUNCAN,
MARISSA SHRUM**
Client: **HSBC**

AMBIENT MEDIA, *SINGLE UNIT*

Creative Firm: **Y&R GERMANY - FRANKFURT AM MAIN, GERMANY**
Creative Team: **UWE MARQUARDT, HELGE KNIESS, ANDREAS RICHTER, DANIEL TRIPP, MARION LAKATOS, WOLFGANG KOENIG**
Client: **COLGATE GERMANY**

Colgate Total Whitening
„Sparkling White Teeth"

The brief

Colgate wanted to more firmly
anchor the performance of its
Total Whitening toothpaste -
which assures sparkling white
teeth thanks to special ingredients - in the beauty conscious-
ness of the urban target group.

The idea

On a midtown Frankfurt office
tower, a mammoth illuminated
display with the Colgate tube
was installed. For this purpose,
it was arranged to leave the lights
on in a coordinated row of offices in the skyscraper. Result:
a sparkling row of teeth that
could be seen for miles around.

Colgate

The challenge was to restore relevance to a formerly iconic brand that, during the '80's, had slipped into retail private-label status.

The solution was to re-launch the Perry Ellis brand by appealing to American men who wanted to dress as adults without becoming overly metrosexual.

To accomplish that, New York creative firm MFP created stories that accurately reflected the lives of the target market. Executed without photography, the engaging stories were told in non-fashion magazines, newspapers and outdoor publications.

Creative Firm: **MFP - NEW YORK, NY**
Creative Team: **NEIL POWELL, JOSH ROGERS, MARK SLOAN**
Client: **PERRY ELLIS**

The (P) *symbol designates a Platinum Award Winner, our Best in Category.*

Mikesology:
How To Change Your Image Without Changing Yourself

Creative Firm: **WE ARE GIGANTIC - NEW YORK, NY**
Creative Team: **NEIL POWELL, JOSH ROGERS, BRAD DIXON, KRISTOFER DELANEY, MARY WILLIAMS**
Client: **MIKE'S HARD LEMONADE**
HTTP://MIKESOLOGY.COM/

Creative Firm: **MFP - NEW YORK, NY**
Creative Team: **NEIL POWELL, JOSH ROGERS, MARY WILLIAMS, ADAM KENNEDY, FRANZ HUEBER, BRANDON**
Client: **GRINCH**

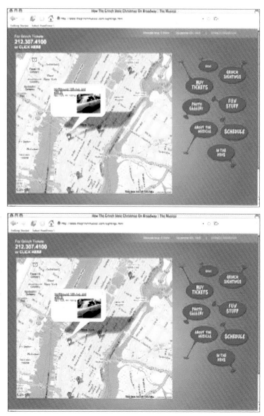

Category: **DEMO/PRESENTATION VIDEO**
School: **TMJ UNIVERSITY, PHILADELPHIA, PA - NEW YORK, NY**
Creative: **JOE DIMARIA**

Category: **BOOK DESIGN, JACKET**
School: **PARSONS THE NEW SCHOOL FOR DESIGN - NEW YORK, NY**
Creative: **JUNGHO WI**

Category: **FOOD & BEVERAGE PACKAGING**
School: **SUSQUEHANNA UNIVERSITY - SELINSGROVE, PA**
Creative: **LESLIE HANSON**

Category: **AMBIENT MEDIA, SINGLE UNIT**
School: **SCHOOL OF VISUAL ARTS - NEW YORK, NY**
Creative: **JESEOK YI**

RISE & F&LL
OF MARILYN MONROE

"she was seemingly destined for tr gedy"

Category: **TYPOGRAPHY, MAGAZINE**
School: **ART INSTITUTE OF NEW YORK - BRONX, NY**
Creative: **JENNIFER RODRIGUEZ**

Category: **AMBIENT MEDIA, SINGLE UNIT**
School: **SCHOOL OF VISUAL ARTS - NEW YORK, NY**
Creative: **JESEOK YI**

Category: **ILLUSTRATION, NEWS & EDITORIAL**
School: **PACIFIC NORTHWEST COLLEGE OF ART**
Creative: **ALLISON BRUNS**

Category: **AMBIENT MEDIA, SINGLE UNIT**
School: **SCHOOL OF VISUAL ARTS - NEW YORK, NY**
Creative: **JESEOK YI**

Category: **FOOD & BEVERAGE PACKAGING**
School: **DREXEL UNIVERSITY GRAPHIC DESIGN PROGRAM, AWCOMAD - PHILADELPHIA, PA**
Creatives: **PATRICK MCKEEVER, SANDY STEWART**

Category: **LOGOS & TRADEMARKS**
School: **IOWA STATE UNIVERSITY - AMES, IA**
Creative: **NATE LUETKEHANS**
Client: **DASTARDLY! GIMMICKS ETC., INC.**

Category: **AMBIENT MEDIA, SINGLE UNIT**
School: **SCHOOL OF VISUAL ARTS - NEW YORK, NY**
Creative: **JESEOK YI**
Client: **THE NATURE CONSERVANCY**

Category: **BOOK DESIGN, JACKET**
School: **DREXEL UNIVERSITY GRAPHIC DESIGN PROGRAM, AWCOMAD - PHILADELPHIA, PA**
Creatives: **MARCELLA ZUCZEK, E. JUNE ROBERTS-LUNN**

SECURITY OF REGULATION

1- You must answer accordingly to my question.
2- Don't try to hide the facts by making this and that. You are strictly prohibited to contest.
3- Don't be a fool for you are thwart the revolution.
4- You must immediatly answer me wasting time to reflect.
5- Don't tell me either about your immorales or the essence of the revolution.
6- While getting lashes or electric not cry at all.
7- Do nothing, sit still and wait. When I ask you something you must do it right away with
8- Don't make pretext about Kam to hide your secret or traitor.
9- If you don't follow all of the ab get many many lashes of electric wire.
10- If you disobey any point of my regulations you shall get either ten lashes or five shocks of electric. Thinking in terms of me or
You must confess if you say nothing beaten with the electric cord.

Category: **ILLUSTRATION, NEWS & EDITORIAL**
School: **PACIFIC NORTHWEST COLLEGE OF ART**
Creative: **ALLISON BRUNS**

Category: **AMBIENT MEDIA, SINGLE UNIT**
School: **SCHOOL OF VISUAL ARTS - NEW YORK, NY**
Creative: **JESEOK YI**
Client: **N.Y. LOTTERY**

Category: **AMBIENT MEDIA, SINGLE UNIT**
School: **SCHOOL OF VISUAL ARTS - NEW YORK, NY**
Creative: **JESEOK YI**
Client: **NRDC (NATURAL RESOURCES DEFENSE COUNCIL)**

Category: **BOOK DESIGN, JACKET**
School: **DREXEL UNIVERSITY GRAPHIC DESIGN PROGRAM, AWCOMAD - PHILADELPHIA, PA**
Creatives: **MARCELLA ZUCZEK, E. JUNE ROBERTS-LUNN**

389

Category: **MAGAZINE AD, CONSUMER, SINGLE UNIT**
School: **SCHOOL OF VISUAL ARTS - NEW YORK, NY**
Creative: **SUEWON CHANG**

Category: **EDITORIAL DESIGN**
School: **THE ART INSTITUTE OF NEW YORK CITY - WOODSIDE, NY**
Creative: **LEE DELGADO**

Category: **WEBSITE, SELF-PROMOTION**
School: **BOWLING GREEN STATE UNIVERSITY - BOWLING GREEN, OH**
Creatives: **BRIAN WATTERSON, AMY FIDLER**
HTTP://WWW.BRIANWATTERSON.COM/

Category: **VIDEO/CD/DVD PACKAGING**
School: **SUSQUEHANNA UNIVERSITY - SELINSGROVE, PA**
Creative: **LESLIE HANSON**

Category: **MAGAZINE AD, CONSUMER, SINGLE UNIT**
School: **SCHOOL OF VISUAL ARTS - NEW YORK, NY**
Creative: **SUEWON CHANG**

Category: **MAGAZINE AD, CONSUMER, SINGLE UNIT**
School: **SCHOOL OF VISUAL ARTS - NEW YORK, NY**
Creative: **SUEWON CHANG**

Category: **EDITORIAL DESIGN**
School: **ART INSTITUTE OF NYC - BROOKLYN, NY**

  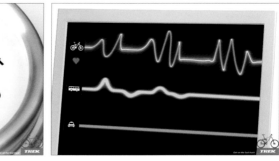

Category: **MAGAZINE AD, CONSUMER, CAMPAIGN**
School: **THE ACADEMY OF ART UNIVERSITY - SAN FRANCISCO, CA**
Creative: **JANG SOON HWANG**
Client: **TREK**

Category: **BOOK DESIGN, JACKET**
School: **DREXEL UNIVERSITY GRAPHIC DESIGN PROGRAM, AWCOMAD - PHILADELPHIA, PA**
Creatives: **PATRICK MCKEEVER, E. JUNE ROBERTS-LUNN**

Category: **MAGAZINE AD, CONSUMER, CAMPAIGN**
School: **SCHOOL OF VISUAL ARTS - NEW YORK, NY**
Creative: **SUEWON CHANG**
Client: **GOLD'S GYM**

Category: **BOOK DESIGN, INTERIOR**
School: **DREXEL UNIVERSITY GRAPHIC DESIGN PROGRAM, AWCOMAD - PHILADELPHIA, PA**
Creatives: **MARCELLA ZUCZEK, E. JUNE ROBERTS-LUNN**

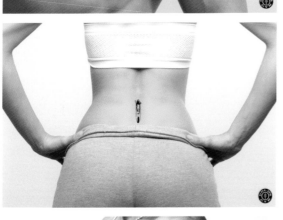

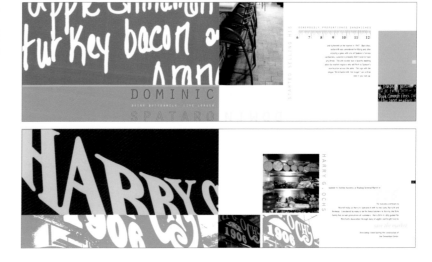

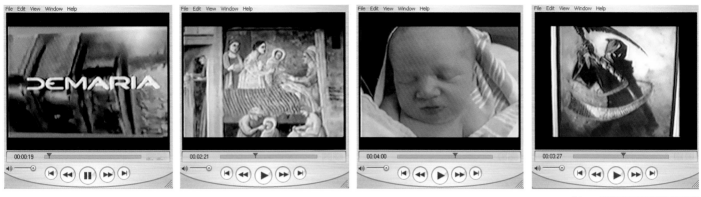

Category: **DEMO/PRESENTATION VIDEO**
School: **TMJ UNIVERSITY - PHILADELPHIA, PA**
Creatives: **JOE DIMARIA**

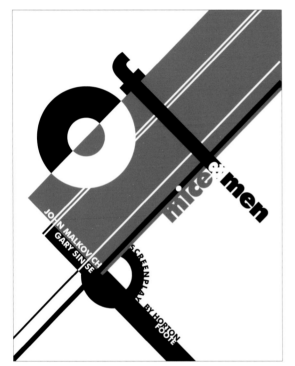

Category: **EDITORIAL DESIGN**
School: **PENNSYLVANIA COLLEGE OF ART & DESIGN - LANCASTER, PA**
Creatives: **STEPHANIE HAMILTON**

Category: **POSTER, SINGLE UNIT**
School: **THE ART INSTITUTE OF NEW YORK CITY - WOODSIDE, NY**
Creatives: **LEE DELGADO**

Category: **BOOK DESIGN, INTERIOR**
School: **TYLER SCHOOL OF ART, TEMPLE UNIVERSITY - PHILADELPHIA, PA**
Creatives: **NICOLE ZIEGLER, PAUL SHERIFF**

Category: **PUBLIC SERVICE TV, SINGLE UNIT**
School: **ART CENTER COLLEGE OF DESIGN - LOS ANGELES, CA**
Creatives: **JENNAVA LASKA, JAMES MANN, MARY DOYLE, JEFF BUTCHER, MARANDA BARSKEY, MARY ANN BRIEWER**
Client: **NATIONAL COALITION AGAINST DOMESTIC VIOLENCE**

Category: **MAGAZINE AD, CONSUMER, CAMPAIGN**
School: **PARSONS THE NEW SCHOOL FOR DESIGN - NEW YORK, NY**
Creative: **JUNGHO WI**
Client: **NINTENDO**

Category: **BOOK DESIGN, INTERIOR**
School: **DREXEL UNIVERSITY GRAPHIC DESIGN PROGRAM, AWCOMAD - PHILADELPHIA, PA**
Creatives: **SHIRA COHEN, JODY GRAFF**

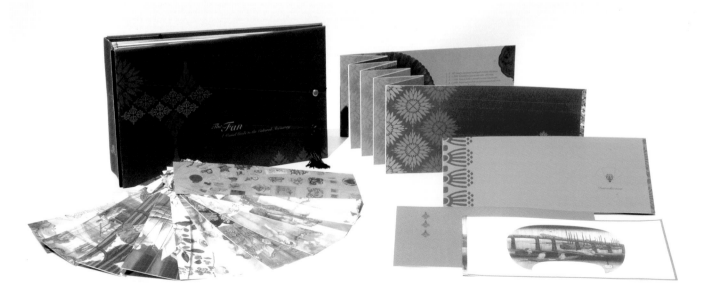